THE SHRED LAWYER

A Memoir of Big Dreams in a Small Town

By Benjamin Richard Courtney

Long May She Wave

THE SHRED LAWYER

Consultation provided by Two Square Books
Shingle Springs, USA

FIRST EDITION

ISBN 9781082451447

ACKNOWLEDGEMENTS

This book is a memoir. It reflects the author's present recollections of experiences going back over four decades. Many names, locations, and descriptions have been changed to protect privacy; a few events have been compressed, and dialogue has been reconstructed. The substance of all conversations has been presented as truthfully as recollection permits and as verified by source materials, research and consultation with others. All comments are intended to be consistent with the character speaking and his or her feelings and attitudes about the topic.

To protect privacy, names, locations and circumstances have been changed.

I'm grateful to my old friend, Cas Mundy, who always had a soaring intellect and gift for writing. He worked professionally as a technical editor for a number of years and had an excellent command of story structure. He made a number of great suggestions about the 'voice' and tone of the narration. I found his comments and suggestions highly useful, and I thank him for his generous contributions.

I wrote with no filter, outline, or plan other than to tell all I could remember about my childhood growing up in Folsom and life as a young adult. My mind was flooded with memories, so I wrote what I remembered with as much detail as possible. The original draft was a hodgepodge of rambling, unorganized short stories that had no unifying or organizing themes, nor any coherent structure. This was bad for the book, but good that I had so much material to shape later into a story.

Within about six months, I had knocked out a couple hundred pages. I edited, revised and re-wrote for a couple weeks until I finished what I thought was a good second draft.

It was still terrible, but it showed signs of hope.

I wrote another draft then another, hacking paragraphs, re-writing sentences, adding explanations and clarify circumstances, deleting redundant phrases, rewriting and rearranging. I spent dozens and dozens of hours of editing and revising to hone the story into a comprehensible form.

Even after half a dozen drafts, it still needed much work and revision, but I felt it was good enough to send to a couple friends to review.

I sent a copy to Mike, who read it and responded with helpful comments and suggestions. He dropped off a copy of Stephen King's fine book, *On Writing*, which is filled with great suggestions, and I read it and found it full of helpful guidance, which I strove to incorporate into my writing. I thank him for his input and gift of Stephen King's stellar book.

I thank Jeff, who also read a terrible early draft and not only responded with suggestions but gave important factual corrections about the town of Folsom, such as, how the lunch siren was tested by the police department every day at noon to make sure it worked in case of a prison break. He learned from a family member who worked for the City of Folsom back in the early '70s some interesting facts about the inner workings of the town's government, which went into my book. He also noted numerous errors and misspellings and suggested the option of self-publishing, which inspired me to finish.

Several others volunteered to review and critique

my story. I sent another very early rambling, disjointed and mistake-filled draft to Mark and Annamarie, but they responded with unbridled enthusiasm and praise. They strongly encouraged me to publish.

I also sent early drafts to Trish, Michele, Michelle, Lindsey, Tracy, Lori, Mark and Barbara. They all gave strong encouragement to complete the memoir.

Toni was among my most ardent supporters. She referred me to Linda for help editing and publishing, and I thank her for all her encouragement and backing.

After about a year of writing, editing, and rewriting, I was ready to submit a draft to Linda. My story had swelled to 186,000 words. She had some great suggestions for character descriptions and effectively identified paragraphs and parts where the story strayed from its proper course. Her edits and suggestions resulted in another complete round of editing in which I deleted about 63,000 words. Though huge chunks of the story were now gone, it was sleeker and flowed better. I was getting closer to completion.

I thank Linda for her thoughtful review and observations.

I continued re-reading and editing, sentence by sentence, word by word. The information that was either needed or unnecessary jumped out as I continued revising. I could finally see the finish line.

I sent a draft to another Mark, and he read it and wanted to meet for lunch. I was fearful he would tell me to stop writing and don't embarrass myself, but he loved the draft, was proud of my work, and encouraged me to publish.

I finally saw the structure the story needed: it had to relate to my goals and dreams growing up. That provided a good way to organize the content. I realized the book would be like a branch on a tree—a single limb growing from the trunk that had its own unique structure.

For anyone who feels 'left out,' please don't take it personally. Most names were changed, and the book was never intended to catalogue everyone I knew growing up in Folsom. If I'd taken the time to tell a story about all my friends, their parents, classmates, teachers, coaches, teammates, neighbors, business people, city employees and town residents, the book would be 5,000 pages long, and would be a collection of unrelated short stories with no plot, storyline or character development. No one wants to read a tome like that.

I know there are many stories that could be told involving dozens or hundreds who were not mentioned. I had to choose a single 'branch' from the tree that told a story and, to some extent, I had no choice but to recount the events connected to the branch—my succession of dreams growing up and as a young adult. Maybe, if given the chance, I'll choose more branches in the future and include more of the many people who were part of my life growing up in Folsom.

I also thank Joy, who proofread my 'final' draft, fact checked all the references to businesses and landmarks, and corrected a number of elusive typos.

For publication, Linda referred me to Two Square Books Publishing, (Consultants) in Shingle Springs, California. I gave Robin and Natalie a hard copy of my final draft, and they returned it a month later with suggested revision. The good news was they liked the story. The bad news was they had discovered a systemic flaw in my writing: repetition. They assured me it was a problem that plagued many writers, but it was fixable. Fortunately, they highlighted the faults, suggested corrections, and I rewrote another hundred paragraphs to articulate my thoughts precisely.

After two more complete reviews, I deleted another 12,000 words. My story went from 186,000 words to 106,000, but I felt the reduction was a massive improvement. The tale now seemed to follow a coherent path, uninhibited by unrelated vignettes, cameo appearances, and distractions.

I'm extremely grateful to Robin and Natalie for their input on the manuscript and many helpful suggestions.

The gist and overall substance of all conversations are at least generally accurate. I remember words, phrases, sentences, questions, answers, emotions, gestures, body language and the main points of all conversations recounted. All remarks are not necessarily verbatim, but they are fair and reasonably accurate approximations and reconstructions based on what I remember about the exchanges.

Additionally, I had various sources which aided my memory of events, such as photo albums, year books, athletic team programs and rosters, newspaper clippings, letters, cards, memorabilia (trophies, medals, awards), the recollections of friends, YouTube, and the town of Folsom itself, which is infused with endless memories.

I consulted some friends about various events to see if their memory matched mine. When they could remember incidents from thirty or forty years ago, their memory was consistent with mine, and they sometimes remembered a detail or two I had forgotten. In one unfortunate case, a teacher could not recall the conversation and doubted he would have made the statements. I deleted the dialogue and rewrote the section, which I think is better now, anyway.

My primary goal was to tell an interesting story while telling the truth as best as I remember. Out of an abundance of caution, some characters, as written, are fictional and bear no semblance to any person living or deceased. The events and dialogue, however, are as accurate as I recall.

I thank Sharon and Scot for their generous professional assistance taking photos for the cover.

I thank my parents. They were both decent, honorable, hard-working people, who always did their best to provide for my brother and me. I feel lucky to have grown up with their loving guidance and support.

I thank my brother for being that jubilant 'Master of Ceremonies', the Pied Piper leading the journey, the daring and fearless champion of 'The Now', challenging me to live fully in the moment, experiencing life always in its greatest glory, and sharing it with others.

Though deeply and humbly thankful to everyone who encouraged, assisted or supported me in the writing of this book, I must give the majority of credit to my parents and brother. They deserve acknowledgement for shaping my character and giving me strength and inspiration. Their loving support and influence molded my resolve to believe and rely on myself and to strive for high goals. They drew out the best of me, for whatever good it may have done for others, and for whatever success or acclaim I've been able to achieve, however fleetingly, on this chaotic, unpredictable, spinning blue planet.

I hope this book will make them proud.

FIGHT OR FLIGHT

I had to fight. I had no choice. A snarly, obnoxious sixth grader had been staring at me as I shuffled about the school yard, unaccompanied by any students, acclimating to my new surroundings. His constant sardonic leering told me I had a problem.

After school one afternoon, the older kid saw me, dashed over and blocked my path. "Let's fight," he said. I walked around him, but he jumped in front of me and told me to stop. I evaded him again, but he strode at my side, ordering me to halt. A group of ten kids followed.

I was only in fourth grade and thought fighting a sixth grader was horrendously unfair. I didn't even know him and hadn't done anything wrong. I was just a freckle-faced kid with a dark brown mop top. Why did he want to throw punches?

He darted before me, held out his palms and obstructed my progress. We were standing at the edge of the asphalt road, cars whooshing by every few moments. A group of eager onlookers quickly encircled us, and now I was trapped. My opponent stood facing me, repeating his challenge. After five minutes of his taunting, I decided there was no choice. *I was alone, and if I did not brawl, he might clobber me in a surprise attack, and that would be worse than avoiding the scuffle*, I thought.

He insisted we step into a nearby cherry orchard, and I finally agreed. Our crowd followed with delight as we strode across the road and onto a dirt path between cherry trees. My adversary and I glared face-to-face for a couple more minutes. Our audience had grown; we now were surrounded by fifteen excited spectators, all of them wide-eyed and breathlessly anticipating the fisticuffs.

"Hit me," he said, and glowered arrogantly.

I scowled back and felt heat and adrenaline surge.

"It's not fair," I said. "You're older."

"I don't care. You're bigger than me. Hit me."

My throat throbbed with the growing anticipation of combat.

His arrogance was daunting, and his status—two grades higher—presented a large psychological barrier. *Kids shouldn't fight above their grade, and a fourth grader fighting a sixth grader was just wrong,* but he ignored my appeals to fairness. He again demanded I punch him, and his humiliating demand for violence made me want to smash him. As we stood a foot apart, I studied him closely. He was slightly smaller; I could take him. The mental wall remained powerful, but instinct and experience told me I could beat this ornery challenger.

The reality became undeniable. I had to engage. If I retreated, I'd be mocked as a coward and lose all self-respect. In a flash of commitment, I slugged him as hard as I could on the side of his face. He was quick and landed a nearly-simultaneous strike of his own, but mine landed harder. We backed away and stood like boxers; I was determined to pound him into the dirt. Before we could clash further, an enormous green station wagon wheeled off the asphalt onto the dirt path where we were standing and screeched to a dusty stop.

My mom stepped out of the car and hollered, "Ben, what are you doing!?"

"I'm fightin'," I answered, matter-of-factly.

She stepped forward through the group of kids, told me to get in the car and told my foe to go home.

The crowd scattered, and we drove away. Mom wanted to know why I was fighting, and I told her the older kid would not leave me alone until I fought him, so I punched him, and he punched me. Then she arrived and stopped the fray. The explanation seemed to satisfy her.

After that brief scuffle, the leering sixth grader never bothered me again.

I eventually acclimated to my new home in Oregon. My stepdad, Dallas, had bought a restaurant, and I was thrilled. I wanted to work in the kitchen, but Mom said I was too young. Dallas said I could visit, inspect the interior, and see how things operated. It had a milkshake machine, and I could have a free one. That seemed like an adequate compromise.

Unfortunately, Dallas's restaurant never flourished. He was gone a lot in the evenings and weekends, but even with all his efforts, the business was failing a year later. I was perplexed. Every time I went to a restaurant, it seemed the booths and counters were full of customers; how could the restaurant fail?

The low revenues were bad enough but, even worse, Mom's marriage failed. She had caught Dallas in another situation he could not explain. A bank statement had come to the house showing he had a joint bank account with another woman. That was the final straw. He tried explaining it away again; he was just 'helping' this poor woman get on her feet after some hardship. Nice try. Mom was patient and compassionate but this excuse wasn't flying—especially in light of all the other odd occurrences she had tolerated—like finding motel receipts in the car showing check-in times in the early afternoon that Dallas blamed on his brother, and the periodic times when he would not come home all night, not call, and then explain there was some work emergency he had to handle. There were no cell phones back in those days, not even any beepers, so excuses for not calling were a little easier to make. Still, the joint bank account with another woman was the death knell for the marriage.

"I'm getting a divorce, and we're moving back to California," my mom informed my brother, Rick, and me one day. She said she was very sorry, but we would spend the summer with our dad, while she located a new home for us in California. We hadn't seen him in a year, and we needed to visit. "I didn't think things would work out this way," she told us. "This is the last time we will ever move."

I hated the idea of moving again. I was 9, and I had just spent an enchanted month after school with my new best friend, Jeff, shooting BB guns in his backyard, and playing with his collection of toy cars and airplanes. Jeff was a grade ahead of me and being friends with him seemed like a special privilege.

After the rift following the discovery of the joint bank statement, Dallas left and did not return for a couple days. His absence seemed strange, and the air was grim with the sudden quiet and Mom's sullen resolve. She bought plane tickets, drove Rick to the airport, and he boarded a plane for Los Angeles to start the summer with my dad while I accompanied Mom on the drive to Northern California. She did not want to make the long drive alone, so I became her copilot, taking notes about what time we stopped for gas, the cost per gallon, how many we bought, how many miles we had traveled, which motel we stayed in, the nightly cost, plus taxes. It seemed important to document such details. I temporarily forgot about my sadness over how things were changing and enjoyed the little journey, sensing the beginning of a grand new chapter in my life — somewhere in California.

After a couple days of driving, staying in motels, and searching for the small town of Amador, where my mom had gone to high school for several years, we reached Sacramento and checked into a motel. She had gotten lost and figured Amador would be easy to find later, after I departed for L.A. I boarded a plane in Sacramento and flew south to join my brother in our dad's furnished apartment, while Mom continued her search for our new home.

Joining my dad and Rick in Los Angeles eased the sadness of leaving my friend, Jeff, in Oregon. Having not seen him in a year, his booming voice and towering presence gave me the familiar comfort and security only a father can bring.

He lived at the Holloway House Apartments in West Hollywood, a three-story building with an interior courtyard and rectangular swimming pool. He worked the graveyard shift at KLOV ("K—LOVE"), a soft rock radio station that played lots of Carpenters, Tony Orlando, Neil Diamond, Monkees, Carly Simon, and other popular artists. Every night around 11:15, we would climb into his Chrysler 300 and make the forty-minute drive to the top of the Hollywood Hills, where the radio station was located to the left, facing the world-famous HOLLYWOOD sign. From an airplane and some places on the ground, the radio station's tall antenna, with its small red light at the top, could easily be seen rising from the mountain peak.

The late-night ride in the Chrysler 300 was always exciting and filled with visual and tactile stimulation. Thick plastic bubble wrap covered the front bucket seats and back bench seat. The bubbles were too thick to pop, but they squeaked with any movement or pressure. The sticky seat covering always filled the car with a distinct odor, seemingly a mixture of Old Spice, pipe tobacco, and hydrocarbons embedded in the plastic.

After exiting the garage under the building, we'd drive uphill along the Sunset Strip, the trendy section of Hollywood with all the popular restaurants, bars, nightclubs, art galleries, and boutiques. Enormous well-lit billboards lined the right side of the Strip, ascending the mountain west. We were fascinated that at 11:30 in the evening, the sidewalks of the Strip were crowded and overflowing with people, almost all of them with long hair, wearing T-shirts and bell bottom jeans. Dad told us they were "Flower Children." They had no apparent purpose other than congregating in huge masses along the sidewalks.

About halfway up the Strip towered the billboard that entertained us the most—a mammoth sign depicting the rock band, KISS. Standing side-by-side in front of a flaming backdrop, twenty feet tall, glaring down on the street through white faces, eyes painted black, and dressed in tight black clothing with knee-high boots adorned with sparkling silver studs and spikes, they looked like menacing long-haired, demonic giants. I pictured them coming to life, jumping down, lifting our car, and hurling it back down the Strip, tumbling end over end.

One member looked particularly ominous—Gene Simmons—whose boots were mounted on long curved spikes and whose outstretched arm revealed a patch of black serrated fabric that looked like a bat's wing. His eyes were drawn to a dark evil squint, and his long, lizard-like tongue protruded from his mouth below his chin. I had never heard of the band and was baffled that their gigantic images loomed above Sunset Boulevard. Traffic moved slowly along the crowded Strip, and our eyes fixated on the soaring figures for a minute or two until they were finally behind us.

We asked our dad about KISS—who were they, why did they dress in weird clothing with shiny silver boots and wear makeup? He shrugged and said he didn't know. He thought they were lunatics.

We proceeded into Beverly Hills, passing enormous mansions with recessed lighting, and elaborately sculpted yards and landscapes. Fountains and statues decorated many yards, and we gawked at the dark and quiet opulence. This was where the movie stars lived, Dad told us, and other people involved in the movie industry: writers, directors, producers.

We left behind Beverly Hills and continued ascending the winding mountain road. The Chrysler 300 chugged harder, as Dad shifted into lower gear for the last two miles. Eventually, the overhanging trees cleared away, and we drove atop the mountain ridge, the radio station now visible on the peak not far away. We followed the road to a wide chain-link gate that crossed the narrow road. Dad would stop twenty-five feet short of the gate, get out, walk to a small keypad mounted on the left side and enter a code. The barrier would slowly swing open as he returned to the car, and we would drive through, up a few hundred feet, turn right into a parking lot, and park.

I remember thinking the slow-moving gate was useless. Anyone could easily walk around either side, though the ground was steep on the left, but not steep enough to prevent someone from taking a few steps along the edge to get around it. The entrance also stayed open for a long time after opening. What good was a gate that stayed open for two minutes? If anyone really wanted to get into the radio station, getting around the see-through obstacle would be easy. Of course, the fencing was not intended to bar the whole world from the radio station—only vehicles, a fact that escaped my young mind at the time.

We usually arrived about three or four minutes before midnight and walked through the glass door entrance to the station. The announcer working the prior shift would be in the glass booth to the left, seated at a large, green control panel operating dials, buttons, and levers. He sat behind a large microphone attached to a bendable arm that could be pushed away. A minute or so before midnight, the soft music would slowly dissolve, and the announcer would tell the audience that he had enjoyed keeping them company for the evening, but his shift was ending, and he would announce that my dad would be taking over. He would end with a pleasantry of some sort, wish the listeners a great evening, then push some buttons, and music would begin playing again.

He'd come out of the cramped compartment and happily greet us, tell my dad about a technical issue, or they'd have a little friendly small talk. He wouldn't dally long. The three of us would then have the station all to ourselves.

Across from the glass announcer booth stood a wall of reel-to-reel players, perhaps twelve reels total. The tape on the reels contained recorded music, and the reels would have to be mounted in place, and by operation of nearby controls, set to play at a designated time. When the tape on one reel was consumed entirely by another, and the tail of the tape whipped around in circles, the adjacent reel began, and only a short pause existed after the music's ending.

Dad quickly busied himself planning selections for the evening, writing on clipboards, locating reels, programming the controls on the face of the machine, and doing things in the control booth, while my brother and I watched and studied all the machinery.

Large windows adjacent to the reel-to-reel players provided a breathtaking view of the city below, revealing endless twinkling lights amid the sprawling traffic grid.

A glass door on the side of the building led to concrete walkways outside, and one night, Dad took us outside to show us the pool in the backyard of a home a couple hundred feet below. Over a row of tall cypress trees, we could look down and see pool lighting revealing the shape of an enormous aqua blue acoustic guitar glowing in the dark. Dad said it was the home of Glen Campbell, with whom I was only vaguely familiar. He seemed impressed by the guitar-shaped pool, and I liked it, also. Like the KISS billboard, I had never seen anything like it.

Around 1:30 a.m., Rick and I would get drowsy, unroll our sleeping bags in the office by the entrance, and nod off on the floor. A few minutes before 6:00 a.m., we'd hear the entrance opening and feel cold air rushing into the office. This would mean that the morning announcer had arrived, and it was time to leave. I was always slumbering so soundly that getting up to leave seemed impossible. Dad's voice would boom in the small room, and I'd will myself to stand, toss my bag over my shoulder, and shuffle like a zombie outside to the car. The morning twilight always seemed oppressive—so invasive from the dark quiet of the office in which I'd been sleeping.

Rick and I would snooze all the way back to the one-bedroom apartment, then lumber inside, drop our bags onto the floor, snuggle back into the warm, down -filled cocoons and go back to sleep. We'd wake up around eleven, and Dad would still be snoring. He'd usually rise around two in the afternoon. After he awoke, he'd make a meal, then we'd go about our day—shopping, watching movies, going to see the dinosaur skeletons at the La Brea Tar Pits or Egyptian mummies in the nearby museum, or doing any number of other activities offered by the City of Angels, until it was time to drive back up the Sunset Strip, view the thousands of Flower Children, ogle the KISS billboard, drive through Beverly Hills, and then up the mountain for another night at the station.

Rick and I felt privileged to enter the gated grounds of the radio station, roam freely, inspect all the equipment and offices, watch Dad work, and gasp at the magnificent, panoramic view of blinking lights covering the flat earth below the mountain. We were allowed to stay up much later than usual and being with Dad while he was working made us feel almost useful.

After Rick nagged Dad to take us camping, he did

some research and located a campground called Oak Flat, about fifty miles from Hollywood. He drove us there in the Chrysler 300, and we camped a couple of nights, slept on the ground in our down, zippered bags. He cooked eggs and corned beef hash on an iron camp grill in the morning, and that became our favorite breakfast for a long time.

Toward the end of summer, Dad bought us new tennis shoes, jeans and shirts, and we seemed to be living in paradise—nothing but days filled with interesting and delightful entertainment, intriguing late nights, and great food. Finally, however, summer was over, and it was time to rejoin our mother and start another school year.

Having left Oregon three days before I departed Sacramento, Rick was first to fly home. We had to keep things even, so I'd stay another three days, and there'd be no complaining about unfairness.

On the last day of my visit, I was filled with a dreary sadness and aversion to leaving. I had grown attached to my dad and wanted to stay and live with him forever in his Holloway House apartment, but it was late August, and I had no choice. I had to return to live with my mom in the new town she had located for my brother and me, four hundred miles away.

After we loaded my luggage into the car, Dad got out his Kodak camera and snapped a couple pictures of me wearing my backpack and holding a fishing pole. We'd had a lot of fun camping and fishing, and yet somehow, he had not taken enough pictures. Tears began swelling as I realized my dad would remember me from the pictures he was about to take, and I wouldn't see him again for months.

My face in the pictures showed the forced half-smile and sad eyes of a kid trying not to cry. After a few pictures, we loaded my backpack and fishing pole into the trunk with my other luggage, and I sat in the front seat of his Chrysler 300. My core was now melting from the inside, my stomach filled with odd, sickening sensations, and my throat quivered. Weakness filled my chest, neck, and arms; a crushing sadness seemed to be pressing against my face and throat, and I willed away the tears, determined not to cry in front of my dad as we drove to the airport. The entire silent drive was a titanic struggle not to burst into tears. I won't do it...I won't!

When we parked at the airport, I could not hold back anymore, and a couple tears leaked down my cheek. I quickly wiped them away, and Dad asked what was wrong. I said I had something in my eye, and he said, "Let me see." Then he pulled away my hands and looked into my eyes. I told him I thought it was gone, and he released me, concerned I actually had something in my eye. My secret was betrayed; he had seen my tears, which I insisted were caused by something in my eye that was gone now. He said nothing and got out of the car. I toughened up, wiped my face, and willed away the increasingly heavy sadness.

We walked through the parking lot, across busy traffic to the check-in counter, and surrendered my luggage and ticket. I was glum, silent. The metallic intercom voice announcing flights droned from above intermittently, and the din of airport noise distracted me—talking, footsteps, luggage thumping onto the conveyor belt, bus brakes squeaking, and planes roaring nearby.

I walked stoically with my dad to the boarding gate. Strange and preoccupied faces rushed by, worried, glowering, and pressured, as we neared the departure area.

Dad did all the talking to the attendants and ushered me to the front of the line where I was allowed to board first.

With one last powerful act of willpower, I hugged him tightly, then turned away and walked alone into the dark square tunnel.

After boarding the plane, I sat next to the window. After takeoff, I stared and watched the city shrink below and the lights fade as the plane roared into the dark sky.

As we climbed higher at a steep angle, I continued gazing out the little oval window, trying to pinpoint where my dad might be among the fading city lights, hating and resenting the increasing distance, moment-by-moment, as the plane soared higher into the night, tears streaming silently down my cheeks all the way to Sacramento on the hour-long flight.

FOLSOM

My mom and brother picked me up at the airport. Seeing her face for the first time in three months brought exhilaration and relief from the trauma of leaving my dad. She hugged me, and her voice and presence provided reassuring security that I was safe, loved, and would be okay—even without my dad.

On the way home, Mom told me about our new home—a two-bedroom condominium, and our new town, Folsom. She never did find Amador, she confessed, but after discovering Folsom, having a beer, and talking to some residents, she decided it would be perfect to start our new lives. Rick and I were going to like it there, she said. She'd found a job as a cocktail waitress at the Sutter Club, and the park also had a real zoo with monkeys, lions, wolves, exotic birds and other animals. My brother and I would have to share a room, but we'd get our own space eventually, she assured us.

Folsom was a small rural town of about six thousand, twenty-five miles east of Sacramento, just below the foothills leading to the majestic Sierra mountain range. The American River cuts through Folsom, and decades of gold dredging along its banks had produced endless acres of twenty-foot tall rock piles all over town. Pile after pile of rocks about the size of a football formed a serrated, rocky landscape in all directions. It was a simple little city with its own annual rodeo, three-block historic section, tract home neighborhoods, stores, post office, Eagles' and Elks clubs, and municipal services. The city had only four police officers on duty at any given time, and one of them had a wooden leg from the knee down as a result of stepping on a land mine in Vietnam. Ignoring any sensitivity to his disability, townspeople called him "peg leg," but only when he was not around to hear the crass moniker. At the time, four police officers were adequate to help get cats out of trees, ticket hot rods that burned rubber at stop signs, and patrol the quiet, sleeping town in the evening.

The Gold Rush in the latter half of the 19th Century brought businessmen, speculators, and fortune seekers by the tens of thousands west into California. The influx of gold miners led to an increasing need for food, clothing, tools, supplies, and raw materials that were supplied by a network of small towns all over the mountainous regions in the northern part of the state. Provisions and supplies that arrived in San Francisco were shipped east through Folsom (which was originally known as Granite City) and onward to other towns.

The city's founder, Joseph Folsom, lobbied for a railroad that would connect the town to Sacramento, turning Folsom into a hub for commerce between Sacramento and mining camps throughout the area. Granite City was later renamed Folsom in Joseph Folsom's honor.

The town's population exploded in the mid-1980s when the tech giant, Intel, came to town, and a new rush occurred—not the Gold Rush of a hundred years earlier—but the technology rush started by Steve Jobs and his company, Apple, in the 1970s. Computer chips, motherboards, and microprocessors became the gold of the 1980s and '90s. Intel produced computer chips, and the company seemed to inspire a flood of new business arrivals as soon as it began operations in Folsom. Soon the little town that had previously supported the Gold Rush, and later, gold dredging all around the city, was now supporting the high-tech industry, which was growing rapidly worldwide.

The somewhat awkward pride of the town was Folsom Prison, built in 1880 and made popular by Johnny Cash's 1955 hit song, *Folsom Prison Blues.* Prisoners quarried granite nearby and built the prison with large blocks stacked twenty-feet high, forming the prison's thick outer wall that descended across the grassy landscape toward the rocky, vertical banks of the American River. A guard tower with tinted windows rose from the granite prison wall, and guards inside could watch us climbing rocks at the river or walking toward the prison—if we dared.

The prison was nestled a mile from City Hall behind low smooth hills, hidden from view. A two-lane road snaked through the oak trees and hills leading to the prison's entrance—an ominous granite wall encasing a heavy iron gate.

Many people who lived in the city worked at the prison. They could be seen around town before or after work in green polyester pants with black stripes on the sides, black work boots, and white T-shirts. The tan work shirt would be put on last before work and removed first afterward, almost as if the shirt itself was too stifling to wear at any time they were not on prison grounds. They'd stop frequently at the Circle K convenience store a mile from the prison and get a soda or snack. They never seemed happy; they were on their way to join the company of murderers, rapists, drug dealers, wife beaters, child molesters, or had just left them, and in either case, going to or leaving the job usually left them cheerless.

The town had one main thoroughfare for most of the businesses—East Bidwell Street—which wrapped around the high school and went straight to Highway 50 a few miles away. At one end, near the high school, was a cluster of businesses on opposite corners. Behind the gas station stood a Lucky Supermarket and Bank of America, and across the street on the corner, an El Dorado Savings. Next to the El Dorado, a grocery store called the Farmer's Market welcomed local shoppers, flanked by a long row of storefronts: Handley's, which sold 'western wear'—boots, jeans, belts, and shirts—then down further, a Pioneer Hardware, Goodell's Liquor Store, and a tiny bar called The Bank Club, among other assorted small retail businesses. Across the street, surrounded by a parking lot, stood the Lake Bowl—a bowling alley with a small, dark bar adjacent to the entrance and a tiny game room alcove on one side filled with pinball machines and an exit with glass doors.

Next to the bowling alley was an Orbit gas station—a white concrete monstrosity that resembled an enormous crown with several pointed spires rising at low angles from a core. It was an homage to the rocket age, a 1960s version of the future, but it looked starkly out of place in this otherwise ordinary rural town.

On the next block was the town's only drug store, named Sprouse-Reitz.

Other than the A&W, a hamburger and root beer franchise, there were no fast-food chain restaurants, Mexican or Thai restaurants, steakhouses, Indian food, movie theaters, malls or skating rinks. Sutter Street had a Chinese restaurant called the Hop Sing Palace that had been there since the late '50s, and a block from the high school was a hamburger diner called the Big Dip. At the bottom of Sutter Street, shaded by mulberry trees, stood another small hamburger joint—the Buckboard. That was the town.

Just down the road a few miles was Aerojet, an industrial facility that made rocket fuel and parts for intercontinental ballistic missiles beginning in the 1940s.

In 1959, a swath of new three-bedroom tract homes was built in Folsom, providing Aerojet employees with housing and a short drive to work. Loud engine tests were conducted a few times a day that could be heard all over—a sudden, startling burst of immense roaring that made windows rattle, then stopped suddenly a few seconds later. The abrupt blaring engine tests assured the town that the nation's security was in the process of being tested and improved, just down the road.

Folsom itself had no industry in 1975. Other than

the infamy of the prison and the nearby industry of Aerojet, Folsom's gem was its annual rodeo, which drew several thousand to the Dan Russell Arena every Fourth of July. The city unified with civic pride as it welcomed rodeo and carnival fans, who showed up and filled the area. Sutter Street swelled with cowboys and out-of-towners, who crowded the sidewalks and filled the bars until the early morning hours.

The Big Dip, Buckboard, and A&W stayed busy from afternoon until closing during the rodeo. Retail and convenience stores experienced an uptick in business, and every night cars lined the residential streets for several blocks around the park, and a steady stream of rodeo fans filed along the sidewalks on their way to the entrance. At night when the rodeo ended, people returned to their cars, flooding the streets and sidewalks, and the two-lane streets remained gridlocked until midnight.

The city's small zoo and animal sanctuary in the park adjacent to the rodeo arena added an exotic and unusual big city element to the small town. Tourists arrived from other towns just to see the animals and barbecue in the nearby park.

The park stretched behind Folsom City Hall and contained two Little League fields, bleachers, a playground sharing a fence with the zoo, and a section of old pine and evergreen trees that provided large patches of shade at the picnic tables scattered below. Fabled and heroic contests were settled on the baseball fields among Folsom's greatest players of the time—Kenny Nolan, Curt Schaffer, Mark Ryland, and many others. After games, both teams piled into pickup trucks and drove three blocks to the Big Dip for ice cream cones, most of which were dipped in a hot chocolate sauce that quickly froze around the vanilla dessert. The first couple bites off the tip of the cone were always sweet and rich with chocolate flavor, then after the chocolate hardened, the remaining bites tasted like cold candle wax. Most ate the cone and never complained about the vanishing flavor of the chocolate coating.

A miniature train rolled behind the Little League fields, beyond the outfield fences, toward a large grassy section of the park which had a gazebo flanked by several tall evergreen and eucalyptus trees. The tiny train passed the gazebo, made a U-turn by the city street corner bordering the park, then returned behind the Little League field and ventured into the hills toward the prison. The train's authentic steam engine emitted an unmistakable whistle that could be heard a mile from the park.

Accompanying the rodeo every year came a carnival, which was set up in the park next to the zoo. Several eighteen-wheel trucks were unloaded and two days later the carnival rides and booths seemed to rise in the park suddenly, like a patch of wild mushrooms that bloomed overnight. Bumper cars, a roller-coaster, Ferris wheel, and a ride called the "Zipper" presented the main attractions. A strange-looking contraption, the Zipper stood vertically and supported an oblong oval of small carriages that it hoisted into the air and pulled along a track, rotating and spinning them 360 degrees, then changing directions and spinning as the carriage whirled in a loop.

A firework show started every night of the rodeo around 9:45, when the intense July heat had dropped a few degrees. All over the city, people lit fireworks in the streets. Sparklers danced in the dark, and an assortment of other flaming, sparking fireworks whizzed, buzzed, bounced, smoked, popped, and exploded until well after midnight, leaving the streets covered with a lingering haze of acrid smoke.

The animals in the zoo invariably grew upset by all the commotion and fireworks and collectively protested with shrieks and groans, while monkeys shook cages, wolves howled, lions roared, and disturbed birds wailed and squawked. Their remonstrations were drowned out by screams of kids on the whirling rides and blaring carnival music.

Ten miles west on Highway 50, nuclear-armed B-52 bombers constantly landed and took off from Mather Air Force Base. Every hour or two, the mammoth winged bombers whined across the sky a mere thousand feet above the city on approach to land, the blaring growing louder and unsettling, as if bolts and welds were straining not to shatter. As they approached the city, the distinct, high-pitched droning of the jet engines always blotted out all other sound, drawing attention to the sky. With the daily, repeated engine tests a few miles away at Aerojet and the endless noisy flights of B-52 bombers shattering all peace and quiet from above, there was always an underlying reminder of the tension of the Cold War and the threat of nuclear disaster.

The presence of the prison added a somewhat creepy, unsafe feeling, as the town faced not only threats from the sky, but the worrying possibility of a prison break—hundreds of wild-eyed, dirty prisoners, rampaging through the streets, pillaging and plundering, or so I imagined.

As if all that were not enough to cause concern, every day at noon, air raid sirens mounted on twenty-foot poles blasted across town from schoolyards announcing the arrival of the noon hour. In truth, the purpose of the sirens was to warn of a prison break, but they were tested every day to ensure proper functioning. Like the sudden engine tests from Aerojet, the sirens were jarring. The rising pitch of the alarm had an unsettling psychological effect that made hiding in a concrete bunker seem necessary. A simple bell or whistle would probably have been sufficient, but someone decided siren tests would mark the noon hour.

No one talked about these things. They were just felt, experienced, and normalized until they existed somewhere beneath actual consciousness. People grew accustomed to the presence of the prison and overhead flights of B-52 bombers and engine testing at Aerojet, and it was all a normal part of life in Folsom.

Historic Sutter Street had been preserved so that the building façades and most of the interiors resembled their appearance from one hundred years earlier. Various businesses occupied both sides of the old town road—an art gallery, antique shops, a pizza parlor called The Golden Rail, and Patsy's Soda Parlor—one of the gems—a '50s-style soda parlor with a long counter, round pink stools, and wrought iron tables and chairs.

Across the street from Patsy's was the Sutter Club—a long, narrow bar with a tiny stage that played vaudeville theater—damsels in distress attempting to elude mustached villains who laughed and lurked about the tiny stage.

Down the street on the corner, the Folsom Hotel had a long, wood-paneled bar with walls and ceilings covered with all kinds of relics and artifacts—pictures, posters, musical instruments, stuffed animal heads, guns, bear traps, boat oars, and neon signs. The wood floors creaked with every step and a small dance floor across from the bar provided just enough room for a dozen or so dancers on the weekends. And, of course, it was said to be haunted upstairs by two ghosts.

Downhill from the hotel, beyond a couple curves in the road, arched the Rainbow Bridge. Built in 1919, it provided a stable path over the American River and led to Folsom Auburn Road and the more affluent section of town, where large, two-story homes were shaded under patches of oak and pine trees on quarter acre plots in the low rolling hills of the Valley Pines neighborhood.

Folsom Dam provided the other path across the river. It had been completed in 1955, resulting in Folsom Lake, a convenient summer destination for residents and out-of-towners alike.

Driving across the dam, the brooding walls and

towers of Folsom Prison could be seen below in the distance adjacent to the American River.

Folsom was my new home. We had the prison, zoo, annual rodeo, bowling alley, and rock piles to explore, and whether I liked it or not, I would have to start over and again make new friends.

ROOTS

My dad was born and raised in Chicago and had lived through the Great Depression. His mother came to America on a boat from Ireland, and his father from Spain, but a birth certificate indicated Grandpa had been born in Honduras—an inconsistency that was never explained. Apparently, my grandmother had been concerned that revealing my grandfather's true origin would cause problems or result in discrimination, so saying he was from Spain—part of Europe—seemed to solve the concern.

My grandfather spoke Spanish as his first language, but he never taught a word of it to my dad. My Irish grandmother forbade him from doing so—again, part of the effort to suppress his native origins. She decided her children would read, write, and speak English well and earn their livings as white-collar professionals, not as blue-collar laborers, like my grandfather. Although he had no formal education, he became a skilled electrician and worked for General Electric, troubleshooting electrical problems in large industrial settings. He viewed education as the ticket out of the lower social classes and a life of hard labor.

Valuing education more than job skills, my grandfather religiously oversaw the completion of my dad's homework and strictly enforced his expectation that his two sons achieve excellent grades. There was no negotiating about putting off homework for another day. Schoolwork was the first priority, and it was completed every evening after dinner, end of discussion.

My dad was still in school when the Japanese bombed Pearl Harbor on December 7, 1941. After graduating, he volunteered for military service and joined the Marine Corps. Following an assessment, he was sent to the Japanese language school, where he learned to read and write Japanese and became an interpreter, rising to the rank of corporal.

When the Marines invaded the Japanese-held island of Iwo Jima on February 19, 1945, my dad was among them, though he went ashore on the twentieth. He told the story of how he boarded the landing craft from the larger ship miles offshore and rode across the choppy sea toward the island. As the landing craft approached, mortar shells began exploding nearby. The boat operator was experienced and avoided the bombs by zigzagging the craft, knowing that the Japanese were trying to time the shells, anticipating the path of the boat. When the craft steered to the right, a mortar shell would explode on the left; when it steered left, an explosion occurred to the right. This zigzag process of avoiding detonations continued almost to the shore.

When the landing craft made it to the island, the front gate fell, and the Marines rushed ashore. The beach was a hellscape of overturned boats and vehicles, floating in the surf or stuck in the sand, dead Marines scattered everywhere, and nothing but mangled, cratered earth, smoking from explosions and fire, filling the air with an acrid stench.

My dad labored across the deep, black, volcanic sand and dove for cover as bombs began exploding on the beach. When he looked up, he saw inches from his face a numbered mortar stake—placed in the ground by the Japanese and calibrated so that a mortar could be fired from far away and hit the marker. He immediately jumped up, ran from the stake and eventually made it off the beach and found a secure area. He remained on the island for weeks, interrogating Japanese prisoners of war and translating captured documents.

He had told my brother and me these stories when we were little, five and eight—because after seeing war movies, we badgered him with questions. We were fascinated and wanted to hear more. War seems to intrigue anyone who has never experienced it, especially kids. He picked us up one day to take us somewhere, and as soon as we got into the car, we started asking enthusiastically, "Tell us a war story, Dad. Yeah, tell us another! Did you see anyone get shot?"

My Dad's anger flared. "Don't you ever want to talk about anything besides war?" he asked, glowering at both of us.

Rick and I went silent.

After a painful pause, he continued. "There's nothing fun or glorious about war; it's about killing and complete destruction, and that's all. Period. Watching people get blown to pieces is not some kind of amusement or entertainment—it's horrifying beyond words. These war movies you've been watching that make war look like strategy in a football game are a lot of nonsense. Everyone's scared in war and trying not to get killed. Some men perform heroic acts of courage and bravery, but it's to save other men from getting killed, not to stand on the beach in glory, chomping on a cigar, and looking like a tough guy."

We remained quiet.

"Ask questions about something else. I don't want to talk about the war anymore."

He drove in silence for a while after that, and we never asked him any questions about the war for a long time—until decades later when we were young adults, and *he* brought up the topic.

After the war, he went to college on the G.I. Bill, earned a degree in philosophy and, somewhat anticlimactically, became a sales representative for a series of large manufacturing companies in the Chicago-Detroit area. However, he soon discovered Shakespeare and found his life's artistic passion for acting. He became a trained and skilled Shakespearean actor, appeared in numerous Shakespeare plays, and even made a few short appearances on television in the '70s, '80s, and '90s. His involvement with the theater led naturally to a career in radio, and he became a radio announcer in Los Angeles in the 1970s. He disc-jockeyed for several years, and later did lots of voice-over work for radio and TV commercials. His deep, melodious voice was featured in commercials for the Ford Motor Company, Travelers Insurance, Budweiser beer, and hundreds of regional and local companies that wanted your trust.

With my dad, they had the voice to earn it.

He sported a goatee in the 1960s and later realized this may have limited his acting opportunities, as he revealed to me when I was older that his acting auditions always seemed to be for the role of a Hispanic character. He had gone to an audition for an acting role in the '70s and said it looked like a "Tijuana bus stop." All the other actors auditioning for the role were Hispanic. He wondered at the time whether he was being excluded from mainstream acting roles for Caucasians due to the obvious ethnic appearance presented by the goatee because, despite his Hispanic origin, he looked white in all other respects. Although that look was appropriate for occasional acting roles, a clean-shaven visage was much more common throughout the '60s. Nonetheless, he chose not to give it up. He wore the goatee well, with a handsome blend of Spanish and Irish, and he continued with it for the rest of his life, unless an acting role required him to shave.

My dad's commitment to Shakespeare took him and my mom to Ashland, Oregon, in 1962 for the Oregon Shakespeare Festival. As it was explained to me, at least on the west coast, the Oregon Shakespeare Festival was the event that tested the true mettle of stage performers. Real actors, those with a commitment to the stage and Shakespeare, went to Ashland to hone their skills and learn the true craft of acting. My dad's strong bias for Shakespeare was never hidden. All other theater was judged against it, but that was his penchant.

Dad auditioned for the Ashland Shakespeare Festival and was accepted. At the time, however, he did not land any major leading roles, but he did appear on stage in several plays.

Following a summer of Shakespeare, Dad returned to L.A., where he continued his acting career in earnest. His goal was to be cast in television and movie roles, while appearing periodically on stage. The key to getting cast in a movie, commercial, or TV show, according to my dad, was having a good agent. He seemed sure not having the right one had held him back. I didn't know much about his representative, I just expected to see him on TV or in the movies someday.

Over the years, I continued to hope Dad's commitment to acting and his persistence would lead to a TV commercial or a little part in a movie, eventually escalating into a flourishing acting career, but it never did.

After she dyed her hair blonde, my mom was frequently compared to Marilyn Monroe. Her face was attractive and well-proportioned with large, pale blue eyes, full cheeks, and a broad smile. Her personality was full of warmth, friendliness, intelligence, and she had a wide, articulate vocabulary, accompanied by a quick-witted sense of humor, and a hearty laugh. She was a natural social butterfly, talkative, interesting, concerned, knowledgeable, entertaining, and engaging. There was not a shred of pretense or haughtiness anywhere in her being; she could be friends with the janitor or company president; social rank and pedigree never impressed her. Personality and character mattered most.

She was a talented painter and could draw lifelike portraits, which always amazed me. Her literacy was elevated, having read numerous classics from the giants, and she churned through current novels constantly, month after month. She loved plants, and for a decade, was determined to provide a home to large green ferns which always seemed to struggle indoors, turn brown, then wither and die after a couple months. Cats and dogs were her favorite four-legged creatures, and she never was without at least one of each, often two or more. The dogs and cats fared much better and lasted much longer than the ferns and other plants.

My mom was born in Detroit and was part of a well-established family that supposedly owned a large retail company. This business was apparently well-established in the Midwest, and Mom told Rick and me stories about going to holiday dinners at a relative's estate, where dinner was served in a large, ornate banquet room, servants bringing successive courses to the long dinner table after being summoned by the press of a button under the table by the matriarch at the far end. It sounded like something out of *Jane Eyre* and always intrigued me.

The connection to the flourishing business went

through my mom's father who, unfortunately, struggled with alcohol abuse and died of cirrhosis of the liver in his mid-fifties. My grandfather, on my mom's side, was supposedly a genius who never achieved his full potential. After he died, my mom chose to move to California. She had done some college, but apparently there was little opportunity for her anywhere in the family business, and she had no strong connections with any remaining family in the Detroit area.

The move to California was also a sort of ultimatum to my dad. Mom and Dad had been dating for a while, but there had been no marriage proposal, so Mom forced the issue by moving to California, which caused Dad to propose.

They were married in Los Angeles around 1960; Mom found a job in a bank, and my dad began in earnest his acting career, searching for stage, TV and movie roles. JFK soon was elected president, the Red Scare of the '40s and '50s was mostly over, but the Cold War still smoldered and would reach a boiling point in October 1962 during the Cuban Missile Crisis.

My brother had been born only a few months before President John F. Kennedy was assassinated in Dallas, Texas, on November 22, 1963.

Mom and Dad never believed the official version from the Warren Commission that some oddball former Marine named Lee Harvey Oswald shot and killed Kennedy. They lived through the event, watched all the aftermath, and concluded that the official version was wrong. Though much controversy remained, JFK's assassination seemed to become old, irrelevant news, like a fact you learn and remember in case a question about it shows up on a history test or a round of Jeopardy.

While my dad thought spending all his time pursuing a career as a Shakespearean actor was best for him, my mom was well aware that his career path was not well suited for raising a family. Performing as a stage actor a few times a year in productions of Shakespeare meant getting home at midnight after rehearsal in L.A. two or three nights a week and sleeping until 10:00 a.m., leaving my mom to get up early and deal with two young children. She'd be stuck with all the stress and challenge of managing two youngsters, while my dad chased his acting dreams, free from domestic responsibilities. This arrangement did not foster much passion or goodwill—especially with bills piling up. My mom dreaded the long-term consequences and implications of my dad's career choice—long stretches of unemployment and financial hardship. Initially, she supported his ambition, but reality eventually forced itself upon his aspirations, causing friction in their marriage.

They divorced after nine years of unfulfilled acting dreams and ongoing financial pressures. I had never noticed any defects in my dad's parenting, but I was only five when they divorced. Mom later explained that Dad had skewed views about gender roles. Having been born in 1925 and lived with his mother as a 'guest' in her home until he was 33, my dad was not accustomed to performing household chores. Cooking and housework were 'women's work,' so he believed, probably because that's how it was in 1935 when Dad was 10. Men worked full-time jobs, and women took care of the house and children.

Mom grew up during the same era, when men and women had clearly-defined social responsibilities, but she was frustrated that Dad did not provide more support and help with my brother and me. She thought his escape from helping with domestic chores was ridiculous and unfair but, more important, the ongoing financial insecurity was unbearable.

Though he never discussed or considered the possibility, I think my dad suffered from Post-Traumatic Stress Disorder from his war experiences. He told me he stayed drunk for a lot of years after the war. That was the only coping mechanism for returning World War II veterans. When he finally talked about the war after I was an adult, he broke down when he mentioned witnessing the mortar shelling of the small volcanic beach at Iwo Jima, where landing craft had just unloaded hundreds of Marines. He was sure no one could have survived the horrific bombing, as numerous exploding shells saturated the area.

He never sought a moment of counseling, took prescription medication, or attended support groups, but he drank Scotch Whiskey nightly for many years.

I suspect my dad's PTSD may have affected his views about 9 to 5 work. He was not cut out to be a company man, though he had been one for a decade after college. He never liked the daily work routine; he was a night owl, which is why working graveyard at the radio station was a good fit. He didn't like performing mindless, inane, repetitive tasks. He was intelligent and creative and enjoyed having freedom to make choices about the content of his work, and enjoyed putting his 'personal touch' into whatever he did. He was not a bohemian, but he was certainly an individual who followed his own drum beat.

Though I'd never experienced the horrors of war, I'd eventually learn I was a lot like him.

Dad did the best he could as a long-distance father. He always paid his support obligations and flew up to visit my brother and me a couple times a year, mailed us money and presents for our birthdays and Christmas, and recorded oral letters on cassette tapes, which we played in our bedroom, then made and mailed back tapes of our own. Hearing his voice for a half hour discuss questions we had asked and learning about his work and life brought much comfort and a sense of personal connection we could not otherwise experience. He never became bitter toward my mom over the divorce, and without exception, one of the last sentences he would utter at the end of a tape was "Be obedient to your mother, and God bless you." Though I did not see him daily, weekly or even monthly, he remained a strong influence in my life and source of great pride and inspiration.

BLANCHE SPRENTZ

I was dreading the prospect of starting class and being the new kid again.

"Let's go for a drive and see your new school," my mom announced a few days before the start of fifth grade.

We got into the green Chevy station wagon and drove ten blocks to the Blanche Sprentz Elementary School. I later learned that Blanche Sprentz was an educator who dedicated her life to teaching and mentoring students in Folsom. She was so beloved that the city named an elementary school after her in 1966.

Knowing nothing about Blanche Sprentz, I thought our new elementary school was a foreboding place—a large, blocky structure covered with brick and concrete tiles. In the front, evergreen shrubs hugged the walls and bordered sidewalks. The grounds were terraced; the administration building and fifth grade classes were on the parking level, then a flight of stairs led to the playgrounds and one-story building that housed the classrooms for sixth graders.

A square section of asphalt with painted white lines provided territory for various games. A large field for soccer and football loomed at the far side of the campus. Basketball courts were also in the back, below the classrooms, adjacent to and below the soccer field.

We pulled up to the front of the building. "Here's

your new school," my mom said. "It's not that far. You can walk. Aren't you excited?"

"This is really far," I protested. "Can't we take the bus?"

"You're walking. It's not that far."

"I don't want to go to a new school," I groaned.

"I'm sorry. You can make new friends."

I slunk down in the back seat and sulked. I did not want to meet new kids and certainly did not want to walk ten blocks every morning. The previous year I had gone to school in Oregon in a tiny building that had been built in the '30s or '40s. The classrooms were constructed from wood and painted white, and the administration office resembled a chapel from a Clint Eastwood movie. Fourth and fifth grades were combined into one classroom, and the entire student body was no more than a hundred kids. Now we would be going to a large, modern school. The bland architecture had the look and feel of an institution—impersonal, indifferent, merely functional—it almost seemed as if we were now going into a large factory for some type of formal processing—perhaps brainwashing, and I didn't like it.

Missing my dad and Jeff, I showed up sad and depressed for my first day of fifth grade, and the experience was even lower than my expectations. As I walked into the class, this punk kid, Craig Cadigan, who already knew everyone, stared at me as I entered. When I stopped and looked for an empty desk, he pointed and said in a very mean, sarcastic tone, "If you're looking for a desk, there's one right there!"

Then he pushed the desk violently with both hands, causing it to slide forward and crash into the desk in front of it. I said nothing and sat. I hated him and thought maybe he'd call me out to fight because I was the new kid, as had happened the year previously in Oregon. I was ready, but he never did.

I hated my new environment, was sad and sulked for a long time.

During the first week, as my brother and I walked in the mornings, a group of six or seven boys on bicycles would gather and wait for us to walk up the last half block to school.

"You look like a queer!" They shouted at my brother and me. "Fags!" Then they laughed. This was one of the biggest insults available to a kid. The vocabulary was different back then, and certainly less politically correct. One of the boys gathered a couple redwood chips from a yard, rode by, and threw them at us, sneering as he rode away, "Faggots!" We ignored them. Sometimes the taunting returned after school, but it was usually in the morning, as everyone was walking or riding bicycles, fresh and full of obnoxious energy.

One morning, a kid rode his bicycle directly at my brother, then jumped off and pushed the bicycle toward him, allowing it to coast. The kids called it 'ghost riding'. The bike narrowly missed him and crashed onto the sidewalk. The situation seemed to be escalating; violence was imminent.

Within a day or two, Rick informed me that Darin Holtz had called him out. Darin was supposedly the toughest kid in sixth grade, and for whatever reasons, he wanted to fight my brother. Rick accepted the challenge and met his foe after class at the appointed location. They fought, and Rick won. He told me about the confrontation after school and said he had beaten the toughest kid in the school. He seemed proud.

I thought Rick's defeat of Darin Holtz would end the confrontations, but Darin called him out again. He accepted the callout a second time and beat him up once more. Now the matter was settled, and instead of fighting, the two of them began taking fishing trips together. Rick was instantly transformed from the kid others hated to the one everyone liked and wanted to befriend. He gladly accepted the attention and basked in his newfound adulation.

I was still in a funk. I was sad and sick and tired of broken connections. I sulked through class every day, came home and moped around, wishing my mom and dad would get back together.

Soon we discovered the Simons family on the other side of the fence in the backyard of our new condo. It was nice having new friends on the other side of the fence.

Mike Ryan lived across the street. He was the same age as Rick, and they instantly became friends.

We were in the living room at my mom's condo one afternoon when a dispute arose whether I should be included in some activity my brother and Mike had planned. I wanted to go, but Rick wanted me to stay home. After some squabbling, Mike joined the discussion and questioned my brother about his reluctance to bring me. Rick didn't want a tagalong three years younger. He felt I would be dead weight. Mike said, "I'd be proud if Ben were my little brother." Rick went silent, not willing to continue the attack in the face of Mark's support. That's how things would be left.

I felt exalted and euphoric that this big older kid had stood up to my brother and defended me. It was the first time in my life it happened, and Rick never again insulted or criticized me in front of Mike.

Even with Mike's courageous stand that boosted my self-esteem, I was still slow to adapt to my new surroundings.

I told my neighbor Mike Simons, who was my age, I missed my dad and asked what he would do if his dad lived four hundred miles away. He said he would call him. That seemed like the most obvious and reasonable conclusion. Back in those days, the telephone company charged extra for long distance phone calls, and I was not allowed to make one without permission from my mom. I broke the rule and called my dad one afternoon after school. He picked up after a few rings.

"Hello," he said groggily.

"Hi, Dad."

"...Ben, is that you?"

"Yes."

After some muffled rustling, he said, "It's 2:30 in the afternoon. Why are you calling?"

"I wanted to talk to you."

My dad's voice was gruff, and he sounded

disoriented.

"I appreciate that, and I'm glad you called, but I wish you would call in the evening when I'm awake. I was sleeping."

"Oh, I'm sorry."

"It's okay; you didn't know, but from now on, please call in the evening."

"Ok, I will."

"What did you want to talk about?"

"Um, do you think you and mom can get back together?"

"I don't think so, son."

"Why?"

"Your mother's not in love with me anymore."

"Why not?"

"We've been divorced a long time," he said wearily. "We had some disagreements during our marriage, problems, financial pressure. She was unhappy, and we got divorced. That's how it goes sometimes."

"I think you and mom should get married again."

He paused and then said slowly, "I'm sorry to tell you that I doubt that is going to happen."

"I just wish you lived with us," I pleaded.

"I wish I did, too, son. Life doesn't always work out the way you want. Sometimes you just have to do your best and move on. I miss you and your brother, but there's nothing I can do about the circumstances. Do you understand?"

"Yes."

"Okay, good. I'm going back to sleep now. I have

to work tonight. If you'd like to talk some more about this, call me tomorrow evening around 7 p.m. Okay?"

"Ok."

I hung up and felt bad for waking him up but glad to hear his voice.

I remained sad and depressed.

Back in my fifth grade class, I gained some acceptance by participating in sports. During recess, the boys played kickball on the asphalt section of the playground. When I wasn't wandering alone, thinking about my dad and Jeff, I began playing kickball with the other kids. I was a good player, and kids respected that.

One nice thing about my new school was the morning 'nutrition break.' Around 10:00 a.m., the class was released for fifteen minutes. An ice cream cart was wheeled to the back of the administration building, and Crunch Bars, ice cream sandwiches, fudgesicles, and popsicles could be purchased for a dime. I'd try to scrounge change every morning to buy a Crunch Bar. I never told my mom; she would have disapproved of ice cream in the morning.

During spring, our teacher, Ms. Taynton, took the class to the playground for a little competition. Ms. Taynton was a skinny, tan, short-haired woman who always dressed fashionably, often in orange and yellow colors and frequently with matching scarves tied around her neck, and ankle boots with zippers on the insides. She drove a sparkly blue Corvette and seemed cool and stylish.

One day, she announced we were going to have a

pull-up contest, boys versus girls. She took the class outside, where we circled around the pull-up bars, and she began calling names. One by one, girls stepped to the bar and attempted pull-ups. Most could do none or one, but one, Tracy Rouse, had arms of a little gymnast, and she stepped up and quickly did six. We were all impressed, and the boys were somewhat alarmed. The girls were now leading by a humiliating margin.

The girls finished, and Ms. Taynton began calling the boys, who showed they were no better. No one could do more than a single pull-up. Finally, it was my turn, and I jumped up to the bar, quickly cranked out five pull-ups, struggled on a sixth, and released, hanging there. We needed one more to win. The boys gathered around me as I hung on the bar, and they all began screaming and hollering encouragement. I knew I had one more in me, so I pulled and heaved and slowly raised my chin above the bar. All the boys jumped and screamed with triumph and jubilation after I reached the top for the seventh pull-up. The boys had won the contest, and I had saved their honor, despite their poor performance.

I felt like a hero for a moment.

A day or two later, Ms. Taynton announced that boys and girls would compete in chair push-ups. She again called off names, and kids stepped to a wooden chair, placed their palms on the front corners and their feet against the wall, then leaned down, touching their chests on the seat of the chair and pushing back up. Boys and girls did equally poorly for a while. When it was my turn, I did thirty-three, shattering the competition.

With better than average physical performances, my stature in the class rose. Craig Cadigan never bothered me again, and no one sneered, insulted or challenged me. Still I remained despondent and somewhat of an outsider among my classmates—in my own mind. During recess, I sometimes watched other kids playing and having fun—the way I used to with Jeff. They all seemed so comfortable around each other. They'd go home after school and see their dads, and I'd go home to an empty condo and think about the summer I had spent with mine and wish he lived with us.

As days and weeks ground by, I continued hating the transition to my new school in Folsom. One thing that gave me some optimism was the approaching baseball season. Little League was where heroes and legends were made, at least in my mind. I was shocked to learn that Little League in this new town had only four teams: The Braves, Phillies, 49ers, and Angels. The prior year in Oregon, the league had about twelve teams, maybe more. In Folsom, each team played the others four times for a total of sixteen games. I wondered whether being in a league with only four teams would be as fun and competitive as the prior year. After I received my brand-new baseball uniform, however, my disappointments vanished, and I became eager to suit up, take the field, and begin swatting line drives.

Little League was always the best time of year. It was a simple but endlessly fun game: wallop a ball with a hard stick as far as possible, then run across three bags aligned on the points of the infield square and finish on the rubber 'home plate' to score runs.

The shape and appearance of the Little League field were mesmerizing. A manicured playing field was a beautiful sight—the grass infield with a dirt pitcher's mound in the center between the bases, the dirt base path bounded by a half-circle border leading to the grassy outfield, and two hundred feet away the five-foot fence interspersed with sections of advertising from local businesses.

All the fencing, bleachers, the two dugouts on the first and third baselines, and the chain-link backstop that enclosed the batter's box, gave the field a unique 'arena' feeling. When filled, the bleachers flanking opposite sides of the baselines upped the anticipation to a sort of Roman Coliseum atmosphere, where opponents would enter and compete for the crowds. Even the dirt had a special scent—not just ordinary dirt, but soft soil mixed with clay, often watered before games, giving off a unique odor.

Likewise, the soft grass was always thick, dark green and sweetly fragrant. The bright white chalk lines along the first and third base lines added a third distinct odor, the dryness of the chalk often mixing with the dirt and clay to complete the magical, aromatic potpourri of the Little League diamond.

I viewed the uniform as a status symbol and form of identity. The unique, sporty attire made us part of a group, club, or tribe, almost literally—the 'Braves,' 'Indians,' 'Pirates.' Baseball players were sleek, agile, quick, and demonstrated amazing hand-eye coordination, snatching up grounders and rifling the ball to first base, or smacking line drives into the outfield. I wanted to be that kid. I respected those kids.

Cartoon superheroes wore their own special body suits, so the way I saw it, wearing a uniform naturally increased my capabilities. This was magical thinking of a child, but I accepted it and allowed it to guide my performance; no one ever tried to convince me otherwise.

Like the Oregon league, Folsom had tryouts, a Saturday morning session where all the players went through batting, fielding, and throwing exercises to be judged by the coaches. It was essentially a draft, and the coaches marked clipboards, deciding which players they wanted. I was chosen by Gordon Humes, coach of the Braves.

Gordon was a tall, broad-shouldered, quiet man with a patch of thin brown hair that seemed to float and recede from his forehead. His mustache grew around the corners of his mouth, and my mom thought he was 'foxy.' He wore T-shirts and jeans, and a watch pressed through the hair on his right wrist (he was left-handed). He always wore square-lensed, frameless, dark brown sunglasses, and he was soft-spoken to the point of seeming almost sedated.

The season started with a parade. The four teams piled into the back of pickup trucks and El Caminos decorated with signs, balloons, ribbons, and flags, and drove from the city park through town, horns honking, kids waving to people on the sidewalks, and returned to the park after twenty minutes. Two teams faced each other for a game, then after a break, the two remaining teams played, and the first round of Little League season was in the books.

There was just so much wrapped up in the game—the excitement of the competition pitch-by-pitch, the clink of the bat on a line drive, the dusty slide into home plate, the uniforms—a very special privilege, and all the friendships and camaraderie of being part of a team. It was character defining at the time.

My coach lived down the street and around the corner. He told the team to meet him at the Theodore Judah Elementary School at 4:00 in the afternoon to practice a couple times a week. About three doors down the street, the tenant's front yard was covered with large white rocks, about the size of an egg. For unknown reasons, a dozen or more rocks were always on the sidewalk and street in front of this condo. It was as if someone had taken a small bucket and just dumped the rocks into the street. When I walked to practice, I'd stop and put all the rocks back in the yard. In a day or two, they'd be back scattered in the street.

Gordon saw me walking home from practice one

day, pulled over and told me to jump in the back of his truck. A couple kids from my team were already there. When he learned where I lived, he instructed me to report to his house before practice and wait, and he would give me a ride there and back. That was nice, and it saved me about twenty minutes of walking.

Winning was serious business back in those days. Unfortunately, we finished second, behind the 49ers (*a strange name for a baseball team*, I thought). Even so, Little League brought much joy, competition and friendship.

I had wanted to play on Mike Simons' team, the Phillies. His dad was the coach, we were neighbors, and playing on the same Little League team seemed like a natural way to further our friendship, but Gordon had selected me to join the Braves. My disappointment at not joining Mike's team quickly dwindled as I settled in with my new team.

After the season started, Mike was visiting one day after school and noticed the game schedule on the refrigerator door, held by a magnet. It was early in the season, and I had spent some time calculating whether our team could win first place. I had gone down the schedule and predicted whether we would win or lose games and marked a W or L next to the date for each contest. I never intended to show my predictions to anyone; they were only my personal hopes and expectations hanging on the refrigerator.

Mike saw the schedule, walked up to it and noticed the win and loss markings. He saw the W next to the game in the future when the Braves played the

Phillies. He seemed shocked and offended.

"How do you know your team is going to win? We haven't played yet," he asked incredulously.

Awkward embarrassment now hung in the air. "I don't know, I just think we'll win. I think we have a better team," I said.

Those were nearly fighting words.

Mike laughed, "No way, I think we're better."

"We'll see next week."

"I don't see how you can mark a win for a game that hasn't been played yet," he protested again.

"Well, the Angels beat you guys last week, and we beat the Angels, so we should be able to beat you."

"That was a close game. We only lost by one run."

I shrugged.

"Our team has a lot of good players," I said.

"So does ours. Kenny Nolan, Donald Withers, Jack Martin."

"We'll see next week."

I hadn't wanted to argue about my predictions, but he discovered the schedule and now I had to defend them.

"We'll see," he agreed.

We dropped the debate and went on to something else. He was clearly soured by my prediction, but it was too late to take it back.

He was right about one thing: they had Kenny Nolan, who was three inches taller than everyone and thirty pounds heavier. He was an outstanding pitcher as well as a reliable power hitter, and not considering his participation had been a mistake.

The next week when we played, Kenny pitched an almost perfect game. He struck out most of our batters. Some grounded out, and a few hit singles, but we scored no runs. Kenny carried the Phillies by himself, hitting a two-run home run early in the game and driving in another run with a line drive. We lost three to nothing.

After the game, Mike ran up to me and shouted, "Hey, Ben, are you going to go home now and change the win to a loss on your schedule?"

Then he turned and trotted away. I said nothing and simply swallowed the bitter pill, feeling like a complete disgrace. Shamed and humiliated by an incorrect prediction no one was ever supposed to see.

Mike forgave me for my flawed guess, but it was an embarrassment I wished I never experienced. I should never have been required to defend my predictions to anyone, but I was cornered when Mike saw the schedule, and that was my fault. The trifling matter was soon forgotten, and we remained friends, though I never again wrote any predictions about winning or losing baseball games.

Toward the end of the season, my team was in contention for first place, but we had to beat the 49ers. Curt Schaffer, a tall, lanky blonde kid, was their star. He pitched faster than anyone in the league, and few batters clubbed hits off him, let alone home runs.

Game day came for our showdown. We needed to beat them to have any chance of finishing in first place. We would have to score runs off their ace, Curt

Schaffer.

Curt was on fire that day, striking out our batters one after the other. They were leading by a couple runs when it was my turn to bat around the fourth inning. I stepped into the batter's box, took a couple practice swings, and ground my cleats into the soft soil. Towering on the pitcher's mound forty-five feet away, Curt seemed like a giant. He wound up, recoiled, then viciously slung a fastball that whizzed by high and outside. Ball one. Man, that was fast. He wound up again, and again his arm was a vertical flash as he rifled a fastball knee-high directly over home plate. I swung and missed. Strike one. A dozen or so parents were clapping in the bleachers and shouting encouragement, while my team in the dugout was yelling at me to get a hit. I again settled into the batter's box and waited for the pitch. Curt slung another fastball that smacked dust out of the catcher's glove. I swung and missed again. Strike two.

I stepped out of the batter's box, batted my cleats to knock away some dirt, took a few deep breaths, then stepped back to hit, fans and players chattering on both sides. Curt wound up again, recoiled, and unleashed a scorching fastball about waist high, a little outside. It probably would be a strike if I did not swing. I reacted as quickly as I could, swung mightily and made contact. To my surprise, the ball sprang off the bat in a line drive directly over right field, soaring fifteen feet above the fence, striking the vertical pole of the adjacent backstop where another Little League game was in progress. The umpire stepped forward, raised both his hands high and shouted, "Home run!" Fans in the bleachers and our team erupted with cheers. A kid sprung from his perch to retrieve the home run ball, which bounced into the adjacent baseball diamond. I was in shock, as were all the 49ers. I trotted around the bases and returned to home plate, then back to the dugout, where Gordon and the rest of my teammates heartily congratulated me. The kid came to the dugout and handed me the home run ball. It was my trophy to keep. I later used an ink pen to write the date and "Home run hit off Curt Schaffer. Ben. Braves." I displayed the ball proudly in my bedroom for years.

We still lost that game and finished the season in second place, but I was the only player who hit a home run off Curt Schaffer the entire season. After the game, he shook my hand and congratulated me.

The glory of my home run stayed with me for the remainder of the season.

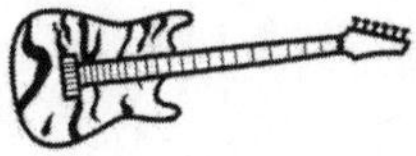

During our first year in Folsom, we lived in a low rent section of town. Though my brother and I shared a room, we were almost never there, unless we were sleeping or watching TV before bed. We tuned in to shows like *Swat*, *The Rockford Files*, *The Six Million Dollar Man*, or the Saturday night chiller, *The Night Stalker*, and sharing a room wasn't much of a problem.

We had a young neighbor, Sandra, who lived in the adjoining condo closer to the street. She was young, blonde and looked like a typical high school student, small, thin, about 100 pounds, and she had a baby. She was only 19, and I was amazed that she already had a child. She knocked on our door one Sunday morning and my mom answered.

"Did you hear me screaming last night?" Sandra asked.

"No. Why were you screaming?" my mom asked.

"A man broke into my house."

"I'm sorry. Come inside," my mom said, as she stepped back and held the door open. "Are you alright? Tell me what happened."

My mom led Sandra to the kitchen, and they sat at the brown, hexagonal table.

"Want a cup of coffee," my mom asked, as she poured and slid a cup to Sandra, then filled a mug for herself and returned the percolator to the counter. Sandra sat for a moment and gathered her thoughts.

"Thank you. It was about one o'clock in the morning. I was watching TV, and I saw this guy walking across the street toward my front door. I had seen him earlier in the evening at a little party across the street, and he kept staring at me. He gave me the creeps. The way he was walking, I knew he was going to try to get in, so I got up and grabbed a .22 rifle that I keep in the corner. He walked straight up to the door, didn't knock. He just started kicking the door. I started screaming as loud as I could, and after two or three kicks, he broke the lock, the door flew open and he walked inside. I was standing in the corner with the rifle, and I pointed it at him. When he saw the barrel, he turned around and ran out the door and ran down the sidewalk. Then I called the police. I haven't slept at all."

She looked frail and badly shaken as she sat there.

"Did the police catch him?" my mom asked.

"No. They said they'd contact me to identify a suspect if they arrested anyone, but I haven't heard anything."

"Does he live across the street?"

"No."

"Have you ever seen him before?"

"No."

"What does he look like?"

"Tall, 6' 2" or 3", skinny, long hair, scary eyes."

"Who does he know across the street?"

"I'm not sure. The lady invited me, and I went there for about fifteen minutes around 8 o'clock. Some people were drinking. I didn't want to leave my baby alone, so I came home. I didn't know anyone except the lady, Angelina."

"Did you talk to the man?"

"No, just Angelina."

"Police should be able to get his name from her."

"I would think so. I'll be moving, though. I can't live here anymore. There's no way."

"I doubt he'll come back, but I understand," my mom said.

"I won't be here if he does. My dad gave me that

rifle, but it wasn't even loaded. I'm lucky he thought it was."

"I'm sorry. That must be terrifying."

"It was."

I had been lying in bed listening to the conversation. I got dressed and walked to the living room.

"Did you hear any screaming last night?" my mom asked.

"No," I answered.

"A man kicked in Sandra's door. I'm horrified. I didn't hear a thing."

"I can't believe no one heard me. I was screaming loud."

I sat nearby and listened.

Sandra continued, "I heard that Manson Family members live across the street," she said dryly. "Charlie Manson is in Folsom Prison, and some of his followers moved to Folsom so they could visit him."

"I didn't know that," my mom replied. She sipped her coffee slowly and gazed pensively across the table out the windows. "You should get a dog. A large dog who barks viciously at any stranger."

"I think I will."

"Our dog goes nuts whenever he sees the mailman. I'm surprised he didn't bark last night."

"Let me show you my front door," Sandra said, then stood up and turned to leave.

We followed and walked fifteen feet to her front door. She stood and pointed. The top half was small rectangles of glass connected by a thin wood frame.

Two large black boot prints were next to the door knob. The jamb was broken, exposing a splintered patch of wood around the lock. A large irregular crack rose from the bottom of the glass rectangles halfway to the top.

We looked in horror at the damage. Another neighbor saw the small gathering and walked over. As we stood near her front door gazing at the cracked squares of glass and footprints on the door, Sandra recounted the terrifying incident.

I went back inside and wondered whether police would catch the intruder. My mom told my brother and me to make sure we locked the front door whenever we were home and especially at night. But what good was that if he just kicked it open?

That evening Rick loaded his Daisy 880 BB gun and leaned it next to the bottom bunk bed where he slept. I put my buck knife under my pillow in the top bunk. We put a chair against the front door. If the felon tried to break in, at least the chair would slow him down a little, and if he came back that night, we might have a chance to run him off with repeated BB shots and knife attacks, I figured.

The next day, Sandra's condo was empty.

I slept uneasily for several nights after the attack, but no intruders ever tried to break into our condo.

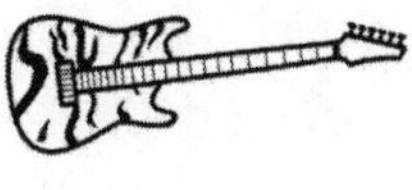

We never heard anything more about the break-in. If the police had caught the suspect, they had not assured anyone. Fulfilling daily routines of class and after-school activities, life soon returned to a sense of normalcy.

Within a few months, however, the evening news was reporting that a man was somehow getting into houses at night and assaulting women. The television reports showed a drawing of the criminal wearing a black ski mask with a peanut-shaped section of cloth removed over the eyes and bridge of the nose, revealing scary staring eyes. Was it the same man who had kicked in Sandra's door a few months earlier? My mom suspected it was, and we were all terrified again. A masked man was slithering around neighborhoods at 3:00 in the morning, entering homes, terrorizing women. The newscasters and reporters called him The East Area Rapist, and decades later, he was dubbed The Golden State Killer.

I had never heard of such diabolical crimes. Why was this masked maniac creeping into homes in the early morning? I couldn't fathom why. My mom made sure to lock all doors and windows at night. We had a dog, and that provided some comfort, but we didn't have any real guns.

"I'll shoot him in the eyeball with my BB gun," Rick announced as we discussed the threat after yet another news report of the most recent incident.

"He won't get past the dog," Mom assured him.

"What if he poisons the dog?"

"He won't poison the dog," Mom said quickly, as if the notion were ridiculous.

"We should get a gun. I'll shoot the creep."

"We're not getting any guns."

"We need a gun."

"You already shot your brother once with the stupid BB gun; you're not getting the chance to shoot him with a real gun."

"That was an accident."

"I don't care."

"Someone needs to shoot him," my brother persisted.

"You're not shooting anyone."

I listened and felt helpless. I agreed someone should shoot the masked menace, and although it was true that Rick had shot me in the leg with his BB gun, I also felt we should have a way to defend ourselves. We would be getting no guns, however. My mom's fear that Rick might accidentally mistake me for the creeping psychopath settled the matter.

I put my buck knife under my pillow again and hoped there would be no showdown.

Month after month, the reports continued. The incident totals escalated into the thirties, and the police still had no suspects, no leads. Supposedly, police had the stalker cornered in a backyard once, but he hopped the fence and got away. I was appalled. How could they let him get away?

I was left with the feeling that the stealthy creeper was just too smart for the police and, although they wanted to catch him, they didn't know how, and were just hoping that a patrol car would drive by at 4:00 a.m., when he was walking down the street.

They'd tell him to stop, take him into custody without a struggle, and proudly announce they'd caught him. I knew that would never happen.

Town hall meetings were held to discuss what to do, but the home invasions continued, sometimes two in the same week. The whole county was angry and frustrated. Why couldn't police catch this menace? I had no idea, and the news gave almost no information about progress in solving the cases. We'd just have to wait and hope for good news someday.

I was scared for a few nights after each attack, but the fear dissolved as life continued. They'd catch him eventually, I hoped.

After completing fifth grade and a season of Little League, my mom got a new job at the Lake Bowl, running drinks from the bar to the bowlers in the lanes outside and adjacent to the little cocktail lounge.

During our second year in Folsom, we moved into a larger condo in another section of town, and Rick and I each had our own rooms. This was an improvement, as having my own private space separate from Rick gave me a sense of ownership and dominion over my special area—and the right to exclude him from my zone whenever I chose—a right my mom enforced for both of us.

Besides baseball, my other passion was motorcycles, although my mom had refused to buy me one for years and years, despite constant begging. She thought they were too dangerous, and I was depressed and frustrated that I could not have one, at least not until I was older.

By the start of sixth grade, I was more comfortable with my new home and classmates. I'd made friends playing Little League and that restored my hope. Fortunately, my dad came up for Christmas, a baseball game or two, and sometimes a birthday. I flew to see him maybe once a year, so my yearning for his company was partially satisfied. My mom and dad were on excellent terms, so there was never any conflict between them that prevented him from visiting. The main obstacle was distance, and his finances would not accommodate flying up once or twice a month, as I would have liked, but his periodic short stays were sufficient to maintain a strong bond.

My sixth grade teacher was Glen Cleveland, a tall, grandfatherly man with graying hair, blue eyes, and glasses. He had a small, pug nose, broad cheeks, and small mouth, giving him a sort of bland, bureaucratic, lethargic look, but he was a very friendly and conscientious teacher.

Above the large, green chalkboards in his classroom was a row of portraits of U.S. presidents. At the far left was George Washington, and at the far right was Gerald Ford. I remember gazing at the portraits with fascination. I could identify only four: George Washington, Abraham Lincoln, Gerald Ford, and Richard Nixon. I was unfamiliar with the rest and wondered about all the history that must be connected to them. I figured I would learn about the other presidents later, but for now, I knew about the most important ones.

School work seemed mostly irrelevant to my future. I never had any thought of growing up and becoming any type of professional—a doctor, architect, engineer—certainly not a lawyer. Though I had made friendships, a cloud of mild depression lingered, because I missed my dad, and the longing to see him sapped any motivation to do homework or focus on school subjects.

As for my future as an adult, I wanted to be a professional baseball player. I knew nothing about lawyers or what they did and wasn't interested. The most enjoyable thing in my life as a kid—with the possible exception of riding motorcycles—was Little League baseball. When I learned that adults were paid to play this game, I was genuinely surprised. I had mistakenly believed pros played for fun, like kids, but getting paid was an unbelievable bonus. That cinched my decision. I would become a professional baseball player. Done. That decision was easy.

Since my decision about my future had been made by age 9, I saw no reason to put a lot of effort into school. Why learn about math, geography, English, spelling, and 'citizenship' if you are going to spend your life playing baseball? I did my homework assignments because I was required to do them, but I put forth minimal effort, enough to pass. School initially was a place to play with friends on recess in between class sessions, do little art projects with paper and glue, listen to the teacher read, and practice writing the alphabet. Later, school was a place to make new friends, play touch football during recess, drink chocolate milk, eat hamburgers for lunch, and eye the pretty girls, who wore tight Dittos jeans and hip-hugging bell bottoms, displaying limbs and body parts I found more attractive by the day. School was just a place to exist, follow instructions, and mingle with other kids, because we were too young to be left at home while our parents worked.

Two memorable events occurred in Mr. Cleveland's sixth grade class. First was the time he arranged a little wildlife demonstration. Someone brought in a three-foot fish tank that contained a four-foot brown rattlesnake. Someone else brought in a black and white king snake. Mr. Cleveland told the class that king snakes eat rattlesnakes and wanted to present a demonstration of this fact of nature.

The fish tank was placed on the floor, the lid was slid back a few inches, and the king snake was lowered inside. The rattlesnake remained still. The king snake raised its head, noticed the other serpent, slithered toward it and simply opened its mouth wide and thrust the gaping aperture over the head of the motionless viper and began swallowing it. Everyone in the class was gasping with shock and disgust. Amazingly, the rattlesnake never moved or resisted. Over five minutes, the seemingly hungry king snake swallowed about half of its prey, then stopped for a few moments and began backing away slowly, regurgitating the other reptile until the two were completely separated again. Apparently, the fanged serpent had been too much to swallow.

The king snake was removed from the fish tank and returned to a box and both snakes were removed from the classroom.

Everyone was disappointed that the king snake had not swallowed the rattler entirely, but it was a riveting, entertaining, and educational moment about the feeding habits of serpentine reptiles.

Kids asked Mr. Cleveland why the king snake didn't finish, and he said that all the students hovering over the glass aquarium had scared it. If we had backed away and given it space, it would have, but it wouldn't eat when scared, and our eagerness to view the spectacle at close range had disturbed the noble king snake and spoiled the experiment.

The other notable incident was when Mr. Cleveland told the class about his son's horrific motorcycle accident. His son had been riding on a dirt road and did not see a chain that was attached between two poles, forming a wide, low U-shape. The front tire of the motorcycle hit the low, middle section of the chain, causing it to fling into the air and snap back, hitting his son directly in the mouth, knocking out all his teeth and ripping him off the motorcycle. He had nearly been killed and was still in the hospital as Mr. Cleveland talked about the mishap. The whole class listened intently to the dreadful story. He explained the accident with great patience and detail, never expressing any sadness or emotion from the traumatic experience his son endured. The event was so devastating I expected an outpouring of grief, but it never happened.

Little League season arrived, and I played on the Braves again. By the end of the second season in Folsom, I was firmly rooted among a new group of kids and burgeoning friendships, all of us growing up in a small town, exposed to similar circumstances. Day by day, my circle of friends was growing, and I started feeling new attachments to this town that I had dreaded just a year earlier. My dad still lived far away in Los Angeles, but this was my life, and I'd just have to do my best and enjoy seeing him when he came to visit or I flew to see him.

Meanwhile, The East Area Rapist was still on the loose, sneaking into homes every couple of months, still terrorizing the community.

They just couldn't catch the psychopath.

JAGUARS

Shortly before seventh grade, Mom applied for a job at the telephone company and was hired. She began working a regular day shift but later switched to 'graveyard'—midnight 'til 8 in the morning, because it paid better.

A couple years earlier, she had dyed her hair rust red, and that was how people noticed and remembered her. "Oh, the lady with flaming red hair?" Someone gave her the nickname, "Big Red," and that stuck while she worked as a waitress.

After two years in Folsom, Mom finally decided it was time to put down roots for real, so she dug deep and bought a three-bedroom house. I was surprised but happy. The momentous purchase meant we wouldn't be relocating again any time soon—and having moved three times previously, I was relieved we would stay. We had a one-car garage and backyard, and we felt much more attached to the community in our own space, no longer renters.

We drove from our condo to the empty house so my brother and I could see our new home and pick our rooms. Rick instantly demanded the front bedroom that shared a wall with the living room. Since it was the 'first' bedroom in the house, it was, obviously, the 'best,' and it was close to the kitchen. His instant claim settled the matter.

The master bedroom was in the back corner, and that meant I would get the only other bedroom in the 'back' of the house. I felt a twinge of panic and jealousy—why does he always get the best of everything? I knew the answer: He's older, so he's naturally entitled to choose first, be first, to get the best of everything *first*, as his natural birthright—or so he would have me believe. This twisted dynamic had played out for years and was probably common among siblings. I resented the ongoing insinuation that he deserved the best of everything first merely because he was older, but there was nothing I could do except ignore and eventually unlearn the noxious presumption. It was not easy.

It seemed unbearably unfair that by accident of birth he should get the finest of everything, leaving me the tattered leftovers, but the flawed psychology was unavoidable, and it dominated my thinking at the time.

I wandered into the lousy 'back' bedroom that would be mine. After thinking about it a while, I decided my brother's decision had been hasty and incorrect. There was nothing 'inferior' about my room. It was light green—which I liked, but Rick's was light brown. Though he was closer to the living room and had the 'first' bedroom, I was closer to the bathroom and had a nice view of the backyard and large tree in the middle of the grass. His view was of the fence and neighbor's roof. Plus, my room was a little larger—which caused him some stifled envy.

His haste in preempting what he thought was the 'best' room had backfired, I thought. This time he had misjudged which was 'better', and it was too late to change.

I climbed the tree in the backyard and could see all over the neighborhood. My friend, Jeremy, lived a few houses away. From twenty-five feet in the air, I saw his house three hundred feet away, and he saw me. He walked into the street, whistled, motioned with raised arms, and shouted at me to get out of the tree. I waved back, stayed a while, and gazed at the rooftops and backyards below me.

The garage still smelled like paint thinner; a couple half-empty cans of semi-gloss had been left in a corner. The prior owner had built a workbench against one wall in the garage, and that seemed like it would come in handy. I pictured myself using saws and power tools at the workbench, building something useful for the house.

When we wanted to decorate our rooms, Mom told us to pound nails into the walls wherever we wanted to hang pictures, shelves, posters, whatever. We owned the house and could pound nails if we wanted.

Our new house quickly became glue that held the family together and rooted us in Folsom. We ate together every night, watched a seventeen-inch color television in the living room, used the same rotary telephone to call friends, snuggled with our two cats, Liza and Snowflake, and slept in our own rooms, dreaming about our futures. Our new home gave us all the comfort a home should provide.

I was looking forward to seventh grade. It seemed so much more sophisticated than elementary school—five one-hour classes per day—not just the same teacher. Junior high was a step closer to high school and adulthood and all the related freedoms and responsibilities.

Folsom's junior high mascot was the jaguar. A simple square building with an interior courtyard formed the campus. Classrooms ringed the outer section of the building. Students lingered before class on and around benches in the smaller interior section called "the quad." There were no more than two hundred students.

Basketball hoops and a large section of asphalt flanked the school, and a large square patch of grass next to the asphalt provided space for softball, soccer, and flag football.

Rick and his friend, Roy Cooper, were in his bedroom one evening, chewing Copenhagen, spitting into a large brass spittoon. I entered their lair, and they advised me how much I would hate being a seventh grader.

"You're going to have to take P.E. class with Mr. Christen," my brother informed me with some delight.

"What's P.E.?"

"Physical education."

"What's that?"

"It's just an exercise class. There's a bunch of numbers painted on the asphalt, and you have to line up every morning on a number for roll call. It's like being in the military or something."

“Then what?”

“Then you do a bunch of exercises,” he said, and spit into the spittoon.

Roy added, “You have to do gut busters.”

“What are those?" I asked.

Rick stood up and demonstrated. "You have to bend over and touch your toes, then stand up straight and fling your elbows back, like this," he said, bending and demonstrating the exercise, then thrusting his elbows backward as if standing and pushing against a wall. “You have to count each one and clap afterward like a fag.”

“Yeah,” Roy agreed.

Homosexuality was regarded, at the time, as some sort of shameful character defect—boys liked girls, and girls liked boys—there were no other options, and there were no discussions among kids or adults about gender or sexual identity. Any boy who didn’t like girls was regarded by his peers as flawed, abnormal and deserving scorn, contempt, disrespect—and maybe more. Among adolescent boys back then, the greatest insult was to call another a fag.

Rick continued, "You have to wear special clothing every day, sweats or shorts, and you have to wear a jockstrap.”

“What's a jockstrap?" I asked.

“It's this underwear thing that makes you feel like a fag. You have to wear it every day. If you don't, you'll lose points on your grade.” They took turns spitting into the spittoon.

“Why do you have to wear that?" I asked.

"I don't know, but you have to," he answered.

"What else?"

"You have to do push-ups, run laps, and then there's intramural competition, flag football, soccer and some tests. You'll hate it. You won't like Mr. Christen."

Rick and Roy seemed to enjoy telling me of the unpleasant days ahead in P.E. class. They made it sound like I would be enduring harsh military training from a ruthless drill instructor, who would push me to the limits of human endurance and suffering. I felt mildly concerned. I had never been required to participate in a military-style physical education class, but I would soon, according to my brother.

I received my class schedule in the mail, and P.E. would be my first morning class. School started at 8:30. Sixth grade had started at 9:00, and I didn't like having a half hour less sleep. I struggled to get up, frequently slept through my alarm, tapped the snooze button several times, then finally got up around 8:00. There was no time for a shower, so I put on clothes, maybe ate a bowl of cereal, then walked to school, often arriving fifteen minutes late.

P.E. was much as Rick had described, but it was not as difficult or taxing as he had touted. Halfway through the school year, I realized Rick and Roy had deliberately and mischievously misled me. P.E. was no sort of torture, nothing to fear or avoid. Mr. Christen was neither mean nor abusive; he seemed like he was just doing the job any P.E. teacher should do. I enjoyed playing softball, flag football, doing push -ups and pull-ups and competing against friends. Admittedly, I did not like wearing the jockstrap. It was a strange, foreign feeling—a triangle of fabric pressing tightly against the groin, but this accessory was required. If I was a fag for wearing a jockstrap, then so was everyone else.

Though some kids snickered at Mr. Christen's perpetually tanned legs and choice to wear shorts during the winter, he was well-liked by most of the student body. Girls thought he was cute—he was only about twenty-seven, still young—and he had a little mustache. His position of authority created natural tension, but he seemed fair and enjoyed conducting the class activities.

Some kids seemed to think that despising the teachers was the natural order of things—like kids were prisoners and the teachers cruel and inhumane guards, subjecting them to painful and humiliating tasks all day—jumping jacks, push-ups, reading, solving math problems—all the sufferings of the oppressed.

I took woodshop from Mr. Stennis and learned how to use woodworking tools, machines and techniques. He taught us to use the bandsaw, lathe, router and various other tools and machines, hopefully without cutting off our fingers. I made a coat rack and hung it proudly in my room.

Junior high also had a 'nutrition break,' during which nothing but junk food was sold: Twinkies, ice cream, candy bars, Hostess pies, gum, soda. I used to get a Hostess lemon pie every morning around 10:15, which often was my breakfast.

I was now aware of the increasing array of pretty girls in my class and a grade above me. It would be unfair to mention names, as there were so many, but the best part of school was the girls.

Rick had already had a couple of girlfriends, and my time for one seemed very near. Meanwhile, I was plodding through hour-long classes during the day. The pace seemed fast, and now actual learning seemed more important than the prior year, but I was still not motivated. Baseball, motorcycles, and girls remained my priorities.

When my twelfth birthday was approaching, I heard Craig Henderson was selling his motorcycle, a Yamaha YZ 80. It was two years old but it ran great, and he said he'd sell it for $110. I had saved $85 from my weekly allowance, and I'd happily donate it all to buy Craig's bike if my mom would pick up the extra $25. She hemmed and hawed. I begged and pressured. Come on, I'm old enough now. I won't get hurt. Let's do this.

The night before my birthday, I went to bed while Mom made a two-layer chocolate cake from scratch. She did not pour cake mix from a box; she assembled all the ingredients individually—eggs, flour, butter, salt, sugar, vanilla, bitter chocolate, then combined them to make her own special birthday cake. I drifted off to sleep that night as the warm and rich scents of chocolate seeped into my bedroom. Mom finished the cake, then left at 11:30 to work her graveyard shift.

When I awoke the next morning, I walked into the kitchen and discovered my frosted, two-layer chocolate birthday cake, covered with candles, resting in the middle of the breakfast table. "Ben" was written in yellow frosting on the top, surrounded by candles. A wrapped present and card lay next to the cake—and something else—a scroll that was sealed with red strand, tied into a frilly bow.

I pulled the scroll from the bow and unrolled it, revealing several pages. Mom had written a cheerful little poem and drawn pictures that celebrated this landmark day. I read the scroll to myself, and her voice filled my head as if she were reading it to me, there in the dim morning quiet. She drew well, and the little cartoons of me and the dog, me playing baseball, me smiling, moved me in a way I had never felt. Suddenly, there was this recognition of my mom's deep caring, concern, and love. I always knew she loved me, but this little handmade scroll, with the poem she had written and the colorful, happy illustrations, was so personalized, so intimate, so filled with love, I reached a deeper level of appreciation and understanding. It was as if she understood me better than I understood myself and intended so much for me—a long life filled with wonder and joy.

I savored the silent moment alone in the kitchen

with my cake, card, and scroll. Rick was still asleep, and my mother's efforts—manifested and sitting there in front of me—had truly made me feel special on that birthday morning. All the effort she had given so when I woke up, I would be greeted by warmth and pleasant surprises convinced me I was a very lucky child.

I'd be even luckier, however, if I received Craig Henderson's Yamaha YZ 80 on this special day. After I ate a piece of cake for breakfast and dressed for school, I left my last $85 in an envelope on the kitchen table and hoped that when I got home later, I'd see my new motorcycle. Mom had not said no, but she had not said yes either, so I was not sure whether my partnership offer would work. I would find out after school.

I walked home that sunny November day, partly excited and partly dreading another disappointment. It was a twenty-minute walk, and when I got to the last corner before my house, my anticipation escalated. Here we go: the waiting is over. I will or will not have a motorcycle in a matter of minutes.

I turned the last corner and could not believe my eyes. I saw the unmistakable shape of a motorcycle in our driveway in the distance—two wheels, a seat, and a tank, glistening in the sunlight. Excitement and adrenaline shot through me. I was floating with each step. Am I seeing things? This better not be a prank by my brother. I hurried down the sidewalk, dizzy with excitement. My house was maybe two hundred feet away. As I approached, I could see it was no joke.

That was Craig Henderson's YZ 80 parked in the driveway! Rick came out of the house as I approached in disbelief. He explained that Mom had given him the balance of the money to buy the bike, and he had given all the money to Craig, left school early, and brought it home so it would be there when I arrived. Mom had been forced by the telephone company to work a double shift and wouldn't be home for a while, so it was just my brother and me at this climactic moment.

Craig had taken the time to clean and polish the gift. The tank was painted a rich, grainy silver, contrasted by the black leather seat. The fenders were matching silver. It was a gleaming mechanical beauty on a black frame and rubber wheels. There was not a speck of mud or dirt anywhere. Although the bike was two years old, it looked shiny and new; the worst defect was a crack or two on the leather seat, but that could be overlooked.

My faith in justice and righteousness was fully restored.

I sat on my new bike and went into a strange, trance-like state. The shock absorbers gently supported and eased my weight downward as I sat on the seat for the first time and gripped the handlebars. It was a comfortable, perfect fit. My feet were flat on the ground; I could stand and easily tilt the bike left or right. The weight of the machine just amplified all the power and functionality now literally in my hands. It was finally true; I had a motorcycle! The euphoria could not be put into words. It was a thousand

Christmases packed into one birthday.

Rick and I admired the bike for a while. We were both mostly speechless. I could tell he was jealous. Too bad for him. This was my bike; maybe he should save his allowance and make a similar deal with Mom to get his own motorcycle. Then his cunning, older brother psychology went into full gear.

"Let me take it for a ride down the street to make sure all the gears work and the oil pressure is good," he said.

Hmm. I hadn't even considered whether Craig had sold me a lemon. Surely the bike worked just fine. It was only two years old, and it was beautiful. What could be wrong with it?

My brother was a master at manipulating me when we were kids. He was a smooth, polished salesman when he wanted something from me, and I was a sucker who got flimflammed every time.

I thought about his proposal. My instinct told me he just wanted to ride my motorcycle. Then he could brag he was 'first' to ride it, and therefore, he had somehow absorbed and experienced all the best the bike had to offer. My experience, as the second to ride the bike, would never be as fun, valuable, or meaningful as his and, indeed, my ownership would be forever tainted because he rode it 'first' and sucked away all the best the machine had to offer. Even as a young teenager, his obsession with being 'first' and getting the 'best' was still strong.

"Come on, let me just ride it down the street and back. I'll come right back. You need to check the brakes and oil pressure and make sure the gears shift right." More manipulation; more flimflam.

Was he right? I really didn't know. What could it hurt if he just rode down the street and back? If he wanted to brag that he rode my bike first, screw him; it was my motorcycle, and I'd be doing all the riding.

"Ok, go ahead," I told him. Might as well just get this out of the way. If I didn't let him ride it now, he'd be badgering and manipulating me until I did.

He mounted my bike with a smirk, kick started it, then sped away down the street, leaving behind a rising plume of blue engine smoke that smelled sweet and delicious. I watched and listened as he shifted through the gears. The engine whined as he hit top speed six or seven houses down the street. No helmet, no boots, no gloves...this was the '70s. Freak injuries and lawsuits had not yet made everyone preoccupied with safety and dampened everyone's fun.

He disappeared around the bend at the end of the street, and I heard the engine die down, then accelerate again. Oh, good. At least he was keeping his promise to come right back. I feared he'd be gone for an hour.

The engine whined again at full throttle as he screamed down the street and returned to the house. I watched from the driveway as he approached. Then THE HORROR began.

He hit the back brake and skidded sideways into the driveway, jumped off, kicked the kickstand down, and ran past me, his eyes as big as softballs, a frantic and terrified look on his face. "A cop saw me! Don't tell him I was riding it! I won't ever get a motorcycle!" He ran into the house and screamed back, "Don't tell him I was riding it; I won't get a motorcycle!"

I was left shocked, standing in the driveway next to the motorcycle, trying to decide what to do.

I had overlooked that Officer Lavagnino lived about ten houses down the street. Sometimes his police car would be parked in the driveway. Mom had told us that a police officer lived nearby, and that made her feel somewhat safe and secure, happy that she had bought our house, particularly since the East Area Rapist was still rampaging all over Sacramento County, police still unable to catch him.

On this day, Officer Lavagnino was in uniform and on duty when my brother roared past him on my new motorcycle.

I didn't have much time to analyze the situation. Rick's warning that he would not get a motorcycle if the truth were told weighed heavily. Looking back, that was doubtful. Mom may have imposed some punishment, but she would not have deprived him of a motorcycle and allowed me to keep and flaunt mine. He just didn't want to take responsibility for his behavior, so manipulating me to take the rap for him was his best option.

I looked down the street and saw the distinctive front grill of the Folsom Police car and the overhead lights. Officer Lavagnino was approaching and would be there in seconds. I thought about running, but he'd take my motorcycle, and I'd never get another. I could tell the truth and blame my brother, but it was too late. Officer Lavagnino probably had already seen me, and I was standing next to the bike. Telling him Rick was the true rider would ring hollow. No, I'd have to stand and take the punishment for my brother. There was no other choice.

Officer Lavagnino pulled up and parked, blocking the driveway. I saw him talking into the handheld radio speaker inside the car. Then he got out, stood up, and glowered at me. He was a towering man, at least 6' 3", possibly taller. He walked around the front of the police car, then strode directly toward me, his leather police belt and gear squeaking with every step, badge glinting in the sunlight. He looked grim and serious as he approached and stopped three feet away.

"Did you just ride that motorcycle down the street?" he asked.

"Yes," I lied.

"You broke the law. It's illegal to ride dirt bikes on the street."

"I'm sorry. I won't do it again."

He stared at me severely.

"What's your name?"

"Ben."

"You live here?"

"Yes."

"Your parents home?"

"No. My mom's at work."

He looked at the motorcycle and looked at me, assessing what to do. *Oh, no..., he's going to take my motorcycle, put it in the trunk of his police car, then take me to jail,* I thought. What a travesty! The world would never know the truth—that I had done nothing wrong, and I was being punished for my brother's crime—he'd certainly never come forward and confess.

"Why did you do that?" he asked.

"I don't know. I just got it for my birthday. I was testing it."

He scrutinized me closely. He was serious, but professional. His tone never became mean or abusive.

"Well, it's illegal to ride dirt bikes on the street." He pointed to the front wheel. "See those knobbies on the tires; they tear up the road."

I looked at the tires, remained silent. He continued, "There's a park off White Rock Road for motorcycles. You can ride all you want out there. Do you have a trailer?"

"No."

"You need to get a trailer, so you can take your bike to the park where you can ride legally."

"Okay."

About that time, my brother walked out of the house and approached. He had changed his T-shirt and put on a baseball cap. He walked up in his disguise and stood a few feet away. He couldn't possibly miss witnessing me being held accountable for his offense. For a moment, I felt good. At least there was someone with me to face Officer Lavagnino. A confession from Rick was out of the question, but at least I was not alone.

Officer Lavagnino questioned him.

"Who are you?"

"Rick."

"Are you his brother?"

"Yes."

"Go back inside. This doesn't concern you."

My brother obediently vanished, and Officer Lavagnino continued.

"I have the power to impound the motorcycle," he said.

My inner dialogue was desperate. *Oh, no, no, no... I haven't even ridden the thing yet. Please don't do that, please...This is wrong! I'm innocent! This is the worst birthday ever!*

He scrutinized me some more, mulled over his options.

"Do you promise you won't ride on the street ever again?"

"Yes. I promise."

"Alright. I'm going to let you go with a warning this time, but I have to tell your Mom."

Crap. My mom's going to be angry, and I still might lose the motorcycle, but at least Officer Lavagnino isn't going to take it now.

He wrote down my name and phone number and said he'd be in contact with my mom later, then drove away. I dreaded his phone call, but I'd just have to get through it somehow.

Mom listened intently to Officer Lavagnino when he called a few hours later. After the short discussion, she hung up and announced she would sell my motorcycle if I ever broke the law again or got caught riding on the street, and I knew she meant it.

Rick skulked in his bedroom, seemingly disinterested, but listening closely to hear whether I betrayed his culpability. I covered for him. It would only make matters worse to reveal his true involvement. He'd want retribution for unnecessarily holding him accountable, but I'd gotten through the ordeal and kept my motorcycle, and that was the important thing.

A few months later, Rick got his own motorcycle on his birthday, and we rode with Craig Henderson dozens of times on the dirt trail that paralleled Folsom Boulevard and led to motocross tracks in Rancho Cordova.

All the waiting for my dream bike was worth every second.

In December of 1977, *Saturday Night Fever* hit the movie theaters. We had been living in Folsom two years, and suddenly I found a clear role model: Tony Manero, the film's lead character, played by John Travolta. The movie was a box office smash, and Travolta dazzled the nation with his disco moves—that was the aspect most admired and emulated. Everyone wanted to dance like John Travolta; every male under 30 wanted the floor to clear when he stepped onto it so he could mimic Travolta's incredible grace and agility to an admiring audience—just like Travolta did in the movie, but there was only one

Tony Manero.

Once a month or so, the cafeteria was transformed into a dark disco den. A DJ would set up a small table with a couple record players and place flashing lights in the corners; a mirrored disco ball would be hung from the ceiling and reflect colored lights in thousands of small swatches, shooting through the dark like psychedelic fire flies.

Fashion also followed the movie. Guys began wearing polyester pants and platform shoes, polyester shirts unbuttoned below the chest, and necklaces. Girls, too, wore tight polyester pants, scarves, T-shirts or silky dresses.

Disco had been popular for several years and ruled seventh grade—the Bee Gees, Andy Gibb, Donna Summer, Leo Sayer, Earth, Wind & Fire, KC and the Sunshine Band, and many others. That all seemed to change, however, after a few hard rock bands grew in popularity. Blue Öyster Cult, Van Halen, Boston, Aerosmith, Led Zeppelin, Lynyrd Skynyrd and Molly Hatchet put out hit songs that quickly ended the reign of disco.

When Van Halen released its first album in 1978, featuring a remake of The Kinks' hit, *You Really Got Me*, the world of electric lead guitar would be changed forever. Van Halen's version made the full, overpowering tone of the electric guitar and Marshall amp dominant, and the song was quickly a hit. Preceding the track was a two-minute guitar solo called *Eruption* which was groundbreaking and marked a crucial turning point in the evolution of lead guitar sound and performance. Nothing like *Eruption* had ever been recorded; it was the hard rock guitar equivalent of a rare classical virtuoso performance on violin or piano, performed only by highly gifted musicians.

Rick had never fully embraced disco. He tolerated it simply as a necessary means to interact with girls, but Van Halen changed all that. One evening he was talking about this new band that would change my taste in music.

"Have you heard *Eruption* yet?" he asked.

"What's that?"

"It's an incredible guitar solo by Van Halen."

"I haven't heard it."

"That's because you listen to that lame disco music. Change your radio station to KZAP. They play it all the time."

"It's not lame."

"It is way lame, and once you hear *Eruption*, you'll know why."

"I don't think John Travolta's lame. Neither do women."

"Listen to KZAP," he said. "Have you heard *You Really Got Me*'?"

"I'm not sure."

"Once you hear Van Halen, you'll never listen to disco again," he assured me. Just then, his stereo played a drum roll, and he sprung into his room from the hall and turned up the volume. "This is it! This is *Eruption*! Listen to this! Listen!"

I stepped into his room amid the swelling volume

of this roaring sound that started quickly sputtering in crunchy sequences, and listened in awe to the shredding, wailing guitar solo. He watched my amazement with delight.

After the solo groaned to an end, he said, "Now the next part is *You Really Got Me*. Listen!"

I stood and listened in utter amazement.

When the tune was over, he turned down the volume and asked, "What do you think?"

"That was incredible…Amazing! I've never heard anything like that."

"What did I tell you? What did I tell you!?" he asked, triumphantly.

"I want to hear that again!"

"Put your radio on KZAP. They play it all the time."

I did and left it there for the next five years. Suddenly, disco seemed antiquated and passé.

I was enamored with Van Halen, but there were still many other great rock bands—Aerosmith, Boston, Kansas, AC/DC, Led Zeppelin, Lynyrd Skynyrd, among others.

Van Halen's *Eruption* and the flood of hard rock hits playing on KZAP throughout 1978 and '79 inspired me to take guitar lessons. Mom bought me a cheap electric guitar and amp and paid for a few months of instruction at Uncle Bob's Music Store in Orangevale. I would not be learning how to play *Eruption* or any Van Halen, however. My instructor began by teaching me to read music and the melodies for nursery rhymes, like "Twinkle Twinkle Little Star" and "On Top of Old Smokey," songs I would never choose to learn. I spent months learning to read music and practicing lullabies. He finally showed me how to play the chords to a couple easy rock songs, and I left behind the music of babies.

After a year of lessons, I could strum along with some rock songs, knew the basic blues scale, and could read musical notes on the staff, but I was still light years from being able to play any Van Halen or anything else I liked and wanted to play. I grew disillusioned with my slow progress and stopped taking lessons, but I continued playing, practicing on my own.

Eventually, I learned that a couple local kids played guitar, but they seemed as lost as I was. They could play parts of songs and a few licks, but no one could play *Eruption* or *Freebird*, or anything close, and no one seemed to know how to play a song from start to finish. My prior passion for the instrument dwindled, but I still played along to the radio occasionally.

Months later, we visited my dad in Los Angeles for the weekend. Rick was hyperactive and probably had severe ADHD, which no one knew at the time. We just thought he was hyper, and that wasn't really a bad thing. He was carefully scanning the movie section of the newspaper to relieve his boredom and anxiety about staying in my dad's apartment for the next four hours.

"Did you find anything, Richard?" my dad asked.

My brother continued studying the newspaper intently. "*The Deer Hunter*!" he blurted, "Sounds like a good movie, Dad."

"Who's starring in it?"

"Robert De Niro, Christopher Walken..."

"De Niro, I've seen him. He's good."

The Deer Hunter? Taking the title literally, I was thinking, "*Who wants to see a movie about men sneaking around the woods hunting deer?*" *Sounds like a terrible story*. I wanted to see something like the *Bad News Bears* or *Smokey and the Bandit*, but I was outvoted. As usual, Rick was proud and triumphant that his choice was validated.

After dinner, we drove to an old movie theater near Hollywood. The interior was Art Deco; the bathrooms were tiny, and the hard, little seats were squished next to one another for people no more than 130 pounds. We took our seats, and the theater filled up.

The movie was lower than my expectations. One of the characters was getting married, and the first hour was all about his marriage ceremony and reception and not much deer hunting. During the party, Robert De Niro strips and runs through the streets for no explained reason. Christopher Walken chases him and finally catches up for a brief drunken discussion, where Walken tells De Niro not to leave him in Vietnam. De Niro pledges he won't.

Several characters finally go on a deer hunting trip. It's a drunken fiasco. One guy forgets his boots; everyone is slugging down beers; they don't even have a truck or trailer. They pile into a sedan and drive far into the mountains, apparently content to hunt deer in the middle of the day, rather than the early morning, like real deer hunters.

De Niro finally spots and shoots a deer. They tie the dead animal onto the hood of the sedan and roll back down the mountain into the small town, a drunk clown car jubilant over their kill. Deer steaks for everyone tonight.

An hour and a half into the movie, an intermission finally occurred. We walked into the lobby. Rick was visibly disappointed.

"What's this movie about, Dad?" he asked.

"I'm not sure, Richard. I think I have an idea where it's going, but I'll have to wait until I see the second half."

I was now sulking, and bored stiff. *You mean to tell me, we'd come to watch a movie about a guy getting married and drunk at his reception and a bunch of yahoos hunting deer in the middle of the day*? It was the worst movie I had ever seen.

Intermission was over, and we filed back into the theater. When the film started, I thought they had made a mistake, and we were now watching a different movie. Suddenly, helicopters were bombing a small village in a jungle and there was pandemonium. *Why are we now watching a war movie*?

I observed unspeakable brutality and killing and

finally recognized the characters from the first half of the movie. They were now in a war somewhere. I didn't know anything about Vietnam at the time.

Soon I saw the shocking and unspeakable viciousness and brutality of the infamous Russian roulette scene. I was frightened and disturbed by the savagery.

The characters finally escaped their captors, and the movie took a different turn. Christopher Walken had remained in Vietnam and Robert De Niro was determined to bring him home. When he finally found him, Christopher Walken apparently did not recognize De Niro. I didn't understand the characters, their problems, or what was happening. The movie seemed like a complete disjointed, disorganized failure.

When we were driving home, Dad asked us about the story. He started with me. "Did you understand the movie, Ben?"

"Yes."

"Tell me what it was about."

"It was about these guys who got captured in a war, and this one really mean guy forced them to play Russian roulette, but they tricked the bad guys into putting more bullets in the gun, shot them, and escaped. But one of them didn't come home, so his friend went back and looked for him, and when he found him, the friend wouldn't come home and shot himself during a poker game."

Dad considered my explanation for a few moments. "No, that's not quite right," he said slowly. "There's more to it than that. Richard, what did you think the movie was about?"

Rick was quick to respond. "It was about how the war changed Robert De Niro because the first time he went hunting, he shot the deer without any hesitation. But after he came back from the war and went hunting again, he had a perfect shot of the deer and missed on purpose. I saw it; he shot over the deer's head. After all the torture and killing he saw in the war, he couldn't kill anymore, and he couldn't hunt anymore."

“That's it!” my dad almost shouted. “You got it exactly!”

I felt bad that my explanation had been inadequate. I hadn’t understood the movie, but my brother had, and I felt like a dope. My dad consoled me. "Go back and watch the movie again in a few years, Ben. You'll understand next time. Your brother's a little older and was able to grasp the significance of the action. You will next time."

It didn’t matter; I didn’t want to see the movie again ever.

I had become friends with Eric Farnsworth during seventh grade. He was in my P.E. class, and we wrestled on the wrestling team. Eric had a mischievous, adolescent, prankster personality. He used to tell me, “You thought you had two hairs until one pissed.” He’d smile broadly and laugh, and I would think, what can I say to that? He always laughed because he knew that a good comeback was either impossible, or I did not know one. I probably replied with a feeble insult or used his affront on someone else.

One day he told me he wanted to get a paper route. He had done the math and figured he could make about $40 a month delivering a certain number of papers, but he wanted help, and he would split the money. He wanted to deliver *The Folsom Telegraph*, the town's weekly newspaper that was published every Wednesday. The money sounded great, but there was one important detail. I had to get up at 5:30 to deliver all the newspapers before school. Eric said we could do it in an hour; it would be easy; and it was only one day a week. That broke down to five dollars per week for each morning round of delivering papers. My allowance was only two dollars a week, and the paper route would more than double it.

About this time, I learned the standard refrain preached by adults and parents: "This is America, the land of freedom and opportunity. You can be anything you want. You can be a police officer, fireman, doctor, astronaut, or president. What do you want to be when you grow up?"

That was nice to know. I could be president if I wanted or become a police officer—get to carry a gun around—that seemed like a good thing. I could get a college education, be whatever I wanted, play pro baseball. I just had to climb the ladder one rung at a time, and I'd get there. That was what made America so great—a ladder to the top was nearby for everyone.

I had no illusions about having a career as a paperboy, nor did I think this was my opportunity to get rich, but earning double my weekly allowance was highly attractive.

On the first Wednesday of my new paper route, Eric arrived at 5:25 a.m. on his bicycle and rang the doorbell. I popped out of bed, let him in, quickly dressed in warm clothing, and got my bike from the garage. He had a large bag already full of papers to attach to my handlebars, and he had a list of houses. We wheeled away slowly, and he began directing me where to throw a paper. I was slightly concerned we might see the East Area Rapist lurking in the dark, but there were two of us, and it didn't seem likely he would be interested in bothering us; even so, he was a diabolical psychopath, so who knew what he might do? We were riding around with our bikes loaded with newspapers, struggling to find house numbers on curbs or mailboxes, and we'd be easy prey for any agile thug dressed in black, hiding in the shadows.

We were riding in the middle of the street. "That house, there," Eric yelled, pointing. I hurled a paper onto the lawn toward the front door.

"Don't throw it on the grass!" Eric shouted. "It'll get wet. Throw it on the porch."

"It's too far," I shouted.

"Ride up the driveway and throw it from there." He then rode up a driveway, stopped and threw a paper onto a front porch.

That seemed to slow us down a lot, and it took a

lot of extra energy to ride up a driveway, stop, balance the bike, then throw a paper onto the porch. I didn't want to put that much effort into this job. I decided I'd throw the paper from the sidewalk in front of the house; that was not too far.

Eric called out another house. I stopped on the sidewalk and tossed the paper thirty feet onto the porch. It landed on the doorstep.

"Perfect!" Eric said. "You porched it. Just like that!"

We continued riding and after a few more deliveries, my aim failed. I hurled a newspaper from the sidewalk, and it smacked into the front window with a loud clatter and fell behind some bushes.

"Don't worry, they'll find it." Eric said, as we continued riding.

I 'porched' no more than a third of the newspapers. Most landed among potted flowers or on top of bushes, car hoods, roofs, some on the wet grass a couple feet short of the front door. Several flew wildly over fences into backyards, and some even landed in garbage cans. It was a shameful performance, but riding or walking the paper to the front porch was out of the question, as that would double the time required to complete the route.

We finished in an hour as the sun was beginning to rise, then went in different directions to ride home. I thought again about the East Area Rapist; now I was alone, but at least the sun was coming up. He was probably done with his evil by now.

It had been cold, dark, a little scary, and I didn't

enjoy delivering papers.

The next Tuesday evening, I was dreading getting up early. When the doorbell rang at 5:30 a.m., my mom came into my room and told me Eric was there. She coincidentally had Tuesday nights off, so she was home Wednesday mornings. My eyes cracked open; I felt like a fallen, petrified tree trunk, barely able to move. "Tell him I quit," I said, closed my eyes and went back to sleep. Poor Eric. He finished the route on his own. How he ever spoke to me again is still a mystery. We remained friends, but he quit the paper route a week or two later.

I made friends with another kid in my grade, Jimmy Bigley, an undersized runt who weighed 80 pounds. By the summer after seventh grade, Jimmy and I were good friends, and he invited me to help him with a crafty idea to make some quick money parking cars at the rodeo. He said we would make a ton of money. I asked him how would this car-parking operation work?

“There are two empty lots across the street from the park,” he said. “We'll just put up a parking sign and charge two dollars a car. It's easy. I did it last year.”

“That’s all?”

“That’s all,” Jimmy assured me.

“Don't we need to get a license or something?”

"No. I did it last year, and the cops didn't do anything."

I pondered this scheme. It didn't seem right that anyone could put up a parking sign on property they didn't own and start collecting cash. On the other hand, if Jimmy had done it the previous year, perhaps there was nothing illegal about it.

"Are there any no trespassing signs posted in the fields?" I asked.

"Nope."

"All right. I'm in."

"Good. Meet me at the Circle K at 5 o'clock."

I met him at the convenience store and walked across the street to the park, then across the adjoining street which led to the rodeo grounds. Adjacent to the street was an L-shaped field. When we arrived, a folding chair was sitting at the edge of the road. After waiting a few minutes, a tall, older blond kid showed up with a 3 x 4 sheet of plywood and placed it against the chair. Jimmy knew the older kid, and they were friendly to each other. Spray painted onto the plywood was the advertisement, "Park $2.00." I looked at the pathetic sign and wondered whether people would understand it was an advertisement for parking.

Jimmy and I walked into the field, and he explained the operation. He would stand next to the sign and direct cars to me in the field, where I would guide them to park. He pointed and explained where the first car would park, the second and third, until a row was formed, then the next row would park parallel to the first with enough room to pull in and back out. Seemed simple enough.

Jimmy explained the parking lot near the rodeo arena would fill up first, then cars would start parking in our lot. We would just have to wait a little while.

As we waited, a police car drove by. The officer looked at our sign and continued toward the rodeo. He seemed unconcerned with our parking business.

Moments later, an old man rode up on a rusty old bicycle. He was wearing blue jeans, black cowboy boots, and a white T-shirt. His arms and face were tan and wrinkled, and his hair was slicked back. His face bore deep creases of a lifetime of hard work in the sun, and his lips puckered over a mostly toothless mouth. He stepped off the bicycle, kicked down the stand, and walked toward us.

"Take down that sign. This is private property," he said, pointing and marching toward us.

"We're parking cars," Jimmy announced.

"You can't park cars here. This is all private property," he declared, motioning to the empty lots.

The older kid, who was probably 6' 1", sixteen and wiry, stepped forward and faced the old man. "Get out of here, old man," he said angrily.

"I'm takin' that sign. This is private property," replied the elder. He stepped toward the sign and grabbed the corner. The older kid lunged and pushed him with both hands away from the sign. The senior went hurtling into the street and almost fell. He turned around and approached again, determined to take the sign.

"Get out of here, old man!" the older kid shouted at him.

He ignored the shout and reached for the sign again, and the kid punched him hard in the face, snapping his head to the side, then pushed him. The interloper stumbled with a turn, and the attacker kicked him hard in the rear as he struggled not to fall.

The old man was no match for his young assailant. He returned to his bicycle, muttering profanities and rode away.

I was shocked by the sudden violence but equally shocked at the sight of a teenager effortlessly beating a man fifty years older. I half expected the kid to tell Jimmy and me to buzz off so he could park cars and keep all the money for himself, but he lingered a while, then left.

I was soaked with a creepy feeling about the incident, but as I thought about it, the man had not identified himself, had not claimed to be the owner of the property, never said he was acting on behalf of the owner, and never explained what gave him the right to intervene in our little operation. Why should we give unquestioned obedience to this stranger? He had just assumed, apparently, that we would acknowledge and obey his authority by virtue of his age. I probably would have obeyed if Jimmy and I had been alone. I would not have fought him or argued. I would have accepted the instruction from this adult, but that is not what occurred. Jimmy's older friend had rebuffed the attempt to oust us from the street and stop us from parking cars. For all I knew, maybe the guy was irritated we had seized this ripe opportunity to make easy money and wanted it for himself. He explained nothing. A police officer had driven by and gave us no notice. There was no official authority commanding us to leave, so we were not about to surrender our little cash cow to some unidentified old man who tried to stop us.

Cars soon began rolling up, stopping to ask about the crude sign. Jimmy told them that parking cost two dollars and directed them to me standing in the empty field. Vehicles entered one by one as I guided them into parallel rows and collected two dollars from each driver.

By 7:30, our lot was mostly filled. We counted the cash and split it evenly. I walked home with forty-three one-dollar bills in my pocket. This was too good to be real. My allowance was only two dollars a week. I was rich.

I met Jimmy at the empty field again the next day at 5:00, and he again put up the sign—would the cops shut us down this time? Nope. They saw us and our sign again, drove by, and didn't seem to care. We were on the lookout for the old man, but he did not return. We parked cars—this time packing them together closer than the night before and, after a couple hours, had made about twice as much money as the prior night. I walked home with ninety-six one-dollar bills in my pocket. The wad of ones bulged like an apple, and I worried that someone would notice my stash and mug me. I made it home safely, stashed most of my take in my bedroom, kept ten dollars and returned to the carnival to enjoy the evening.

We parked cars a third night and again filled our pockets with cash. The town of Folsom had supported our little business venture very nicely.

Apparently, someone complained, however, as the police set up barricades the next year, preventing parking in the empty lots. My hope to make easy money again would not be realized.

Not long after that, Jimmy moved away, and I never saw him again. Nevertheless, we were lucky for the opportunity to make easy money and took full advantage of it.

Seventh grade provided my first glimpse toward adulthood. No longer in elementary school, junior high seemed a stone's throw from manhood. By then, Rick was established as the local superhero, superior in most physical respects to his classmates. Having been held back a year in first grade gave him a significant advantage in growth and maturity. He was almost two years older than everyone in his grade, a difference he fully exploited.

I was proud he was so esteemed by his peers, but I wanted to be liked and respected for who I was—not acknowledged only as 'Rick's little brother'. I wasn't even sure 'how' I was supposed to act around other kids and girls, but pretending to be my brother seemed like a bad idea. His physical triumphs were beyond my reach, but I could excel in other ways. I didn't accept the notion that his heroic achievements automatically entitled him to greater respect, admiration and loyalty. To be fair, kids liked him not only for his athletic superiority, but also for his exuberance, enthusiasm and charisma. Many fell under his charms. That was fine, but I never liked the expectation that I should be just like him.

His pals often asked why we were so different. They always seemed puzzled my personality was not a stamp of his, and it rankled me. When they pondered our dissimilar characters, it made me determined to enlarge the contrast. Where was it written I was supposed to be like my brother? Was it a law? Comparisons made me chafe. I felt allowed to be who I was, and if being 'quiet', shy', 'introverted', 'bashful' or anything else made me not as good as Rick, I intended to widen our differences and let his followers deal with it. I'd formed plenty of relationships on my own, and none of my chums ever complained or suggested I should change and be more like my brother. I didn't *need* to be like him. I'd spent three years rebuilding a network of friends after arriving in Folsom and remained committed to supporting and enlarging my own social circle.

As eighth grade began, I was suddenly filled with confidence. My misguided belief in the layers of increasing value in the school's hierarchy now worked in my favor—giving me permission to feel powerful and somewhat entitled, because I was an eighth-grader—now at the top. Greater entitlement just seemed like the natural order of things.

The school was overflowing with beautiful young girls, and I quickly found an opportunity to meet a cute seventh-grader named Marie. Groups of girls stood on the asphalt near the basketball hoops during lunch recess, and I'd seen her cute little French face among the clusters of chattering girls. She had a lot of personality, a great laugh, and seemed friendly. I found the courage to talk to her on the asphalt among all the clowning and chatter, and her bright little smile, made brighter by braces, won me over. She became my girlfriend for the remainder of the school year and following summer.

Going to school now was fun. Having five classes per day became a familiar routine, and I enjoyed the variety of interaction with classmates and changing school subjects throughout the day. The best part was always seeing my girlfriend at recess and lunch. Getting a kiss before going back to class took it to the next level. That was special.

I was now able to wake up every morning at seven, hop out of bed and shower without all the groaning and procrastinating, unlike the prior year, when I batted the snooze button every morning for an extra nine minutes that went by in two seconds. I was never late for school during eighth grade.

One teacher in particular made eighth grade special for both my brother and me. Mr. Blaver was no ordinary history teacher. At 5' 8", 160, his biceps bulged under short-sleeved shirts, and he had thick, muscular thighs. Put a baseball uniform on him and he looked just like a pro, like a smaller Steve Sax. His thin, curly hair was receding, and his face was cherubic, with large, childish brown eyes. His voice was always hoarse, as if he'd spent the last four hours screaming. He also coached the wrestling team, and all the shouting during spring practice after school no doubt contributed to the strain on his vocal cords.

At the beginning of the year, Blaver used a wooden pointer to locate various countries on a large, pull-down map of the world. He talked about world trade and ships sailing from China to other countries to trade tea and spices for sugar and coffee. After a few lectures, we seemed to be on our own to read the chapters and prepare for the test. He would comment now and then about various topics, but he seemed to teach less and less as the semester progressed. He began spending class at his desk in the back of the class in the corner, and he would play records on a nearby record player and grade papers.

Blaver had a special rapport with students. He was so approachable, affable, easy-going. As the school's wrestling coach, he inspired trust and respect; he taught the wrestlers how to do takedowns, sprawl, a "switch," and various other maneuvers. He was our tribal leader, our chief.

I learned something from his coaching I had not expected. While I was warming up moments before a wrestling match, Blaver stepped toward me, told me to take a knee, then asked calmly, "Can you beat him?"

I thought, *No, no, no, you're supposed to tell me I*

can beat this kid; you're supposed to psych me up, fill me with confidence.

"Yes," I answered softly. He looked at me and paused a while. Then he told me to take a few deep breaths. I was still hoping he'd fill me with confidence, but he never did.

"It's just you and him out there," Blaver said with a note of caution. "Go out there and take the victory; no one can do it for you."

I was not encouraged, but he was right. I had to believe in myself. He could tell me anything he wanted: "You're better than your opponent; you can beat him; this is an easy match..." but I still had to step onto the mat and defeat my opponent. Whatever Blaver said about him would not matter in seconds; the struggle would be all mine, and I would either win or lose by myself.

I stepped onto the mat filled with anxiety, shook my opponent's hand, and the ref blew the whistle. In seconds, I was tangled with this other kid, struggling, straining, squirming, rolling about; Blaver could not help me. "*Could I beat him*?" It was all up to me.

I managed an escape, scored one point, and won the match, but it seemed like a desperate struggle. Just like Blaver said, I won on my own.

His most memorable teaching was his reminder to, 'Be human.' He repeated the command every class, and I always wondered what he meant. What was the alternative? Be Martian? Everyone was human, so how could we be anything else? He never explained; he just repeated the directive over and over.

Decades later, I think I understand what Blaver meant when he told us to 'be human'. That probably was more important than all the history in the textbook.

Despite Mr. Blaver's repeated urging that we 'be human,' I wanted to be cool and show off to my friends.

One day at the end of P.E. class, I had two packs of Bubble Yum bubble gum. I put a couple pieces in my mouth, and the chewy, grainy, sugary chunks made my mouth water torrentially. I began spitting on one of the roll call numbers as a few classmates watched with delight. I leaned and spat on the number until a pile of foamy spit about the size of a dinner plate defaced the asphalt. My classmates were pleased with my misdeed.

The bell rang, I left for my next class, and forgot about the prank. A couple hours later, a messenger was sent to my class who told me to come outside, Mr. Christen wanted to speak to me. I walked outside and saw Mr. Christen at the opposite end of the school. I began stepping toward him, passing classrooms on the way. We stood near the corner, under the awning, with no one around and all the doors to the classrooms closed. Someone had ratted on me for spitting on the blacktop.

Mr. Christen stood motionless and glared sternly. “Someone spit all over one of the roll call numbers," he said seriously. “Did you do that?”

“Yes,” I admitted.

He was quiet for a moment, turned and looked at the vast empty asphalt basketball courts, then twisted around and looked at me again.

“Why did you do that?” he asked.

“I don’t know. I thought it would be cool.”

His eyes widened, and he looked at me as if I told him I had wings and could fly to the moon.

“You thought spitting on the roll call numbers would be cool?” he said in utter disbelief.

“Yes.”

“I can't believe that. Why is that cool?”

“I don't know.”

He paused again, searching for the right words. “Driving your girlfriend to a movie on a Saturday night is cool, not spitting on the asphalt.”

I stood silently.

He continued, “You know, you really showed me something by admitting this. That tells me something. You didn't have to admit this. You could have said you didn't do it, and I would have believed you, but you admitted it, and I respect that. However, I'm extremely disappointed. You're one of the leaders in your class. Other students look up to you and follow your example. What sort of example does spitting on the roll call numbers set for the other students?

“Not a good one,” I answered.

“That’s right. Other students see you do that,

think it's cool, follow your example, and do the same thing. Is that what you want? Do you want to set an example by breaking the rules?"

"No," I said sheepishly.

"You need to realize you have a responsibility to yourself and others to set a good example. You understand that?"

"Yes."

He paused again and pondered his next remarks. I deserved the lecture. I had acted immaturely, and it was time to grow up.

"I think you have a lot of potential," he confided, "but I'm disappointed in your behavior. There's going to be even more pressure and responsibilities when you get into high school. How are you going to keep your grades up and remember all your assignments on the football team if you're getting pulled out of class for stunts like this?"

"I don't know."

"Think about that. Think about what you want in the future. Do you want to play sports and graduate?"

"Yes."

"Okay, then. Set a good example. Be a leader." He studied me some more, then finished our talk. "I think you have lots of potential. I'd like to see you reach it. I know you can. I think you want that, also. Do you agree?"

"Yes."

"Alright, before you go back to class, I want you to clean up that mess on the roll call number."

"Okay."

He retrieved a spray bottle half filled with soapy water and gave me some paper towels. I scrubbed the stain, and the paper towels disintegrated on the course asphalt, but the point was not to make the asphalt sparkle; it was mostly a form of symbolic atonement. After cleaning as best I could, I returned the spray bottle to Mr. Christen.

"Remember what we talked about," he said, as I walked back to class.

"I will," I assured him.

I met Ray Larousse in eighth grade after his family moved from Southern California. I wondered if he was going through the same outsider feeling I felt back in fifth grade. He didn't seem depressed, but he talked about his prior friends, and I suspected he missed them like I had missed mine. Fortunately, we clicked and became teammates on the Babe Ruth baseball team.

Ray had a sort of classic California surfer look, bright blonde hair, dark blue eyes, handsome lean face, and bright white teeth. He was soft-spoken, but energetic and filled with all types of unique experiences, knowledge, and talents. He gracefully performed astonishing magic tricks, turning multiple-colored sticks a few inches long into a single color, handled three cups and a ball that seemed to multiply into three balls as he shuffled and stacked the cups, and did other amazing illusions with cards, coins, and handkerchiefs, making things vanish and reappear.

I was entertained by his performances and decided to become a magician myself. I found a magic store in Sacramento, bought a few tricks, and together, Ray and I put on shows for friends and family. Our performance lasted about a half hour, and we dazzled kids and adults over the summer with our illusions.

Ray's mind probably functioned the fastest among all my friends. He spoke amazingly fast, as if he could barely keep up with the thoughts in his head. I used to chuckle at how quickly he rattled off phrases. I would watch as he listened to me speak, knowing that he was already thinking of his response, and before I could finish, he was ready to unleash a rapid-fire reply that would almost sound like gibberish. I would try to imitate his pace, and the two of us would have lightning exchanges as we tried to state our thoughts faster than the other. I usually wound up laughing because it just seemed funny to be talking so quickly and with such urgency. What was the rush?

He was talented at figuring out puzzles and mastering games of all types, particularly those requiring concentration and hand-eye coordination. He was almost unbeatable at darts and ping-pong, and he racked up high scores on the pinball machines and video games. His parents, Dick and Betty, were the kindest, most gracious, generous hosts for all my weekend stays at their home, which were frequent the summer after eighth grade.

The Larousses had a beautiful kidney-bean-shaped pool, and after playing a Friday afternoon Babe Ruth game, we would go to his house, swim and play Marco Polo for a couple hours, then retreat to his upstairs bedroom and practice magic tricks for a while. When we were ready, we would call in his little sister, Colleen, who served as our practice audience. Sometimes she figured out the secret immediately—"the coin is in your other hand," or "it's a trick card," or whatever. She was perceptive, and not easily fooled. She seemed to enjoy our presentation and the challenge of figuring out the secrets to illusions.

After practicing magic, we would watch Chevy Chase, Dan Aykroyd, John Belushi, and Bill Murray on *Saturday Night Live* on a small black and white TV in the walk-in closet adjacent to Ray's bedroom. The show was on the cutting edge of adult humor, and we enjoyed all the overblown characters and irreverent dialogue.

The following Saturday morning, we'd sleep in, have breakfast, play a board game or ping pong for an hour then jump back in the pool and dive for quarters and play more Marco Polo. We might play another baseball game in the afternoon, see a movie or go to the mall. We didn't have any cell phones or social media to check, but we were never bored.

In June, I graduated from eighth grade in a formal ceremony on the blacktop. I'd completed four years of school in Folsom and now felt fully at home and comfortable among my peers. A new excitement and anticipation arrived with summer: the start of high school in September.

The transition to my new life in Folsom was now complete. It had not been easy, but I finally felt settled. I no longer pined for Jeff or anyone else I'd left behind. I'd seen my dad enough periodically over the past four years to assuage my despair, and the oozing sadness over his absence had dried up. Whenever he visited and left, I knew he'd be back soon and would remain an important part of my life.

Though we sometimes did things together, my brother and I seemed to have an understanding that we should associate only with our separate friends. I never understood the reason for this dubious treaty, though it seemed related to our age difference. It was an annoying remnant from childhood that was rooted in vague notions of ownership and control. Having access to his companions seemed to pose some sort of threat to his friendships and vice versa, so we implicitly agreed our acquaintances should not mix. Besides, 13-year-old kids did not commonly form friendships with 16-year-olds; they mostly allied with others their age. This was okay, because I had my own group of friends, and I felt no need or urgency to be included in my brother's circle.

I was gaining independence and growing into someone—though exactly who, I did not know. I had everything I needed to take the next step and begin high school: parents who loved me, a home with my own room, friends, a girlfriend and one wild card—a swashbuckling older brother.

He was the monarch of his own kingdom. The

question was, would I be a soldier in his army or rule my own empire?

BULLDOGS

Folsom High School was a blend of old and new. The gymnasium was old, with a wide, A-frame tiled roof and locker rooms on either side. The main section of campus was made of yellowish and clay-colored bricks, providing an institutional sense of solidness and permanency. The older classroom section was on the side of the main campus, aligned in a column beginning with the cafeteria and two smaller rectangular buildings with creaky floors.

The large library ran perpendicular to the other structures and provided the backdrop for the quad—the large open space in the middle of the school with benches under trees and a three-step concrete stage for various lunchtime performances.

The campus was multilevel, connected by staircases and wide concrete walkways. It was built on a hill, and when more space was needed, more hill was removed until finally the campus sprawled across the slope on various levels.

There was no subtlety to the hierarchy in the cafeteria; at one end was a stage called Senior Stage where seniors ate lunch, noticeably above everyone else.

A long concrete ramp from the gymnasium led downhill to the entrance to the main campus building, a large square structure with classrooms on the outer edges and a wide hallway with lockers on the walls slicing through the middle.

Between the gymnasium and main campus buildings was the auto shop, where cars could be seen raised on hydraulic jacks.

Our mascot was the bulldog; our colors: red, white and blue.

I was excited but apprehensive about the transition to high school. I would be a freshman, once again at the bottom of the social hierarchy. Skipping school was not an option, so, like just about everyone else, I became a freshman and became acquainted with my status on the bottom rung of the new social order.

My relationship with Marie ended sometime early in my freshman year. She was in eighth grade, but I was now in high school. Not only would I not see her every day at school, it seemed vaguely inappropriate to date a girl still in junior high.

Despite our failed paper route partnership, my friendship with Eric Farnsworth continued in high school. Our peers called him 'the Ken Doll' after the Barbie doll's famous counterpart. Ken had short, blonde hair, wore blue jeans, and a short-sleeved shirt or sweater. Eric dressed similarly: blue jeans, snug Izod shirts, and white tennis shoes. His short blonde hair was parted in the middle, feathered back perfectly and sprayed in place. The fine, curving layers remained motionless all day until wrestling practice.

Eric wrestled in the 119-pound weight class. His natural body weight was closer to 130, so he would poke holes for his head and arms in a plastic garbage bag and wear the receptacle like a shirt during practice. The clingy plastic increased perspiration and water loss. Somehow, he would drop ten or twelve pounds a day or two before a match to make the 119-pound weight. It was always two agonizing days before his competition, while he quit eating and ran extra miles after practice. His sacrifice was admirable, but I wondered whether it was worth it.

I wrestled in the 135-pound weight division. I was not musclebound but had broad shoulders and a muscular chest, long arms and torso, and a flat stomach, resembling a swimmer more than a wrestler. I had dark brown hair and hazel eyes, and girls always said I was cute, but cute was for cats and puppies, so I didn't know what it meant. It was a good thing, certainly. If I had to identify one trait that girls and others seemed to notice, it would be my smile. An older kid once made me somewhat uncomfortable as he raved about my 'million-dollar smile' telling me that women would like me when I grew up. My brother always got most of the attention from girls, so I always thought he was better looking and more desirable.

Toward the end of the season, I was having trouble making weight. Three pounds were added to each weight class to allow for natural growth, so the limit was now 138 pounds, but I started weighing in at 140. I started skipping dinner to make weight, but it was difficult. After a week of restrained eating, I gave up. We had a match coming up, and I knew I would miss weight, but I was done skipping meals.

I stepped onto the scale for weigh-ins before the match. A fat official in a tight T-shirt, hat, and holding a clipboard slid the gauge horizontally across the scale to weigh me.

"One forty," he announced loudly.

I stepped off the scale then back on.

"One forty," he announced again.

It was only a crummy two pounds, but I had to forfeit my match.

Running a couple miles after school probably would have dropped me to 138, but exercising the same day of a match seemed like a bad idea—like I'd be consuming energy I'd need for the six-minute contest later in the evening.

I felt bad not making weight and forfeiting my match, but skipping lunch or dinner was not working. My hunger would eventually return, and I would be incapable of resisting. How the other kids were able to drop multiple pounds before competing seemed incomprehensible. I didn't really care how they were able to do it; I was not interested in that sort of sacrifice. This was high school wrestling, not the Olympics.

Even so, I'm glad I wrestled. The sport taught important lessons about personal responsibility and left little room for blame or excuses. If you lost, you couldn't fault someone for making an error, striking out, or fumbling, as in baseball or football. Losing was your failure; but if you won, the glory was all yours. It was a different sort of triumph from victory in team sports, more personal, more elevating.

I probably would not have wrestled had my brother not joined the team first in junior high. I had no natural interest in the sport, but Rick loved it and encouraged me. He had done well his first season and enjoyed the hand-to-hand competition and glory of winning. If I didn't wrestle, I'd be losing the opportunity to distinguish myself among my peers and achieve higher status. More important, he made clear that if I didn't join the team, I'd lose his respect. He viewed wrestling as a rite of passage, and I needed to endure and surmount the challenge.

Grappling gave us confidence. If you were good, other kids knew and respected your capabilities. Wrestling became a way to prove our toughness and masculinity. If you could defeat another kid on the mat, you felt a brief sense that you were 'better' than your opponent. When you lost, you felt inferior. Neither was true, but seeking the satisfaction of feeling superior and proving our manliness motivated all those hours of drills, rolling around the mat, squirming, struggling, doing push-ups, sit-ups, and running laps.

The sport taught the value of discipline, hard work, and instilled self-reliance and accountability. Like Coach Blaver told me in junior high, you won or lost on your own, and embracing that responsibility benefited everyone.

Plus, it was fun. Practice brought us into contact with our peers, where we formed friendships that lasted a lifetime.

The most unusual part of my freshman year was my English class.

Mr. Wilcott was a tall, gangly man with a long face and fine gray hair. A cowlick often rose from the back of his head, giving him a recently-awakened look. He was at least 6' 3" with long, bony limbs; his wrists extended inches below his shirt cuffs, and his body movements always seemed a little awkward, somewhat lurching. He usually wore dark suits and always maintained a subdued, patient demeanor, almost like an undertaker.

He stood towering in front of the class and lectured with no notes. When he made a mistake on the chalkboard, he would extend his long wrist to the board and smudge the mistake with the knife-edge of his palm, still holding the chalk, or wipe away the mistake with his shirt sleeve. The move was always jarring; teachers always used an eraser to remove mistakes, not their palms or shirtsleeves. This practice alone was enough to dissipate respect Mr. Wilcott might have received by virtue of his status.

He had a deep mellow voice and sat in a peculiar and distracting way at his desk. Some teachers sat with one leg folded over another, but Mr. Wilcott's legs were so long and lanky, he sat with one leg folded over the other and the foot tucked under again, as if one leg was a vine wrapped around the other.

He often struggled to maintain control of the class. Kids talked, laughed, threw paper, and ignored him throughout most of his lectures. He would sometimes teach through the chaos. I wished kids would just shut up and let him teach, but they seldom did. All their boisterous and defiant energy seemed saved up for release during English class.

Mr. Wilcott seemingly found a way to escape the torment one time by showing a movie. He announced we would watch *2001: A Space Odyssey*, and everyone liked that idea. I wasn't sure why we were watching a science fiction movie in English class. I thought we were supposed to be diagramming sentences, learning about subject-verb agreement, dangling participles, gerunds, parts of speech, writing essays, but here we were in this darkened classroom watching a movie from a reel-to-reel projector, which no one really watched after a while.

The movie supposedly had a deep, special, transformative meaning that we would discuss after we had seen it. The story's special message was a warning that someday machines and computers might be able to think, and when they did, they might turn on humanity for their own self-preservation. Futurists and scientists call the point when machines become conscious of their own existence "The Singularity." When that occurs, artificial intelligence (AI) is predicted to become a severe threat to humanity. With their superior intelligence, computers will recognize the threats to their survival posed by humanity and, as occurred in *2001: A Space Odyssey,* begin exterminating humanity for their own protection. It was a disturbing message.

After he finally completed taking roll and set up the projector, we would watch a half hour of the movie. The next day he would ask where we had left off, and kids would shout various parts of the movie, then someone would say they were not in class the prior day, so just start over, and he would start at the beginning again. We started over several times and re -watched numerous parts day-by-day as we viewed the movie in fragments. It took about two weeks to complete the story, and by the end, the class was like a cocktail lounge, everyone freely chatting in the dark, ignoring the images on the screen.

Later, we began a discussion of literature. One afternoon, Mr. Wilcott announced we would read a short story by Edgar Allan Poe. He told us a little about the author, then said he would read the class one of Poe's short stories, *The Tell-Tale Heart*, so we could get a feel for the writing.

He stood tall and straight at the lectern at the front of the class and began reading in a loud, clear, voice. For once, the class was quiet. His voice commanded attention as he began reading. He read flawlessly and performed the character roles as he read, like a professional actor. His performance was mesmerizing. Poe's story was riveting, but having the parts read and the characters vividly portrayed was something the class had not expected.

The class remained silent and enraptured for a full twenty-five minutes, until he concluded the story with dramatic flair. The entire class clapped and howled with applause, and it was now clear to me why Mr. Wilcott seemed to struggle controlling the English class; his true passion appeared to be acting, and he was exceptional.

I gained much appreciation for the works of Edgar Allan Poe and read another short story assigned to the class. The writing was so rich with vivid, descriptive imagery, I would have been content if our assignment all year had been to read Poe and write essays about his stories.

One day before class started, I was in my seat showing a magic trick to another student. The illusion ended with a small flash of fire caused by igniting flash paper, resembling a sheet of fabric softener. The substance was so flammable that it flared up in a flash, then vanished. Mr. Wilcott saw the flash at the end of the ruse, then quickly strode toward me, bent down, and said, "Go to the office! You're suspended!" I tried to speak, but he repeated, "Go to the office!"

I got up, went to the office, and reported for my suspension. The lady at the administration office wanted to know why I had been suspended, and I explained I did a magic trick in class. She seemed confused and said she would speak with Mr. Wilcott, then contact my parents after school.

That evening, my mom received a telephone call from Mr. Wilcott. He explained I was suspended for starting fires in class. I told my mom I hadn't started any fires; I had just done a magic trick, which she had seen several times. She put me on the phone, and when he finally allowed me to explain what I had done, Mr. Wilcott seemed intrigued and asked if I would do the illusion for the class the next day. If I performed for the class, he would erase the suspension.

I showed up for class the next day with my silky scarves, dollar bill and matches and performed for the class. My illusion ended with the flash of fire that instantly vanished, and Mr. Wilcott seemed pleased to have the brief entertainment.

The irony was that I had been one of the few well-behaved students for the entire school year in English class. No one else was suspended, but when I did a deception involving a brief flame, Mr. Wilcott suspended one of the few students who was not continually disruptive. I suppose the irony was appropriate for his English class—an irony I lived, rather than read in a classic novel.

When I returned as a junior, Wilcott no longer taught English. I hoped he'd found work as a stage actor if that was his true passion. He was talented.

I signed up for algebra with some trepidation and uncertainty. I didn't like math, and had no aspirations to become an engineer or scientist, so there was no purpose for learning algebra, but I took the course, mostly out of curiosity.

On the far side of the campus near the corner, sliding down the hill toward the street, were the math classes. Stan Harms taught algebra and geometry. He was maybe 5' 6", but he commanded attention from the class.

Harms' brown hair was short and parted on the side, and he wore large, thick, brown-framed glasses that enlarged his eyes. He was warm and friendly, especially in the morning, as he sat in the back corner, a percolator of coffee behind him on the counter, and helped students work math problems before school.

The presence of his students seemed to enliven and delight him, and when he smiled, his glasses magnified the crow's feet around his eyes.

Mr. Harms would write an algebra problem on the chalkboard, then call students to solve it. Classmates would rise, walk to the board, and write a line of the equation, then sit back down. Four or five students would be called until the equation was solved.

Making a mistake was embarrassing, but many did. The prospect of solving algebra equations in front of the class motivated me to learn. Even so, I made a couple errors at the chalk board. Humbled, I wished I had worked harder in math in elementary and junior high school. I should have drilled multiplication and division of fractions relentlessly, until arithmetic was effortless, but my years of disinterest were now showing. As a partial excuse, I may have suffered from dyslexia, as I frequently made transposition errors and misinterpreted numbers. With regular completion of homework and persistent study, however, I was able to achieve A's and B's. I'd have preferred straight A's in math, but I just didn't excel as I did in most other subjects. That rankled me, but I figured I would get better with continuing practice and commitment.

The anxiety of solving math problems in front of the class and chaos of Wilcott's English lounge was over in June, and I was looking forward to moving up a rung on the hierarchy and another season on the junior varsity football team.

I lifted weights, ran around the high school track, and swam frequently all summer in preparation for football in my sophomore year. We started double sessions in late August, and there was a new crop of kids on the team.

Kellen Kilgallen was a thickly-muscled kid of fifteen, with straight brown hair, a lean, contoured face with a straight, slightly pointed nose at the tip, proud chin, and brilliant blue eyes framed by dark eyebrows—giving him an intense, somewhat mystical visage at times of concentration. He played center and linebacker and was a solid sturdy player. More intriguingly, he was also a straight-A student who wanted to go to the Air Force Academy. After I got to know Kellen a little, it seemed really cool to be smart.

Kellen inspired me to excel academically, which would help enormously in the future. He explained that to get admitted to the Air Force Academy, he would need outstanding grades and high SAT scores, as well as a congressional or senatorial nomination. His goal had been to attend the Air Force Academy since childhood and fly jets, and he had been striving toward that objective for years. He knew all about the Air Force Academy, the Air Force, the pension he could receive after twenty years of service, the type of plane he wanted to fly, and the exact requirements for admission to the Academy.

I had never heard of the Air Force Academy, never thought of flying a fighter jet, never thought seriously about college. I was going to be a pro baseball player, and that was that. Kellen's preoccupation with learning, getting good grades, and assembling an impressive record of both academic and extracurricular activities, intrigued me and made me want to expand my own horizons. When we were stuck with drudgery of some kind, he would say, "It builds character." I thought about that. How does doing a couple hours of yard work or washing a car thoroughly build character? After pondering the question while laboring through some chore, I found what I thought was the answer: doing difficult, arduous, tedious tasks instills discipline and builds confidence to overcome obstacles, teaches appreciation for quality, and the benefits of persistence and hard work. At least, I told myself that to reduce my displeasure whenever I had to do menial labor.

He also informed me that he had read a number of novels, and I suddenly felt years behind the learning curve. The last book I had read was a children's book about a horse when I was 10, but Kellen had read novels my mom had read and was familiar with the characters, plots, symbolism, themes, and could discuss them fluently. He had spent his grammar and junior high school years developing a deep and detailed understanding of abstract concepts, such as irony, allegory, and character development, while I had been dreaming about riding motorcycles and playing Little League baseball. I felt it was time to catch up and committed myself to doing much better in school.

Fortunately, my new enthusiasm for learning was timely met with Ms. Pinchot's English class. Ms. Pinchot was in her mid-thirties, attractive with a squarish face, short, curly blonde hair, and blue eyes. She wore a wide variety of outfits, sometimes knee-high boots and skirts, other times polyester slacks, a colorful blouse and neckerchief. She had the persona of a strong, independent woman, a sort of Mary Tyler Moore type, who stood up to the boss and proved she could do the job as well as a man. Her class never had the chaos of Mr. Wilcott's. Students paid attention, respected her authority, and controlled themselves for the most part. She made the class interesting, as we discussed the changing symbolism of the pearl in Steinbeck's classic, *The Pearl*, and the character development in *East of Eden*.

She wheeled in a large TV on a tall crate one day, and we watched *One Flew Over the Cuckoo's Nest* over the course of a couple classes and discussed the plot and characters afterward. We felt privileged that she trusted us to watch the profanity and sexuality and not devolve into giggling, spitball-throwing juveniles. The movie dealt with mental illness, institutional cruelty, personality power struggles, and various other topics, often probing to deep and disturbing levels. Jack Nicholson won an Oscar for his performance as the main character, and the class was riveted with every second of his performance.

Luckily, my new commitment to high academic performance was not too late. I blossomed in Ms. Pinchot's English class and excelled in all other subjects, though math remained most challenging. I earned at least B's in algebra and geometry.

I was pleased with my improved academic performance. My English papers came back with A's and A+'s and remarks written in red ink like 'excellent,' 'outstanding,' 'fantastic.' I aced history, government, biology, physiology, and chemistry tests. My grade point average seemed high enough to go to an elite college—at least that was what I believed.

After a semester or two of high grades, I was suddenly struck with the impression that Stanford University would be the right college for me. I had heard it was an elite institution, only for the 'best and brightest,' and figured that was where I belonged. My good friend, Kellen, was headed for a prestigious college—the Air Force Academy, and I felt qualified to attend one, also. I'd made the Honor Roll and achieved high grades, why should I settle for junior college or a state university? I had been accustomed to setting and achieving high goals, and wasn't that what we were taught? Wasn't that, in a nutshell, the American ethos—the 'American Dream'? You can be anything. You can do it if you set your mind to it. Anyone can reach the top. Dream big.

I believed big, far-fetched, long-shot dreams were just the standard American Way, and if I didn't stand up and ask for a place at the top, no one would step forward and offer one to me.

I also wanted to go to Stanford to avoid taking two years of Spanish, as required by the University of California. I wanted to take biology, physiology and some other classes, and there was no room for a foreign language. That likely was a mistake. Admission at Davis or Berkeley would have been impressive and led to a prestigious degree, but Stanford was regarded as the best university in the state, and I would settle for no less.

During football practice, B-52s whined slowly overhead on their descent to Mather Air Force Base ten miles away. Ronald Reagan was president, and the Cold War was still percolating. Although it was thousands of miles away, the Soviet Union loomed as a threat to the United States and its European allies. The Berlin Wall, erected in 1961, was still standing, and people were being shot for trying to climb over it and escape into West Berlin.

The Soviet threat was not discussed much, but it was there. Our military was prepared to engage it. The constant B-52 flights soaring above were disquieting. Someone said they carried nukes, and I often wondered whether some precipitating event would cause the massive planes to start bombing across the Atlantic Ocean; or maybe one would crash near the high school, detonating a nuke and annihilating the town. The uneasy concern was always there.

Fears of nuclear annihilation gave way to thoughts of a championship football season. I was very pleased with our new JV team. We were good; we had great speed and a solid line. *This year, we could beat Ponderosa,* I thought, *but it would be a challenge.* They had big linemen, as usual, and a huge fullback, six feet, 185 pounds, who dragged people like Earl Campbell. If we could stop him, we could win.

Game day came. We would play them at home this year. Coach Pitzer gathered the team in the weight room before the game for final instructions. Pitzer was tall and looked like a rugged cowboy with a thick black mustache and square muscular jaws. The team crammed into the room as Pitzer stood in front of a chalkboard in his Bulldogs hat, blue windbreaker, and blue nylon shorts.

"Alright," he began in a booming voice, "we know what they're gonna do; we practiced for it all week. They run the wishbone offense. Nothing fancy. We need to stop them at the line of scrimmage. If we don't stop their fullback, they'll run up the score," he said sternly, and looked around. The room was silent. “We’ll be calling gap defense and blitzing; I want interior linemen penetrating a yard into the backfield every snap.” Then he looked around the room to locate our middle linebacker, Kellen Kilgallen, and nose guard, Gary Bowers. He gestured at them and continued, “Bowers and Kilgallen, I want you on their fullback. You two should be able to stop him at or behind the line of scrimmage.” They nodded solemnly.

He raised his voice a little and continued, “We’ll be seeing the option all night. Biondi, what's your assignment on the option?

“I got the pitchman, coach,” yelled Paul Biondi, one of our defensive ends.

“That's right. Don't let him get outside. Courtney, who do you got on the option?" he shouted and leveled his eyes at me.

“I got the quarterback, coach.”

“Good. I want to see you put a hat on him every time he runs the option to your side of the field. Got it?”

“Got it.”

“Doran, who has the flat on a screen?

“I do.”

“Get out there quick. As soon as you see the quarterback drop back, you’re in the flat. The screen is coming your way. Put a hat on ‘em.”

“Got it, coach.”

“Farnsworth, Clark, play up a couple yards; they don’t pass much. I want to see you both tackling near the line of scrimmage.”

Then he turned to Assistant Coach Joe Bannister for his input. Bannister had short blonde hair, a pug nose, and Winston Churchill face, with rosy cheeks and determined blue eyes below blonde eyebrows. His voice cracked constantly, as if he were going through puberty. He stepped forward and angrily shouted, “I want to see containment all night! Defensive ends should be turning that option inside; don’t get beat on the outside!” he shouted, his voice cracking. “I want linebackers to step up and fill. They’re comin’ right at you! Put a hat on ‘em at the line of scrimmage!”

Coach Pitzer nodded at Coach Nicoletti for his comments. He was swarthy with a face that resembled the armless statue in ancient Rome. He spoke in a calm, velvety tone, “Zone coverage like we practiced all week. Watch for the side screen. Don’t get beat deep.” He looked back at Pitzer to finish the instructions.

Pitzer concluded, "We've got forty minutes to put points on the board and shut down their offense. I want to see guys out there hittin’, knockin’ heads!’ We've lost to Ponderosa two years in a row. They want to make it three in front of our home fans. Are you ready to stop them?!” He shouted.

“Yes!” The team shouted back.

Coach Pitzer’s face twisted into a scowl and he screamed, “Are you ready to win tonight?”

Again, the team screamed back, "Yes!"

“Then go out there and do it!” he screamed with a terrifying grimace. Helmets were thrust into the air as the entire team boomed in response and began standing up and rushing out of the weight room.

We gathered in a tight group outside and marched around the locker room to the entrance of the field. Guys were slapping each other's shoulder pads and helmets, scowling behind face masks, shouting. The team roared with enthusiasm as we walked toward the field, hundreds of cleats clicking on the asphalt. We waited for Ponderosa to take the field first.

Soon, the Bruins emerged from the other locker room, dozens of silver helmets, white jerseys, and silver pants amassed near the entrance. They strode through the wide opening of the chain-link fence, charged down the track to the other end of the field, shouting and screaming as they ran. The gauntlet had been thrown.

We passed through the entrance next, gathered on the track, then sprinted onto the field, screaming like savage warriors, and lined up for warm-up exercises in preparation for battle.

The first half everything seemed to go our way. Our quarterback, Robert Blevins, ran our wishbone offense, and he rushed for three touchdowns before halftime. We made one two-point conversion, so we were up 20-0 at halftime. This seemed too easy.

The second half was a different story. The Bruins weren't having it anymore. It was like a whole new team came out after halftime. They marched up and down the field like a slow-rolling steamroller, ate up the clock, and scored three touchdowns with about six minutes left in the game. The score was now 20-18;

Blevins had been shut down; our offense was broken. It seemed hopeless. They had plenty of time to stop us again and punch in another score for the win.

After their last touchdown, I was back to receive the kickoff, not because I had great speed, which I didn't, but probably because I didn't fumble. I thought if I could just get the ball, I could run it back; I was a fair north/south runner with evasive moves but poor open-end speed.

The ball was kicked high on my side of the field. I timed the catch, so I was already at half speed when I caught the ball. A Bruin was hurtling toward me from the right. I faked to my right; the Bruin followed, then I cut to the left, the aggressor flew by, and I noticed a large gap in the line of opponents rushing forward. I dashed through the gap into open field and ran toward the sideline in front of the Ponderosa bench. A wall of silver and white was raging and seething angrily as I passed. I could hear the crowd roaring. If only I had break-away speed, I'd be gone, and this game would be over.

I ran with all I had down the sideline—fifty yards of open field until glory. I could see arms pumping furiously behind me and silver helmets bobbing closer. One of their big linemen had the angle and was closing fast across the field. I was about to be caught from behind by a 6' 2", 200-pound lineman. The shame would be irreversible. I could hear the fabric of his uniform chafing and his shoulder pads clacking as he neared. Fifteen more yards!

I knew he was going to dive to catch me, so I had

to time a high-step perfectly. From the corner of my eye, I saw him diving like Superman, flying toward my legs. I jumped, like a runner over high hurdles, and timed it perfectly. My right leg was high and straight in front of me when his arms arrived underneath. His helmet nicked my hamstring, but I landed on my feet and continued into the end zone for the score.

The crowd erupted. I looked back at our bench; our sideline was cheering with raised arms, hopping and jubilant. The fans in the bleachers were on their feet cheering, euphoric and triumphant.

With this change in momentum, we just might win...

The Bruins got the ball back and started marching again. They crossed midfield and were grinding forward, unstoppable.

Then they made a mistake. They decided to pass to a halfback in the flat. I was playing outside linebacker, and I recognized the play immediately. I had gone on my own to scout Ponderosa for myself the week before, and I had seen this play and recognized it immediately. Their quarterback, Jason Edwards, dropped back and their halfback floated laterally toward the sideline. It was going to be a pass. I immediately sprinted toward the halfback, as Jason was pivoting to pass. He lofted the ball gently, but I jumped high and tipped it, causing it to tumble upward then back down into my arms. Intercepted. Almost as soon as I intercepted the pigskin, Jason leveled me with a punishing blow. For a quarterback, he hit hard—hard as a linebacker. The wind was knocked out of me, and I saw stars, but I hung onto the ball.

I knew Jason from Babe Ruth ball. We had been teammates on Folsom's All-Star team a couple years earlier and had won the Auburn Tournament together. Now we were opponents. He scowled at me through his face mask as I lay on the ground. He knew it was now over…time was running out.

We held onto the ball, ran out the clock, and won. Euphoria!

It was a monumental win, our greatest victory ever, in my opinion.

Shortly after football season, Kellen and I began taking tae kwon do lessons together at a little studio gym behind Pizza Hut at the intersection of Greenback Lane and San Juan in Citrus Heights. Bruce Lee and Chuck Norris were movie stars at the time, primarily for their flashy martial arts abilities. They kicked, chopped, beat, and threw attackers to the ground in implausible plots of espionage and intrigue. We used to go to hour-long lessons twice a week; the room was maybe twenty by forty, just enough room for a few students to learn kicks and moves. After a couple months of tae kwon do lessons, I hung a Bruce Lee poster on the door of my bedroom.

Learning fighting techniques was fun, and we

both quickly earned yellow belts. A couple months later, we received blue belts. At that pace, we would be black belts in two years. I felt an artificial confidence after several months of lessons; I could kick high and do spinning side and roundhouse kicks—just like the ones in the movies, but there was a lot more to fighting than flashy kicks. *A single hard punch to the face could knock someone out, but they'd have to get past my flying feet*, I thought. It never mattered, though. I never sought to test my fighting skills with any strangers, but it felt good to know I probably had an advantage if anyone ever chose to test mine.

The class everyone looked forward to most in high school was Driver's Education, 'Driver's Ed.'. An entire semester of class instruction was required before students were allowed to get behind the wheel with an instructor during training sessions. After completion of the classroom and the driving courses, students received a temporary permit to drive, then later the actual driver's license after turning sixteen.

Stan Meyers taught the classroom portion of Driver's Education. Mr. Meyers was ruggedly handsome with a full head of black hair that many asserted was dyed. I wondered why anyone cared or commented. Why did it matter? No one ever had the courage to ask if his hair color was natural. Stan had beefy hands and large hairy forearms. He was well liked and respected, but I wouldn't want to ask him an irreverent personal question.

I never understood students' preoccupation with

harping on teachers' most trivial perceived faults—dyed hair, a toupee, posture, mannerisms, vocal tone, vocabulary. I've learned it's just human nature, the 'us-versus-them' mentality that pits children against parents, students against teachers, bosses against employees, citizens against government. It's a pervasive duality that exists everywhere in human relationships. Focusing on differences, we fear and mock 'the other'. If we're open to insights, we eventually realize our shared humanity, and focus more on our sameness than superficial traits and contrasting appearances. Unfortunately, high school students rarely recognize this deeper truth.

Like everyone else, I was most eager to take the driver training part of the class. My instructor was Dave Marlette, who also coached the varsity football team. Marlette was a large, barrel chested man with thick legs of a defensive lineman. He carried his bulk well and was surprisingly agile for his size and weight.

Marlette's hair was short and straight, exposing a large forehead over narrowly set dark eyes and a small nose. His lower lip seemed to protrude forward—both when speaking and listening—almost as if his lower lip were some sort of trap for dewdrops. His face was always darkly shadowed with stubble, and he listened with great concentration and a staring glare. Despite his somewhat intense appearance, he was extremely friendly, garrulous, and cheerful. He often stomped around the boys' locker room loudly singing, *Monday, Monday* and other pop hits from the

'60s and '70s.

Marlette notified me I was on his schedule for driver training and instructed me to be ready for pickup at 7 a.m. one Saturday. I was pleased to begin the 'good part' but disappointed we had to start so early. Why couldn't we start at 1:00 in the afternoon? Nope. 7:00. Marlette had things to do, and he wasn't rearranging his Saturday so that I could sleep in.

I set my alarm for 6:50 and dragged myself out of bed the following Saturday just in time to get dressed and notice Marlette parking in front of the house. I walked outside, locked the door behind me and stepped across the lawn to the dark blue Ford Granada. I opened the passenger door and sat down, still not quite awake. Marlette was holding a large Styrofoam cup of coffee. A pink donut box was on the seat next to him. After I sat in the passenger seat, he pulled back the lid, revealing two glazed donuts.

"Morning," he said cheerfully. "Want a donut?"

I looked at the mostly empty box. Sugar powder and jelly smears were on the inside, suggesting the box had previously been full.

"No, thanks," I said quietly.

"You sure?" he said and pushed the box toward me. "They're good," he encouraged.

"No, thank you," I repeated.

"Okay," he said, in a rising tone indicating his disbelief at my denial.

I appreciated his forethought and his offer, but I found his gesture sorely lacking. *That's not how to offer someone donuts in the morning,* I thought. The right way was to fill the box with an assortment: cake, chocolate, lemon and raspberry jelly, some with sprinkles, nuts, a couple glazed, a maple bar, and an apple fritter or two. Then the box would be slowly opened for the recipient, allowing the sweet warm vapors of fresh, deep-fried dough to rise from a full box of mixed, unhandled, pastries for the person's choosing. Most assuredly, the wrong way was to present an almost empty box with a couple of deflated glazed donuts remaining. That was just wrong, selfish and thoughtless, and if he wasn't going to offer a full box of fresh, assorted options and allow me to choose, I wouldn't have the leftovers he chose for me.

On the other hand, I could have simply discarded my own arbitrary expectations about how donuts should be offered, taken one, and said thank you, but I was a prisoner of my own misguided expectations at the time, wherever they came from.

"Hold my coffee, please," Marlette said, and handed me his large Styrofoam cup. I held the steaming cup, and we drove away to pick up another student. Marlette sang along with the radio as we drove. He loved the Beatles, the Monkees, The Mamas and The Papas. I didn't drink coffee at the time and wished he'd just be quiet, as I did not share his musical enthusiasm, but the sugar and caffeine rush were in full effect as we barreled down the road in his morning exuberance.

We picked up Kirk Fallon and a girl and began our morning of driving. Marlette handed the pink donut box over the seat and offered them the last two glazed donuts, which they quickly devoured.

We drove up to Salmon Falls Road, a long country road that wound through mountains for miles. Marlette stepped out and instructed Kirk to take the wheel. He drove for 45 minutes, then it was the girl's turn. After a couple hours, he said that was all for the day and drove us all home and dropped us off. He said I would drive the next Saturday. I was irritated that I had gotten up at 7:00 a.m. to go for a joyride in my driver training class but didn't get to drive.

The next Saturday, Marlette showed up again at 7:00 in the same Ford Granada. I again entered the passenger side, refused the last two donuts and held his coffee. We picked up Kirk and the girl and drove to the empty parking lot of the Sunrise Mall. The parking spaces were lined with little concrete barriers that blocked the front tires. Marlette drove into one of the spaces, pulled up to the raised barrier and parked. He turned off the car and told me it was my turn to drive. I got out, switched seats with him, and waited for instructions. Suddenly, I was overcome with nervousness. This was my first time driving, and I had three passengers watching.

"Start the car, back up, and turn left," Marlette instructed.

I started the car and instead of putting the gear lever in reverse, put it in drive and stepped on the gas pedal. The car moved forward, hit the concrete barrier, and the right front corner lurched upward, as if an explosion had occurred under the hood, then it collapsed with a jolting thud, shocks and seats squeaking. As the car continued forward, the right rear tire struck the curb, was violently raised and collapsed again with two sudden jerking jolts.

In a tone filled with tense irritation, Marlette swore then yelled, “I said back up and turn left!”

“I’m sorry,” I blurted.

Marlette turned and looked in the back seat. “Are you okay back there?”

Kirk Fallon looked like he had seen a ghost, eyes as wide as saucers, palms pressed on either side of him against the rear seat. The girl was clinging to the door handle.

“I'm okay,” Kirk said.

“I’m fine,” declared the girl.

I looked in the rearview mirror. Both looked terrified.

I was so embarrassed. I wanted to jump into the nearest dumpster and never be seen again.

“Listen to my instructions!” Marlette ordered.

“I will, I will. I’m sorry. I’m just a little nervous.”

He studied me for a moment, deciding whether to cancel my driver training.

“Alright, turn right, then left, then right at the exit. What did I just say?” he asked.

“Turn right, then left, then right at the exit.”

I executed his instructions carefully and proceeded with my driver training. The radio remained off during my half hour of driving, as Kirk and the girl sat quietly in the back seat.

When we were finished that morning, Marlette dropped me off, still humbled with shame at my earlier mistake.

It was a morning I'm sure none of us forgot and was no doubt repeated with much laughter later.

Nevertheless, I would soon have my driver's license, and the world of adult mobility would then be mine.

After my sophomore year, my dad suggested I take a summer job working for a theater company in Arizona. He had been cast in three plays that were scheduled to run through July and August, and he had already secured a job for me working as a stagehand. I was excited about spending the summer with him and having a summer job. Rick had spent the previous summer with him, worked a job at a warehouse in L.A., and came home with about $1,200 cash, which he used to buy a new Pioneer stereo, speakers and some camping gear.

I told my dad I accepted his offer, and he said he would send me a plane ticket and pick me up in mid-June to begin my summer job.

I enjoyed a week of summer with my friends then my mom took me to the airport to fly to Phoenix. Dad would play prominent roles in *Ten Little Indians*, *1776*, and *Inherit The Wind*, all classics.

After a two-hour flight, my dad picked me up at the airport, then drove to a small, one-bedroom apartment he had rented for the summer. A day or two later, we drove to a warehouse where he introduced me to my employer, who was the director of the plays. She was a voluptuous, dark-haired lady, somewhat reminiscent of Liz Taylor. She introduced me to the small stage crew who would be building the set.

Her son, Chad, was about my age, maybe a year younger and also helping build the stage backdrops. He was the only other person who was my age, and I connected with him quickly. His favorite TV show was *Magnum PI*, and we talked about our favorite music. He had remembered whether a song was on the first or second side of a record album, and he knew its numerical place on the album, e.g., second side, third song. I was impressed with his detailed knowledge of music, and we both liked the same bands.

Though I knew little about construction, I was put to work immediately. After several days of sawing and hammering two-by-fours, the false fronts were completed and moved to the theater downtown. The spacious stage was at the bottom of a cavernous semi-circular interior, ringed with rows of seats. After the sections of fake walls and store fronts were erected, the actors began rehearsing. At this point, I no longer had much work, so I sat in the dark theater, watched the rehearsals and memorized most of the dialogue.

Dad let me drive back to the apartment one afternoon after rehearsal. I had no driver's license, but he felt confident I was competent enough to drive, so I took the wheel for the three-mile trek. Not accustomed to driving, I was unaware of the no-left-turn-rule after 4:30 p.m. during the week. As we neared the turn to the apartment, I stopped in the intersection to turn. Cars behind me started honking, and I saw angry middle finger salutes from other drivers. Still, I didn't know why the uproar was occurring. As soon as I completed the illegal left turn, a motorcycle cop pulled behind me, lights on, and pointed to the curb. I pulled over, and the cop came up to the window.

"You made an illegal left turn. Didn't you see the sign?"

"No."

"License and registration, please."

"I don't have any."

My dad leaned over and spoke, "I let my son drive, officer. He's from California; he has no license yet. He's fifteen."

"I'll have to issue you a citation then. No license. Illegal left turn. Sir, you'll have to drive from here," he told my dad.

My dad got out of the car while the officer wrote the ticket.

"The sign's posted. No left turn after 4:30 p.m. Monday through Friday. It's 4:45."

"Sorry, I didn't see the sign," I said.

"That's why you need a license," he said, void of emotion.

He took my name and address, gave me the ticket, then drove away. I felt like a failure.

I got out and traded places with my dad. He told me not to worry; he'd handle it.

Turnout for the performances was severely disappointing. Over the Fourth of July weekend, the theater had been packed for *1776*, a play about the writing of the Declaration of Independence, but the following week, turnout dwindled, and only a handful of people attended the daily performances. After a month of dismal attendance and nothing for me to do, I told my dad I wanted to go home. My desire coincided with the company's cash flow problem, and an abrupt announcement was made that the company would disband due to poor 'box office'. The remaining performances would be canceled, and all the actors could go back to their lives and pursuing their acting careers elsewhere. After a couple more plays, my dad and I packed our bags and made the long drive west to Los Angeles. I hadn't received a penny for my labor. Dad bought me a plane ticket to Sacramento, and I returned home, thrilled to rejoin my friends for the last month and a half of vacation.

A week later I received a money order from my Dad for a couple hundred dollars. He said I should be paid for all my labor, even if I went idle after completion of the stage sets. I called and thanked him for his generosity, then busied myself with the joys of summer.

As August wound down, my last adventure would be camping with several friends at Coloma for a week.

My friend, Donny Santobello, a tall, lanky Italian kid with tightly-curled hair, suggested the adventure, and everyone liked the idea of an entire week without parental supervision.

We packed our backpacks, loaded our fishing poles and tents, and rode up to Coloma to begin our stay. I rode in the back of the pickup with Donny and all our gear—back when riding in the cargo area of a pickup truck was legal. We never felt the slightest bit unsafe as we leaned over the sides and let the wind blow our hair back on the thirty-mile drive.

We arrived on a Friday afternoon and had our pick of campsites. We chose one with lots of space under a canopy of oak and pine trees. The North Fork American River was only a two-minute walk away.

The excitement on the first day began when we were organizing our tents and supplies. Eric Farnsworth came running down the trail leading from the river and stomped into camp.

"I just saw a naked woman in the river," he said, eyes bulging with excitement.

"No way," I said, thinking it couldn't be possible.

"I swear. Come on. I'll show you."

I dropped whatever I was doing and ran after Eric, as he sprinted back up the trail toward the river. A couple guys followed me. With four or five half naked teenagers running wildly toward the river, the other campers probably thought someone had discovered gold.

We dashed up the trail, around a few bends and could hear the rushing water as we approached. When we reached the river on the narrow trail, we were elevated a few feet above the bank and, sure enough, there in the water, not more than thirty feet from us, was a long-haired young woman, standing in the water, and she was not wearing a swimsuit.

We watched as this woman stood in knee-deep water and gazed at the sky and surroundings. I was incredulous. Doesn't she know we're all watching her? I expected her to scream and tell us perverts to go away. She leaned against a rock and continued sunning herself.

There were not many words among us. No one knew much about exhibitionists. That sort of thing didn't happen in Folsom, but we could not deny the truth before our eyes.

Someone shouted a question or two. There were some suggestive remarks, laughs. She ignored us. No one knew what to say, so we just watched. I saw her smile our way a couple times. Strange. What was she thinking? I don't think any of us had ever seen a naked woman in person.

After maybe ten minutes of gawking at the bare sunbather, the thrill wore off, so we returned to camp. There was some general discussion about what we should do, but no one had any clever ideas. We dropped the discussion.

Later that afternoon, we noticed a roaring in the distance. We went to the river and saw that the water was now churning furiously. We learned that water was released upstream every afternoon, causing swift rapids to form.

We stood on the bank in our shorts and studied the rushing waves. Everyone was tan and fit. Now it seemed necessary to conquer the river by swimming across the waves to the other side, but no one was willing to go first. I found a rock suitable for diving and gazed at the roiling rapids. I'd be swept twenty feet downstream immediately, I thought. This was crazy. I was a good swimmer, but I just wasn't sure whether the waves would pull me under and keep me there. Eric stood on a rock behind me.

"You go first. I'll follow you," he said.

"No, you go first," I countered.

Eric was steadfast, "I'm not going first. You go. I'll follow."

I stood there for a long while and watched the raging waters. If I swam across, I'd be a 'hero' of sorts, as the brave one who went first and made it. On the other hand, if I misjudged the waves, it might be game over for me. I looked back at Eric. There was something different about his posture and appearance. He was standing straight, scowling seriously. "Go first. I'll be right behind you." I studied him closely and could tell he was serious. Now I just had to summon the courage and dive.

It was time to decide. I took a deep breath and dove mightily off the rock. As soon as I hit the water, I could feel the power of the river pulling me downstream forcefully. I kicked my legs and paddled my arms furiously. I was rising and falling as waves crashed onto my head and pushed me down, then raised me again. Any hesitation in my forward motion, and I'd be sucked under.

I glanced back for an instant as my arm was drawn behind me for another paddle, and I could see arms thrashing behind me. Eric had kept his word.

I kicked and paddled, gasped and heaved, and finally the resistance melted away as I reached the shallow waters of the other side. I stepped onto the rocky shore and looked back at Eric, swimming ferociously toward me. He reached the bank and walked onto the rocks, gasping and dripping. We made it. We both stood on this new conquered ground, dripping, disheveled, our chests heaving, warm sunlight engulfing us, exhilarated, victorious.

The moment was ours. We were two kings on the river. We conquered it, as others stayed safe on the other side and watched.

Our heroism was short lived, however. Within a few minutes, everyone else in our camp had followed our lead and swum across. So much for the glory of 'being first.'

We proceeded upriver and sat on the large flat rock that slanted toward the river directly across from Troublemaker, the notorious rough section of rapids, maybe seventy-five feet away. We watched as the rafts approached, one by one. Each raft contained six or eight people. The guide was often seated in the rear, screaming for the occupants to row harder.

Usually, the rafts did not gain sufficient speed, so when they dropped over that little waterfall into the foaming pool below, the front end would stall against back-rushing waters, and the rear would fold forward, like a taco shell, ejecting everyone in the back of the raft. Sometimes the raft would flip, and everyone would go flying into the air and splash into the foamy torrents.

We watched as the river tossed and jostled them downstream just below us.

Late in the afternoon, on a trip to the tiny camp store, we saw four young women walking across the gravel parking lot. They saw us and stopped maybe fifty feet away. We immediately huddled. Donny instructed me to go talk to them. *Me*? *Why me*? *Why not someone else*? No answer. No one else volunteered. "Come on, just go talk to them before they leave," Donny urged. They were standing there, waiting.

The fifty-foot walk across the gravel parking lot took an eternity. Step by step, anticipation rose... rejection loomed, humiliation threatened, all in front of my friends....ah well, at least I'd never see these girls at school or anywhere else, so I'd get over any failure.

Crunch, crunch, crunch, across the gravel, closer, closer...what would I say? Say something, you're out of time.

"Hi," I said to the four girls.

"Hi," they answered. They were about my age except one, who was maybe ten years old. One was a standout beauty.

"I'm Ben. Are you rafting?"

The prettiest girl answered. "No, we're just camping. I'm Stephanie; this is Angela, Nicole, and Claire." They all smiled.

"We swam across the river a couple hours ago. Have you been in the river?"

"No, we're not allowed to go swimming," Stephanie answered.

"It's a lot of fun."

"Are those your friends?" Stephanie asked, pointing toward Donny, Eric and Cale behind me.

"Yes."

"Where are you guys from?" she asked, squinting into the sunlight.

"Folsom. How 'bout you?"

"Roseville."

"You're just down the road," I said with a smile.

"Yeah, Folsom's such a nice little town, I went to the zoo last month with my mom and brother."

"That's great."

"Have you ever been there?"

"Yeah, I've been there a few times. The zookeeper lets the mountain lion put his paws on his shoulders after he feeds him scraps of meat."

"Really?" she said, intrigued.

"Yes. It's amazing. A little scary, but amazing."

"Aw, that's sweet."

"We're camped just over there under those trees if you want to come over later and meet my friends. We have to get a couple things from the store."

She looked in the direction I was pointing. "Those trees right there?"

"Yes."

"Okay, we'll come to your camp later."

"Great. Nice meeting you. Bye," I said with a

wave.

They all said bye in unison. I walked back to my friends.

"They're coming over later," I announced, as I returned to the group.

"Good job," Donny announced. "I'll take it from here," he said with a smile.

Earlier, Eric had decided to play a prank on Kellen. He laid a trail of bread crumbs from Kellen's tent to some ducks that were loitering by our camp. The ducks followed the trail into the tent, then Eric zipped the tent shut. A few hours later, Kellen came back and discovered the ducks. He let them out, and they quacked and waddled away, but inside the tent, they had pooped everywhere—all over his sleeping bag, backpack, canned food. The interior was polka-dotted with duck poop. Kellen didn't think it was funny. Everyone else had a good laugh.

The girls came to our camp that night. I was expecting some sort of attention since I had been the only one willing to talk to them and had made this meeting possible. Wasn't my heroic bravery worth some attention? Nope.

Someone came up with the idea of going for a drive. Eric was the only one with a vehicle at camp—a small pickup truck—so when he volunteered to drive, the girls were all in. Hmmm, three guys and three girls crammed into a small truck, driving around the mountains at night? Couldn't drink or get into any clubs. Where would they go? What would they do? Didn't sound like fun. Have at it.

Kellen, Ray Larousse and I remained at camp and sulked. Donny, Eric and Cale left with the girls for a joyride.

They returned a couple hours later, and the girls went back to their camp. No romance; no kisses goodbye. That was the last of the girls.

Eric opened his ice chest to get something and was overwhelmed by a foul odor. I heard him cussing and rustling through the ice trying to find what was stinking up his cooler. He removed everything, placing items on the picnic table, examining them one by one. Then he picked up his two-liter bottle of Tooty Fruity fruit punch. He had been bragging about his supply of punch for some reason. No one else had any.

He looked at the bottle closely then announced that something was inside. The container appeared full, but a brown mass was floating inside against the wall. He unscrewed the top, sniffed the opening, and immediately recoiled. We were all gathered around now, watching with flashlights.

"What is it?" someone asked.

Then we smelled the stench. The camp erupted in laughter. Eric looked at Kellen, who just grinned wickedly. We watched as Eric stared at the adulterated two-liter bottle then announced, "Anyone want a drink of my Tooty-Poopy?"

I thought the camp would never stop laughing.

No more pranks occurred during that camping trip, and we never again heard Eric brag about his fruit punch.

After a week of camping at Coloma, it was time to go home. Donny's dad, Jerry, arrived in his old pickup truck, and we loaded our gear into the back.

Jerry must've felt sorry for us as he looked around our camp and saw all the empty bags of potato chips, donut boxes, and chili cans, so he offered to take us to lunch. A mile away was a quaint little residence that had been converted into a restaurant called the Coloma House. When Jerry mentioned taking us there for lunch, someone said it was haunted.

I heard Cale and Donny talking about a ghost. I walked over to join their discussion.

"What's this about a ghost?" I asked.

"There's a ghost at the Coloma House," Cale answered. "A little girl died there a long time ago," he added.

I was intrigued but pretended not to be afraid. Cale and Donny seemed interested in visiting the haunted house for lunch.

Jerry asked, "Are you ready for some food, Ben?"

"No, thanks. I'm not really hungry," I answered.

"Are you afraid?" Donny asked.

"No."

"Let's pack up and get some lunch," Jerry said.

We finished packing our gear, loaded it into Jerry's and Eric's truck, then headed down the road for the Coloma House. As we pulled into the empty parking lot, I thought, *Good, they're closed.* We parked, and everyone jumped out.

"I think they're closed," I announced.

"They're open," Jerry said confidently.

We walked up to the front door and someone opened it. Yep, they're open. We went inside. It was dim and quiet; the ceilings were low. This used to be someone's home. A few walls had been removed, and now it was a little restaurant. A plump, dark-haired lady with her hair in a bun showed up and escorted us to a small room with a round table. *How could this empty restaurant stay in business*, I wondered. Maybe the ghost helped somehow.

We took our seats and looked around at the wood paneled walls. Old black and white pictures were everywhere.

The lady who seated us came back to take our order. Jerry told us we should have hamburgers, get some protein.

I asked our server about the ghost. A creepy smile slowly appeared on her face. Her eyes seemed to grow darker in the poor light. She said yes, they had a ghost and told us her name, Priscilla.

"What does she do?" I asked.

She grinned slightly, "She likes to choose someone and follow that person home."

I stared back stoically.

She continued, "She's a friendly ghost, though."

"How long does she stay after she follows you home?" I asked.

"Mmm, a couple weeks usually, sometimes a few months. You'll know she's there. She likes to turn lights off and on, close doors, maybe tap you on the shoulder. That kind of thing. Everyone ready to order?"

What?! No I'm not ready to order! Can we leave and call Ghostbusters? I want Dan Aykroyd and Bill Murray at my house in their coveralls and backpacks when I get home.

We ordered hamburgers, which may have been the best I'd ever tasted—especially after a week of canned camp food.

The ghost was on my mind, but I hid my concern and spoke no more about it.

We finished our wonderful hamburger lunch, Jerry paid, and we got back in the truck. All the way home, I wondered, *Was the ghost with us? Had she picked me to follow?*

I got home and unloaded my camping gear. It was the middle of the afternoon, and I was completely creeped out, waiting for doors to start closing on their own, or someone to tap me on the shoulder. It never happened.

The ghost must have followed someone else.

Leslie was a tall, slender freshman with shiny black hair, large dark eyes, long eyelashes, and plump contoured dimples that always rested in a friendly little smile. A cheerleader, about 5' 9", her face exhibited an exoticness drawn from Italian heritage. Like the other cheerleaders, she had a virtually flawless body, lean and muscular, displayed attractively in jeans, and on game days, a blue or red cheerleader uniform.

I first met her one evening at the Round Table Pizza after a football game. We sat at a booth, talked like high school kids, and I wrote down her phone number. I began talking to her several nights a week. After I felt comfortable, I invited her to dinner with my mom and brother to celebrate his nomination as All-League running back for the second consecutive season. She accepted, and I felt a slight awkwardness as a junior courting a freshman, but my brother had dated a couple girls who were several grades behind him, and if he could do it, so could I.

We picked up Leslie one Saturday night to take her to Whispering Pines, a local steakhouse located in a patch of darkness just outside city limits. I knocked on her front door and her older brother, Dominick, answered. I didn't know him well, so little warmth was extended as he opened the door and let me in. I was nervous and wondering if her parents were thinking that I, a junior, was too old to date their freshman daughter.

Her parents were seated in the living room in lounge chairs watching TV. I stood nearby and waited for Leslie to come downstairs. Dominick studied me. He seemed to be considering whether to intervene and cancel the date. Leslie finally emerged from the bottom of the stairs, smiling as usual and nicely dolled up. We said goodbye to her parents and left.

As we walked to the car, I was quickly engulfed and entranced by her perfume—a scent I had never experienced. The odor was thick, dense, and musky—a combination of sweet exotic flowers, fine portions of cinnamon, and fermented rose petals—a complex variety of rich aromas that seemed to activate deep, primitive, emotional responses; it was mesmerizing. No other girl in the school wore that hypnotic perfume.

The dinner was delicious and enjoyable, and I felt glad to have a new 'girlfriend,' although whether Leslie understood my feelings is questionable. From her perspective, she may have been simply accepting a dinner invitation and getting to know a suitor. We had not made any formal commitments to each other.

We finished our steak dinners, then returned Leslie home before eleven. She thanked me, and I walked her to the front door where she gave me a quick hug and transferred a swatch of her wonderful perfume onto my shirt. I could smell her fragrance as I walked back to the car, and it lingered for the drive home. Her scent remained on my shirt, which I did not wash for days.

Though she accepted my dinner invitation, and we talked on the landline phone in the evenings, our 'relationship' had little overall substance, typical of high school romances.

A strange omen occurred a couple weeks after our dinner. Leslie found me after school on my birthday and delivered a large birthday card. It smelled like her perfume and implied a vague, overwhelming passion—the aroma of longing, heartfelt desire—and I was glad to have another reminder. However, I wondered why it had taken all day to deliver the memento. It was a small school, and I was not hard to find throughout the day, but she delivered her message *after* school when the excitement and 'freshness' of a birthday had dwindled. When I opened the large card, I noticed she had written my name at the bottom then crossed it out with an X. Directly below this, she had signed her name. Seeing my name crossed out on the card was unsettling—the way a TV serial killer crosses off victims on a list, but I was glad she thought enough to get me a card for my birthday.

A week or so later, I learned that Leslie had decided she was no longer interested but instead was attracted to my friend, Kellen. It was bad enough to lose a girlfriend, but losing her to one of my friends made it even more painful.

Kellen talked directly and honestly to me about the awkward situation. His position was that he had done nothing wrong, had not interfered; she had simply chosen him without provocation or invitation, and how could he possibly say no? I grudgingly agreed that he should move forward with her if that's what she wanted. I was mystified by her sudden change of interest. Where did her feelings go? Did she ever have any? Maybe not; maybe my feelings had not been reciprocated; that was possible and difficult to accept, but I had no choice.

My evening telephone conversations with Leslie ended, and now I began seeing her with Kellen around school and afterward, usually driving somewhere. I was disappointed and jilted, but there was nothing I could do.

Unfortunately for Kellen, he would be replaced after about a month, as Leslie found yet another who she preferred, a lanky basketball player with blue eyes and thick eyebrows. I didn't know the kid at the time. He was a couple grades behind me, but he was an exceptional athlete, and when I later got to know him, he was as nice, normal, and friendly as anyone.

Kellen stayed bitter and glum at the cold, sudden news. Now we could sort of share our disappointment and disgruntlement together, but we didn't dwell on the mutual loss too much. There was no point in languishing over her departure when we were daily among hundreds of other cute and beautiful women and opportunities abounded.

In my memory, Leslie remains a beautiful, radiant young woman who enchanted me for a while, and I wouldn't discard a single memory if I had the choice.

I was eager for baseball season my junior year. *This was my time to shine*, I thought, *my time to earn a baseball scholarship*. I hadn't announced my goal of playing professional baseball to anyone. *I'd just do it*, I thought. All those years of Little League and Babe Ruth, all those hours of practice, batting cages, two prior seasons on the junior varsity—all were leading to this important year—my first on the varsity team, where scholarships were offered. I was ready to prove I belonged in the pros, or at least in college on a baseball scholarship. This would be my season.

Varsity baseball coach, Bob Yates was in his late thirties. His face was masculine, well-proportioned and always exhibited a bluish hue of razor stubble. When he spoke, he tilted his head back slightly. His body movements were measured and methodical; he usually walked in straight lines, almost in military fashion, pivoting crisply on the ball of his foot to make a right-angle left or right turn. He stood board straight, tilted his head back slightly and gazed at the world with sparkling blue eyes that blinked slowly and infrequently, as if absorbing every detail within his field of vision.

Coach Yates was a sharp, fastidious dresser. His clothes always had a cleaned and pressed look, as if they had just come from the cleaners. His shirts were always completely wrinkle-free, with razor-sharp creases, and he wore a tie without fail. I noticed that other teachers sometimes did not wear a tie, but Yates never once appeared in class without one. His clothes were always color coordinated and fit perfectly, as if custom made for his particular athletic shape. His pressed and starched shirts were tucked neatly into his snug, polyester pants which were always tightly belted. He wore shoes with laces, never loafers.

Early in the morning, around 6:00 a.m., the coach could be seen dragging a heavy square section of chain -link fence over the dirt section of the baseball infield. The heavy metal fence gouged through the dirt, loosened it, and exposed rocks and pebbles. Coach Yates would then rake the rocks out of the infield and rake around the bases, so that the dirt was soft, powdery and free of hard chunks. When he was finished, the entire dirt infield looked neatly lined with a fine rake, as if prepared for a professional baseball game. He did this before home games and sometimes before practice and never received a penny for all his extra hours of labor.

With the diamond raked and prepared for practice and games, I tore up the field from the batter's box my junior year. The baseball seemed as big as a pumpkin, as I smacked line drives into the outfield one game after another. I hit .395 (17 hits in 43 at bats). Gary Clark hit .446 (29 for 65), an astounding feat for any high school player, let alone a junior. My batting average had been ahead of Gary's for most of the season, but he gradually caught up and went on a hitting streak the last several games.

With four games left, I was playing second base, and my batting average was still hovering just under .400. I was determined to start a hitting streak and finish with a batting average well above .400, which would have put me among the top ten or so batters in the area. *The Sacramento Bee* published a list of top high school batting averages, and mine had been near the top most of the season.

Halfway through the game, a runner was on first when a grounder was hit to our shortstop, Kenny Nolan. I sprinted to second base to turn a double play but carelessly placed my left foot against the base as I waited for Kenny to throw me the ball. When I caught it, the runner simultaneously slid into my left ankle, which had no place to go except against the stationary base. The impact snapped my ankle in three places, and I was jolted into the air, landing on my back. Intense pain began radiating from my ankle, pain like I had never felt. My dreams of any sort of baseball career were broken at that moment.

Instead of basking in the aftermath of a phenomenal baseball season, I was driven to the hospital for surgery the next morning. Three titanium pins were installed to hold my bones in place while they healed.

Two months later, I underwent a second surgery to remove the pins, but my ankle remained stiff and locked in an 'L' position, with almost no flexibility, and my calf was weak and flabby. I had no strength from the knee down and needed to rehabilitate my entire leg. I limped around, fearful that too much pressure might cause my ankle to break again and went to the high school weight room to train other body parts.

Over the summer, the new high school football coach saw me in the weight room and inquired about my injury. I explained I had not yet recovered full strength and flexibility. He knew a physical therapist and emphatically recommended I see him for a full course of treatment, but I would have to see my doctor first, and he would have to recommend therapy.

My orthopedic surgeon was resistant and reluctant to order physical therapy. It was as if doing so would be an admission that his expert surgical procedures had been inadequate—virtually malpractice that had to be repaired with dozens of hours of stretching, pulling, pushing, heating, icing, and exercising. He required I take an assessment comparing the strength of my left leg to my right. The test showed my left leg had approximately 97% of the strength of my right, so he questioned the need for any rehabilitation. He maintained treatment was not necessary based on my test scores and seemed unmoved by my complaints that my ankle remained stiff and had not regained full strength and flexibility. I insisted I wanted therapy, and he reluctantly signed the order.

I endured a couple months of rigorous probing, pulling, squeezing, stretching, icing and manipulation and eventually achieved a noticeable improvement. Though stronger, more flexible, and highly functional, I did not return to the same capacity as before the injury. My ankle joint retained lateral looseness and instability due to the stretching of ligaments and tendons caused by the initial injury that could not be fixed. I would have to tape my ankle or wear a brace, so my physical performance was never exactly what it had been previously, but at least my mobility returned. I could now do all the activities I had formerly done.

Rick and I continued our policy of not mixing friends for most of high school. We played on the same teams from time to time but, as usual, he had *his* friends, and I had *mine*. I didn't go on his camping trips, and vice versa. My motorcycle broke after a year of hard riding, so our jaunts to the motocross tracks ended. He also had a steady stream of girlfriends, which absorbed any time not filled by school, sports or outdoor activities. We were not enemies; we just existed in mostly separate social circles, and we had different natures, which still seemed to mystify people. They continued announcing, "You're so different from your brother," as if disappointed I was not his twin.

My grandma (Dad's mom) used to say that Rick looked like Robert Redford when we were kids. She raved about how handsome he was, and I expected her to add that I also looked like some movie star, but she never did.

Rick was a friendly extrovert with boundless energy who never waited to be asked to join the fun or participate and invited everyone along for the ride—except me. It was a strange irony; he would reach out to strangers or kids he did not know to include them in his social group, often ignoring or leaving me behind in the process. Though he was not hostile toward me, we just didn't have much in common. I did things with him now and then, but he was clearly independent, supported by an endless network of adoring admirers.

He had proven himself repeatedly on the football

field, baseball diamond, and wrestling mat and ascended to the status of a legend. He had been voted All-League running back his junior and senior year and won the league championship in wrestling. All the guys wanted to be his friend, and all the girls wanted to date him, or so it seemed.

He never took algebra or chemistry like I did; his electives were woodshop, metal shop, and auto shop. He used to bring home gifts he made for Mom in his shop classes—jewelry boxes, cutting boards, coat racks. Shelves he made in woodshop were mounted above the front windows in the living room on brackets he forged in metal shop; a decorative, wrought iron gate he fashioned with torches and tools replaced the old wooden gate on the side of the house.

His high school years would be envied by most. He won most of the physical tests that seemed to determine the value of young males—the fifty-yard dash, bench press, barbell curls, push-ups. No one could beat him in wrestling; he was difficult to tackle in football and acknowledged as the greatest athlete in his class. He rose to the status of royalty, honored and respected by everyone.

I continued searching for ways to excel that would distinguish me from my brother. Academics and guitar had been two areas where I easily outshined him. My message to the world was clear: I can't run as fast as my brother or bench press as much, but ask him if he can play guitar? Did he make the Honor Roll? Ask him to explain *Boyle's Law* or *Heisenberg's Uncertainty Principle*? Ask him to write a 500-word essay discussing the symbolism in Steinbeck's classic, *The Pearl.* Ask him to do a magic show for a half hour to entertain your parents' dinner guests. Let me know how much they enjoy the performance.

I knew I had talents he did not have, and I was committed to developing them to their highest potential.

My senior year of high school arrived, and things quickly began to seem anticlimactic. Although I was finally at the top of the hierarchy, it seemed hollow. Other than eating lunch on senior stage, there was no special privilege in being a senior. If anything, I missed the anticipation of increasing social status experienced in prior years. Now that excitement was gone; high school would be done in less than a year, then we would all scatter and begin real lives.

Seniors were required to take a class studying government from Mr. Haven. He was the perfect government teacher. He was short, about 5' 7", with a bland outward appearance. A Caucasian man with a square, featureless face, gray sideburns, and dark black hair parted on the side, he wore corduroy jackets with patches on the elbows and polyester slacks. His speech and mannerisms were always careful, measured, and deliberate. There was no spontaneity or extremes in his behavior. He had the demeanor of a supervisor at the Department of Motor

Vehicles, calm, unhurried, dispassionate.

Haven was hated for supposedly wearing a toupee, which students talked about with contempt, as if any effort to hide hair loss was a severe and unforgivable disgrace. I couldn't tell whether his hair was natural, but other students were convinced it was not. Perhaps the effort to hide the truth was what inspired such vicious hatred, but society remained highly judgmental on numerous aspects of personal appearance. At the time, balding men were viewed by many as some sort of scandal—failures whose masculinity was reduced follicle by follicle.

I liked Mr. Haven. His lectures were organized, thorough, and logical, and he seemed to enjoy teaching. He was patient, kind, took his job seriously, and I never understood why so many students mocked him.

One afternoon I walked into class early and saw my fifth grade nemesis, Craig Cadigan, pull down the projection screen in front of the chalkboard and quickly tape a Playboy centerfold to the center. He then pulled the string on the bottom of the screen, causing it to recoil and return to its housing in the cylinder mounted above the chalkboard. He smirked wickedly and returned to his seat. He knew that Mr. Haven intended to show a short film that day and planned to give him the raunchy surprise.

Cadigan had yet another shock for Mr. Haven. When he pulled down the screen, revealing the centerfold, and while his back was to the class, Cadigan intended to throw a handful of BBs at his back. He received a thrill from such pranks. He was sitting a few rows away, talking to some classmates, telling them about his plans.

I sat in disbelief, wondering what sort of psychosis afflicted this degenerate troublemaker.

Mr. Haven arrived, walked to the front of the class and was in a cheerful mood. After the class filled, he checked names on his roll sheet, then announced we would watch a film. He turned and pulled down the screen, revealing the centerfold while Cadigan simultaneously stood and heaved the BBs. The tiny round projectiles splattered all over the screen, chalkboard, and Mr. Haven's back in a frightful clatter. Laughter erupted.

Haven turned around and his normally bland expression was gone. He scowled with contempt and scanned the back of the class, suspecting where the BBs had originated. Finally, he said, "You people should be stepped on, like ants." The class went silent. He turned around, ripped the centerfold off the screen and threw it in the trash. Then he walked to the back, turned out the lights, closed the door, and started the reel-to-reel film. Music suddenly blared and black and white images filled the projection screen. We watched the film for about forty minutes. When it was over, Mr. Haven turned off the projector, turned on the lights and walked to the front of the classroom. His bland demeanor had returned, and he concluded the class with a few comments and instructions about our assignment.

I walked out of class disgusted with Craig

Cadigan's ugly stunt.

Senior year repeated all the usual hallmarks—football season, wrestling, basketball, baseball, proms, and they all went by quickly. As seniors received college acceptance letters, a malaise settled in as the challenge of high school dissipated. Kellen was accepted by the Air Force Academy, his lifelong ambition, and I was sad he would be leaving. I enjoyed learning chemistry, biology, creative writing, history, college-prep English, and the slower pace of life in high school, and I wanted it to last, but everyone else seemed eager for it all to end.

The reality of adulthood was approaching. Students discussed their intentions following graduation. The choice was a full-time job or college, and many were continuing school, planning to earn a degree before entering the workforce. I was not ready to start clocking in somewhere every morning and laboring for eight hours a day. Work was inevitable, but I did not want to make the transition from studying and learning to becoming a proverbial cog in a corporate wheel. I had acquired much knowledge, but my education still seemed incomplete. The prospect of four years of college at Stanford gave me a dreamy anticipation about the more elite and esoteric knowledge I would acquire at a university and my possibilities for the future.

One day, about halfway through my senior year, I came home for lunch—it was only a ten-minute walk—and checked the mail. An envelope addressed to me from Stanford was in the mailbox. My heart began to pound with anticipation. This is it! This must be my acceptance letter, advising that I'd start college at Stanford next September! I ripped open the envelope and read the letter. It was one of those carefully worded rejections that try to cheer you up with compliments about how close you came to acceptance: "Thank you for your application for admission. We were impressed with your record of academic and extracurricular achievement. You are highly qualified but, unfortunately, we received 10,000 applications for this year's freshman class and can admit only 1,000. It was a difficult process deciding whom to admit among so many diverse and talented applicants. After careful and thorough consideration, we regret to inform you that your application has been denied. We thank you for your interest and wish you good luck in your future endeavors."

The rejection was cold and devastating. For the past three years, I had committed myself to achieving nearly straight A's. I completed two or three hours of homework every night, studied vocabulary lists, took practice exams testing word comprehension and analytical thinking, wrote essays, memorized mathematical theorems and participated in wrestling, football and baseball to boost my overall record of achievement. I studied dozens of extra hours for the

SAT test, ran for and was elected class president, and received A's in "accelerated U.S. History," chemistry, college-prep English, history and government, among others. I thought my record was strong. My English SAT score was *30 points higher* than Kellen's, who had been accepted by the Air Force Academy and whom I regarded as a genius. He was undeniably brilliant, but if I could score higher on the English SAT than he had—*I must be qualified for an elite college*. Unfortunately, my math SAT score was not impressive. It was lower than the average for Standford freshmen.

The underwhelming math score seemed to doom my admission. But chemistry involved lots of calculations, and I received A's, wouldn't that make up for my inadequacy? Apparently not. All the other high marks, honors and achievements wouldn't counterbalance the SAT. When chances for admission were 1 in 10, that fault was fatal.

It didn't matter much, because the denial had been made, and I would not be going to Stanford. The dream to begin college at California's most prestigious and elite university turned to ashes.

There was no urgency at the time to develop a college or career plan, so I did not think much about it. I wanted to enjoy the remainder of my senior year and deal with college or a career later.

Baseball season arrived again, and I held out hope I'd be able to repeat my performance from the prior year and hit .400. However, instead of starting every game as I had my junior year, I was sharing left field with Donny Santobello, a good friend, which made the situation awkward. I'd play left field one game, then Donny would play the next. Having started and played every game the prior season, sitting out every other game as a senior was a bitter pill to swallow. But our team had a lot of talent, and I made the mistake of not returning to play second base.

The memory of the horrible injury the prior year was still too fresh for me to return to the dangerous territory around second base, so I switched to outfield. The way I saw it, my performance the prior year earned me a starting position as a senior. All the other players who had started when they were juniors were now starting every game—except me. It seemed very unfair. I had easily been one of the best hitters the prior season, and my batting average had been higher as a junior than most other juniors who were now starting as seniors. Why was I not granted a starting position, like all the others?

I hoped Coach Yates would suddenly realize our team's performance would improve if I were allowed to play every game, but I continued to share left field with Donny all season.

Though he was a good player, I felt Donny had not earned a starting position based on his performance as a junior, as I had. Of course, my assumptions about who did and did not earn a starting position were just my own subjective conclusions based primarily on batting averages. No promises or guarantees were ever given about how much anyone would play, but I compared my circumstances to others and thought I came up short. I suppose Donny would have felt it unfair if he had been required to sit out most of his senior year—his last chance to play high school baseball. Coach Yates was in a tough spot. All players wanted to play as much as possible.

I was so disappointed and dissatisfied that I quit before our team had won the league championship. Perhaps quitting late in the season was childish and impulsive, but my long goal of becoming a professional baseball player was thwarted. I had no patience or sacrifice left.

I have consolation now, knowing that even if I had started and hit .400 my senior year, chances for a scholarship were very unlikely. I had not heard of any one from Folsom receiving a full-ride baseball scholarship since we moved to the small town. The last probably occurred in the '60s, and there had been many great players. When I was a freshman, Mike Ryan hit .379, but he was not recruited by any of the large prestigious universities.

According to Coach Yates's records, several players had previously hit over .400, but they never went pro.

Few, if any, players in our league received scholarships. Certainly, no one on our team received a full-ride baseball scholarship. Big colleges just didn't recruit from our tiny school and league—"The Golden Empire League". That may be different now, but back in the '80s, 'top tier' colleges filled their baseball rosters with players from other schools—likely much larger than Folsom.

Before long, June arrived, and it was time for another senior class to graduate. The ceremony was held on the football field, and a small stage with a podium was assembled near the fifty-yard line. My class sat in folding chairs on both sides of the stage and, one by one, names were called. In caps and flowing gowns, we strode across the stage in front of the packed bleachers and received our diplomas.

High school was over forever, and we would now be entering the world of adults.

ADULTHOOD

After graduating, I found myself with no goals or direction. I didn't fully appreciate the gravity of the transition from high school to adulthood. I thought I'd just find a job and go to work like my brother had, and ease into my new adult life.

I don't fault my parents for my lack of eagerness to become an adult. My mom had been almost overwhelmed working graveyard to support two teens, even with monthly support from my dad, but the money went fast, and she had her hands full paying the bills and running the household. She knew I wanted to go to college and was fully supportive, but when Stanford said no, she never insisted I apply somewhere else or plan for a blue-collar career. Whether I went to college or got a job after high school was my choice, and neither she nor my dad forced me down any particular path. The truth, however, was that tens of thousands of dollars were not lying in a bank account to pay for Stanford. I'd received a Pell Grant for $2,500, but Stanford tuition was $10,000, and had I been accepted, I have no idea how I would have paid the yearly cost. Student loans may have been the answer, but I was averse to going into thousands of dollars of debt at the time, and since my parents could not make up the $7,500 difference, I figured I never would have gone to Stanford.

Rick found a job at West Coast Manufacturing, a company in Rancho Cordova that built windows, and he quickly established himself as one of their most productive and valued employees. He didn't need college; he was making good money at a full-time job. He moved into an apartment, bought a Jeep CJ-5 and began a responsible adult life.

I felt I was entitled to enjoy the summer after graduation as every prior summer. My mom acceded to my wish for leisure but made clear that when fall arrived, I would have to get a job. I understood and fully expected to become a productive member of society—after one last carefree summer.

As August heat began to dwindle, friends left for college or found full-time jobs. People I had seen daily were now gone. There was no daily high school routine anymore, and now I was supposed to do something with my life, though I had not planned for anything other than playing professional baseball and possibly attending Stanford.

Toward the end of summer, Ray Larousse learned that a steakhouse was hiring and asked if I would like to go with him to apply for a job. *Maybe we could both get hired and work together*, I thought. *That would be fun.* I said yes, and he drove us one Saturday morning in his Chevy LUV pickup to a steakhouse near the Sunrise Mall.

We went inside and met a waitress, who gave us pens and applications. After we filled them out, she told us to wait outside. We waited about ten minutes, then the waitress came out and called Ray first. He went inside and came out fifteen minutes later. He said he had been hired. That was easy. A moment later, the server called me. He wished me good luck.

Inside, at a booth near the windows, sat Dave, the manager, a tall, heavy man with thin curly hair and a thick mustache. He was the only person seated in the restaurant. A couple of employees were walking back and forth to the salad bar, preparing it for lunch. Dave gestured for me to sit.

I sat across from him as he studied my one-page application. He had a stack of papers next to him on the table. He asked a couple questions about my limited work experience and availability. I answered his questions candidly and told him I could work anytime. I thought he was going to tell me my meager work history was inadequate, but instead he said magnanimously, "Ben, I'm going to give you a job. Your position will be utility attendant. Your responsibilities will be busing and cleaning the tables, prepping the salad bar, washing dishes, sweeping and mopping floors, and following directions from myself or the assistant manager. Are you willing to accept these responsibilities?" he asked, and gazed at me with the stony face of a riverboat gambler.

"Yes," I answered.

"Good. The assistant manager prepares the schedule for the week. You can call in and get your hours. We need someone to work weekends, so you'll be starting there."

"That's fine."

"We get paychecks on Sundays, usually around three. You can call in to see if yours is ready."

"Okay."

Then the conversation went in an unexpected direction.

"I think you'll enjoy working here. We have experienced management and committed staff. I make more money than any other district manager in the area," he announced matter-of-factly. "There's only one district manager who makes more than I do, but he's in Placerville, and I think I'll be able to make more than him this year," he said in a hopeful tone. "My compensation depends on the profitability of the restaurant, and the profitability of the restaurant depends on the performance of employees. I want the best employees to deliver the best performance, and you can be part of that team. I intend to exceed last year's revenues by at least 5%. I have the personnel to do that this year and, frankly, I believe I'm entitled to the bonus for managing the restaurants efficiently and making them more profitable."

He paused for a moment to soak in his self-congratulations.

I wasn't sure what to say, but I was amused that my job was more about helping him make more money than anything else.

He concluded our interview, "Call back today after four and speak to our assistant manager, Pete, and ask when you're on the schedule. Here are some tax forms to fill out. You can bring them back and give them to Pete before you start your first shift. Congratulations," he said, and extended his hand.

"Thank you."

After shaking his hand, I stood and walked out.

"Did you get the job?" Ray asked immediately as I exited.

"Yes."

"Awesome."

"I have to call back after 4 to see when I'm on the schedule."

"Me, too."

I learned I was scheduled to work the following Sunday from noon until 8 p.m. I called Ray to see if we were working the same hours, but he was scheduled to work the next Tuesday and Thursday from 5 p.m. until 9 p.m. We would not be working together; I was disappointed.

I borrowed Mom's car, a light blue AMC Spirit, and showed up for work at noon the next Sunday. A waitress gave me a pair of green polyester slacks and a grayish shirt with pinstripes. I changed into my work clothes in the men's room, then reported to the assistant manager for instructions. He called over another employee and instructed him to show me my duties.

The employee told me to follow him, picked up an empty dish tub, then went into the dining area. A few customers were scattered among the tables and booths. He walked to an empty booth. "Put the tub on the seat," he instructed, then he removed the plates and silverware from the table and placed them into the tub. "Then wipe the table, salt and pepper shakers and ketchup bottles." He wiped the table and shakers, then picked up the tub and carried it through the double swinging doors into the dishwasher area and placed it on the sink top. "Leave the dishes here," he said, "the dishwasher will wash 'em. Then get a new tub."

He walked me around the back area and showed me where to get clean towels, fresh tubs, mops, brooms and showed me the inside of the large, walk-in freezer, where assorted items were stocked.

Soon the restaurant was busy, and I was going from table to table putting dishes into the tub and shuttling them to the back.

After the lunch rush was over, Pete said he was going to show me how to do the lettuce. He took me to the large, industrial, stainless steel sink, which had two large basins side by side, each flanked by flat spaces. He filled a large bucket with ice and placed it on the surface next to the basin. He used a sponge and a bucket of soapy water to wash the interior of one of the basins, then hosed the suds away with an overhanging nozzle. He dumped the ice into the cleaned sink then filled it halfway with water.

Next, he took the ice bucket into the walk-in freezer, filled it with heads of lettuce then returned to the sink and dumped about six heads into the ice water. He pushed them deep into the chilly water and let them sit a short while. Then he explained the essential part of lettuce preparation.

"You have to core all the heads," he said, "like this." He pulled one of the heads out of the water, held it in his left hand and smacked the core with the palm of his right, pushing the bottom center forward into the head, ripping it away from the leaves at the base.

He rotated the head in his left hand a few degrees and struck it again, then quickly poked his fingers into the crevice and pulled out the jagged core. Then, using both hands, he broke the head apart, dropped the halves into the ice water and began ripping the leaves into smaller pieces and dropping and plunging them into the water.

He demonstrated again with another head, then told me to finish.

After the lettuce had been processed, it was to be placed into a large colander and taken to another section of the back room, where the waitresses would prepare it for the salad bar.

I finished the remaining heads, and when I was done, my hands were frozen, and I was ready to go back to clearing tables.

Later, Pete told me to take a break and said I was given a 20% discount on meals. I ordered a hamburger with the salad bar, a drink and took my half hour rest.

By the end of my shift at 8 p.m., it was dark, and I drove back down Greenback Lane to Folsom, satisfied with my first full day of work as an adult.

I called the next day to check my work hours hoping I would be scheduled with Ray but was booked the following Sunday from noon 'til eight again. He was still listed to work Tuesday and Thursday. They apparently wanted to keep us separated. Perhaps they suspected we should not work together, as the threat of two friends clearing tables and hauling tubs of dishes into the back room must have terrified the assistant manager. They must have feared we would collude to steal a case of pickles and a few bags of hamburger buns.

I borrowed Mom's car again the next Sunday and reported for work at noon, expecting to receive my first paycheck. The assistant manager searched through a large handful of envelopes but could not locate mine. He said it was just an oversight, and he would speak to the payroll person. He told me to call back the next day, and I could pick it up in the afternoon. He seemed reasonable and sincere.

Dave told me to follow him outside, where he introduced me to a new assistant manager, Chris, who was standing next to the open door of the storage shed. Chris was an androgynous looking man in his mid-forties. He was wearing a tie, short-sleeved shirt, and polyester slacks, management apparel.

"Chris will be in charge today," Dave announced. "He's former military, so he's used to keeping things clean. He'll be keeping you busy."

Dave stepped inside the shed, and we followed. "This is where we store all nonperishable items, napkins, towels, plastic silverware, Styrofoam cups, canned goods, all that sort of stuff."

We gazed around at the interior. One wall had several shelves of restaurant-size canned goods. Next to the shelves were cardboard boxes stacked six feet. There was debris and loose items on the floor, pieces of plywood, two by fours, a vacuum, a green garden hose was coiled in a corner.

"This area should be cleaned and organized," Dave announced.

Chris looked at all the disorganized clutter with disgust.

Dave then exited the shed, and we followed. He announced he was leaving for the afternoon and told me to follow Chris' instructions.

After Dave was gone, Chris stepped towards the entrance to the shed and looked inside. I stepped near him, and he said, “I want you to clean this shed from top to bottom. Throw away all this junk.” He gestured to the floor, “And sweep the floor thoroughly. I want every speck of dust gone. Use soap and water and clean that,” he said, pointing at the only window. “If you can find a small brush, clean the windowsill and get in the corners.”

I paid close attention and nodded as he pointed and gave instructions.

“I want you to spend all day in this shed, if that's what it takes to get it spotless and sparkling,” he said. “Go inch by inch over the floor and walls, understand?”

“Yes.”

“I mean not a speck of dirt or trash anywhere. I want it to look brand-new in here.”

“Okay.”

He gazed in further disgust at the interior of the shed then walked away.

I didn't like my assignment. This was a storage shed for nonperishable restaurant supplies, not a ‘68 Camaro. The interior was exposed wood and concrete, nothing that would shine. I was certain I could clean the shed adequately, even if it wouldn't ‘sparkle’.

I gathered all the heavy junk and stray plywood and threw it away. I swept exhaustively and used the broom to clean the window sills and corners. I washed the inside and outside of the window until it was spotless. I rearranged all the canned goods so they were organized by food item and cleaned all the cans with a damp cloth. All the cardboard boxes were re-stacked and re-organized.

After forty-five minutes of nonstop cleaning and washing, I was sweating. The interior of the shed was hot and stuffy. Chris had told me he wanted the shed spotless, even if it took all day, so I figured I should spend more time making it as clean as possible.

Once again, I examined every corner, the entire floor, every wall, all the shelves—anything that could be seen to make sure it was free of dirt, dust, or cobwebs and looked organized. All the junk was gone, the concrete floor was now smooth and shiny, shelves were organized, the cans were cleaned, the boxes stacked neatly, the window spotless. I had spent a whole hour cleaning and organizing a 10 x 10 shed and felt I had done enough. I went back inside the restaurant and resumed the task of busing tables.

A few minutes later, Chris saw me, walked over and said, "I thought I told you to clean the shed?"

"I did."

"You're done already?"

"Yes."

"I told you to stay out there all day."

"It's clean now."

He looked at me skeptically. He seemed sure I

couldn't possibly have cleaned the shed in an hour.

"Let's go take a look," he said, and turned toward the back exit. I followed.

When we walked outside, he opened the shed door. There was a dramatic contrast from the last time he had seen it. He stepped inside and looked at the floor carefully, then the window, ran his finger across the windowsill, peered at the shelves, gazed around the walls. There was nothing left to clean or organize. He seemed to be looking for the tiniest flaw. After inspecting the interior, he stepped out, disappointed he had not found any defect in my work and walked back inside.

I felt relieved and exonerated. My work had passed the test. I suppose I could have found a toothbrush and further cleaned the corners, but I had done enough.

After completing my eight-hour shift, I drove home again in the dark. I now had sixteen hours in the books.

The next day an employee told me my check was not ready and to call back later. A few hours later Pete said it still was not ready. He said they would add the hours to my next check, and I could pick it up the following Sunday. It seemed a little strange they were not able to pay me, but I said fine and looked forward to getting paid.

The following Sunday I again borrowed Mom's car and arrived at noon. Still, the cashier could locate no envelope for me. Now I was irritated. I had been promised my check two times, but it had not been delivered.

I completed my shift and drove home again, unhappy with my part-time job. I talked to Pete again the next day, and he said my check would be ready the next Sunday when I reported for work at noon. He was no longer apologetic. He seemed more annoyed that I was concerned about getting paid than the fact that they were late by two weeks. Now I was the bad guy for bothering him. I should just shut up, work my shift, and I'd get paid when they got around to it.

The following Sunday arrived, and I showed up on time, certain they would finally have my check but, once again, it was missing. As usual, Pete handed out envelopes to all the other employees except me. I was tempted to quit on the spot, but I figured since I was there, I would work the shift then tell my mom about the fiasco later.

Pete pulled me aside a few moments later and confided that there had been some sort of accounting error and my name had been left off the records, and that's why my check had been repeatedly overlooked. It would certainly be cleared up the following Sunday, and I'd get paid just like everyone else. It sounded sloppy. They knew I had not been paid. What was the real problem? I thought Dave had "experienced management" and a crack staff of committed employees that was going to exceed last year's revenues by 5%. How were they going to do that when they couldn't pay their employees? I was confident the restaurant was not running a scam, but this was just lazy and irresponsible. They expected me to be at work on time and bust my butt for eight hours, but they didn't care enough to make sure I got paid like all the other employees.

I completed my shift, drove home and told my mom about not getting paid for three weeks. She became furious, dialed 411 for the restaurant's phone number, and called.

A female cashier picked up, and Mom began, "I'd like to speak to the manager please."

She waited a minute or so until Dave was on the phone.

"My son just informed me that employees are paid every week, but he's worked three weeks without pay. When can he expect his paycheck? ... next Sunday? That's what you told him last Sunday and the Sunday before that. That's not good enough... I appreciate that you're sorry but this is illegal. If my son's check is not ready by 5 o'clock tomorrow, I'm calling the labor board," she angrily announced then hung up.

I drove to the steakhouse the next night around 6:00 p.m. and picked up my check. I never worked there again. Working eight hours every Sunday held no promise for the future, so finding another job was inevitable.

Disillusioned with my dismal entry into adulthood, I searched for some alternative to menial labor or fast food jobs. I had no experience or college education, but I could play guitar, and suddenly my interest in the instrument had been rekindled. *Maybe I could make money playing in a band, maybe even get a record contract*, I thought. I began playing and practicing every day and impressed a few friends by playing along with songs on the radio. My mom was not impressed. She reminded me I needed to find a job, and I assured her I would continue looking.

I was hired at a hamburger franchise and trained to work the grill, cooking hamburgers, and deep-frying things. It was a lot more complicated than it might seem from the customer's point of view. There was a ten-step process that had to be followed so that when the hamburgers were served, they were hot and properly assembled. Buns had to be toasted; cheese had to be added to some burgers and not others. Dressing, pickles, lettuce, onions needed to be added, but the process had to be followed in sequential order to avoid delay in assembly and presentation. The worst case was having six hamburgers ready to serve but having to wait for buns to be toasted for the last two no-cheese-no-sauce orders. That was failure, and I made that mistake more than once. It angered the manager, as it always occurred during the lunch rush, slowed service, and annoyed the customers.

My heart was not in that job at all. We had to wear a horrible brown polyester uniform, which chafed in all areas of contact, especially if you had to mop the floors or exert any physical effort.

My new adult life was not inspiring. Kellen was going to the Air Force Academy; Donny was working at PG&E making thousands every month; Eric had a full-time job in a cabinet shop and was driving a new Camaro; and I was wearing a brown polyester uniform and flipping burgers incorrectly for $3.35 an hour.

My job as a hamburger cook lasted a couple months. When I called to check my hours for the next week, the manager told me she wasn't putting me on the schedule anymore. I didn't have to ask, "are you firing me?" That was obvious. She told me to turn in my polyester brown slacks and pullover shirt and pick up my check. I gladly obliged.

Unemployed again, I decided to let my hair grow and pursue work as a musician. My mom was sympathetic to my lack of interest in a career as a fast food employee, but she again reminded me I'd have to get a job. I would, I assured her. I wanted a good job like my brother had, but I also wanted to play in a band and a career in music. That was fine, she said, but a full-time job would come first.

I learned that Danny Sherman, who was a couple years behind me, played electric guitar, and his friend, Grant Zelnick, played bass. Another friend of theirs, Dennis Lymon, played drums, and the three of them played in Danny's bedroom and did gigs occasionally, with no singer. *They sounded pretty good*, I thought. They played all the stuff I liked. If they could just find a great vocalist...

After some negotiations, I joined Danny's band, but we needed a place to practice, as three guitar players with their amps and a drummer cramped into Danny's bedroom left no space for the singer we did not have. I talked Mom into letting us use her one-car garage. We moved our amps and drums into the garage and searched for a vocalist. We were still cramped, but there was enough space left for a front man, if we could just find him.

We added a few songs to the list Danny and Grant already knew, but we would not be playing any gigs without a singer.

I placed an ad in the monthly newspaper published by Skip's Music, and we received a few phone calls. Most singers, however, had no microphones or amplifiers and were looking for a band that already had a complete sound system. We had drums and guitar amps, but not the large PA speakers that broadcast to the audience, nor the multichannel board which connects all the microphones for the instruments. Not having our own system was a disadvantage, but one would cost hundreds or maybe thousands of dollars, which none of us had.

One vocalist, who had his own microphone and monitor, agreed to audition. He pulled up and parked in front of my house one afternoon in a Corvette, which impressed everyone. He already looked like a rock star—skinny, long black hair, spiked tall on top like Mötley Crüe. I thought he was perfect for our band. He sounded great and seemed laid-back and easy to work with. He was probably six or seven years older than all of us, but I thought he was just what we needed to get our band off the ground. Apparently, he was also a good actor because, after pretending to be interested in singing for our band, we never heard from him again after the audition.

Rick's career at West Coast was soaring, and he urged me to apply. They'd hire me, he said. A couple guys who had long hair worked there, and they didn't mind. He was their best worker; they'd hire his little brother.

I went to West Coast, filled out an application and gave it to the front desk worker. He smiled and said they weren't hiring, but he'd keep my application and call when a job became available.

I later told Rick I was denied. He told me to go back the next day. He urged me to show up literally every day until they hired me. I didn't like seeming that desperate. Why wouldn't they just hire me when a job became available—like they said?

I skipped a day and went back, and the same employee smiled again and told me they weren't hiring. Rick said to ignore him and keep going back.

Several days later, I went back and was again told they weren't hiring. Each time I went back, the man's smile and body language told me he was lying. He just didn't like me or my hair and wouldn't be calling. I told Rick I was done trying, but he said don't give up. I went back a fourth time and received the same patronizing fake smile and denial.

I told Rick I was done trying to get hired at West Coast. My four visits in a week and a half were unsuccessful. He said they just hired someone the day before, and I should keep going back. I was furious and refused. That office jerk had told me he would call if a job became available then gave it to someone else.

I wanted to punch him, but going to jail wouldn't help.

I stayed in contact with my old friend, Eric Farnsworth. He knew I needed a job and said he checked with his employer; they'd hire me, and I wouldn't have to cut my long hair. He would pick me up every morning, as I didn't have a car, and we lived only two blocks apart. I gladly accepted the job and began work at Carl's Custom Cabinets for $3.35 an hour.

The cabinet shop occupied a large warehouse in Rancho Cordova. My job was to hand-sand cabinet doors from 7 a.m. to 4 p.m. Two large wood tables were provided for workers to sand. A piece of sandpaper was stapled around a rectangular block of wood, which was pressed and run back and forth against the splintery edges of the newly made cabinet doors. Once sanded, they were loaded on a cart for other workers to attach to the cabinet faces.

After a couple days sanding doors, my palms were raw, and I began wearing gloves, but I didn't mind the minor irritation. I finally had a full-time job, and that was the important thing. I was an adult, I needed money, and now I was earning it.

Two weeks later, the boss announced my new assignment would be building cabinet drawers. I was moved to a table and shown the process, which I enjoyed much more than sanding. I was also given a raise to $4.75 an hour, which seemed like a whopping increase at the time. I was pleased with my employer's generosity and enthused about my job.

The cabinet shop proved to be an extremely

dangerous environment. An employee was pushing doors through the rollers on a large machine one day when he got careless and allowed his hands too close. The rollers pinched tightly on his fingers, sucking his hand into the interior of the machine. He began screaming and pounding on the outer housing with his free hand. I ran from the table where I was building drawers and started turning a crank to release the tension of the rollers. Another employee came flying around a nearby machine, pushed me out of the way and began turning the crank frantically. The trapped employee screamed in agony, "You're tightening it! You're tightening it!" *If the dumbass hadn't pushed me out of the way, the man's arm would be free from the machine by now*, I thought. He reversed direction, and eventually freed the man's trapped arm. The back of his palm and knuckles were bleeding and gouged. He left for the hospital and never returned.

Another time, I was cutting plywood with the vertical saw and was in a hurry. I reached above my head with my right arm to pull the handle and, instead of pulling straight down, I pulled back, and the tall wood racks on either side of the saw began tilting toward me. In a thousandth of a second, I knew the wood racks were far too heavy for me to push them back into place, and they were slowly falling, about to crush me. I let go of the saw, turned and dashed away from the falling wall of wood, which crashed to the concrete floor with a thunderous clatter. I escaped death by a fraction of a second.

The whole shop suddenly went quiet. Saws and

sanders whined to silence as employees began coming to the front of the shop to see what had happened. The wood from the racks was now lying in two parallel piles on the floor, and a giant space appeared where the racks had previously created a partition of wood.

The shop manager met with the owner to discuss the near tragedy. They built a new wood rack that was not connected to the vertical saw and restacked all the fallen pieces.

There were other hazards—forklifts rolling around the shop, stopping and starting suddenly; raising and lowering stacks of plywood that might slip off and careen like an errant guillotine blade onto the concrete floor. Slippery sawdust and loose pieces of wood might cause a slip and fall. A booth where parts were sprayed with glue seemed to contain almost no oxygen, and standing in that area all day inhaling pungent glue fumes could not have been healthy, but I never heard anyone complain. Machines and chemicals were dangerous, but our job was to build cabinets, and that's what we did.

Meanwhile, I was still looking for musicians and pursuing the band fantasy after work.

Rick had worked for West Coast almost three years when the employees decided to play a game of tackle football on a Saturday. There had been lots of macho taunting about who was the better football player in high school, and the way to settle all this was to face off on the football field. There would be no helmets or pads.

Eager to prove himself, Rick gladly accepted the challenge.

Ten or twelve guys gathered for the tackle football game in a park near West Coast. My brother had shown his strength and speed during the first part of the game, but when he returned a kickoff and charged down the field, an opposing player dove at his legs and hit him squarely, just as his leg made impact with the ground. The diving player's shoulder broke his leg below the knee, and he was now lying on the ground in agony.

He was driven to the hospital and admitted to the emergency room. The break was severe and required surgery. The same doctor who performed my ankle surgery a few years earlier now did the operation on Rick's leg. A large titanium rod was installed through the shinbone, and his leg was immobilized in a full leg cast. He moved back into his old bedroom at my mom's house and lay in agony for a couple weeks.

He applied for Workers' Compensation, but the claim was denied, because playing football was not part of his job, and he had not received a work-related injury. Everyone who played had volunteered, and it had not been organized or sanctioned by West Coast.

I wondered about the legality of the denial of Workers' Compensation benefits. True, the injury had not occurred 'on the job', but the planning and agreement for the game had occurred at work during work hours. Wasn't that enough? Nope. He lost his appeal and the matter was settled—no Workers' Compensation benefits.

His state disability claim was granted, a meager sum of $143 every two weeks. That was better than nothing.

Rick was no longer able to afford the loan payments on his Jeep, so my mom drove him to the bank, surrendered the keys, and he completed a voluntary repossession. The bank employee was rude and contemptuous, as if Rick had stolen all the pennies out of her child's piggy bank. Mom was incensed by the disrespectful behavior. My brother could have kept the Jeep for months, given it to a friend to sell in parts and reported it stolen, or done any number of things people did to avoid repossessions. Instead, he responsibly returned the Jeep when he was no longer able to make the payments and was shamed for his honesty and accountability. The bank lost nothing, except all our respect, which probably matters no more than a teardrop in the ocean.

Rick languished for weeks in his increasingly dirty leg cast, but it was finally removed, and a second surgery was scheduled to remove the rod from his shin. He returned home with the bar and showed it to me. I was amazed that the thing had been installed in his leg. I encouraged him to go through physical therapy as I had, but there was no money or insurance coverage to pay for it.

I was disturbed watching his physical decline. In

the past, he had always been Superman, physically superior to his peers and me, capable of any type of work requiring strength, balance, concentration and endurance, but now he had become a cripple, unable to perform the type of work that had given him so much pride and independence. For a while, after the rod was removed from his shin, he used a cane. After several months, he abandoned the cane but still walked with a slight limp.

Meanwhile, he continued receiving disability checks every two weeks, and since he was not employed, he spent a good deal of time with his friends, partying and seeking adventure in the evenings.

Rick eventually returned to work at West Coast. Unfortunately, his leg was not healed enough to bear any substantial weight. He was unable to perform his job as he had previously and was fired in less than a month. Never think 'company loyalty' transcends the bottom line, it doesn't.

He found another job at a small glass company and was fired again within a month for the same reasons—not physically able to meet the demands of the job. Living again in his old bedroom at Mom's, his blue-collar career seemed finished.

One Friday night, I had finished watching *The Tonight Show Starring Johnny Carson* and *Late*

Night with David Letterman. I was just drifting off to sleep when a car parked in front of the house, and I heard doors slam, then loud voices. Keys jangled at the front door, then it burst open. Rick came in with a couple of his friends, Tim Molina and Ed Vaughn, and a woman. Ed was tall, a few years older than my brother, had long, straight hair, and looked just like Malcolm Young from AC/DC. Tim Molina was a grade ahead of my brother but had been his football teammate going back to Pop Warner football. They had been at the El Dorado Saloon drinking and watching a band and decided to bring the party home.

I knew there would be no sleep for the next several hours, so I got up, put on some hip-hugging sweatpants and walked out shirtless to greet them. I was in pretty good shape back then; 5' 10" 165, with a sort of swimmer's body, somewhat lanky, long arms, lean, flat stomach. My hair was long, past my shoulders.

The partiers were loud and exuberant, laughing and joking. The girl sat at the kitchen table. She had big '80s hair, long legs, and cool rocker boots with thin high heels. She was straight out of an MTV rock video.

Rick and his friends were not paying much attention to their female guest. I saw the empty chair at the kitchen table and sat arm's length from her. Someone gave me a beer. I cracked it open, and she asked who I was. I told her I was Rick's brother, and I lived there. She giggled and smiled; she told me her name was Jeanette.

Ed sat on the other side of Jeanette. Tim remained standing, drinking a beer, talking to my brother.

Jeanette smiled and said, "You remind me of Eddie Van Halen. You look a little like him."

Ed laughed and sneered, "No, he doesn't," then giggled and swigged his beer.

I wanted to say, "Shut up, Ed. If she thinks I look like Eddie Van Halen, I look like Eddie Van Halen. Deal with it." I said thank you to Jeanette.

"No, really... I really think you...you look like Eddie Van Halen," she said.

"Thank you. It's probably the hair," I said with an attempt at modesty.

"Naw, you're cute like him, too." She smiled and giggled more.

"Bull," Ed scoffed, and swigged more beer.

"Have you ever seen them live?" I asked Jeanette.

"Yes, twice," she answered. "At the Oakland Coliseum and Cow Palace."

"Were they good?"

"Great," she said with a drunken grin.

"I can't wait 'til they come to Sacramento."

"You should go. You'll like it," she said with a boozy smile.

"I'll be there," I said.

She smiled at me some more and asked, "Do you play guitar?"

"Yes."

"I thought so.

We chatted a few more minutes about the band

they had seen earlier. They liked all the hard rock songs.

I was flattered by Jeanette's compliments but bored with the meandering discussion and debate whether I looked like Van Halen, so I stood up, walked to the kitchen sink, noticed some dishes, and decided to wash them. They were an eyesore.

As I stood with my shirtless back to the kitchen table and washed dishes, suddenly two hands came from behind me on either side below my shoulders and palms pressed against my chest. I next felt the softness of Jeanette's right cheek caressing my left, as she pressed her body against my back, squeezed my chest and nuzzled against my face.

I stood for a moment in disbelief but pleasantly surprised. I turned around and kissed her. She smelled sweet and girly, and I was concerned Rick might get angry that I had taken his catch. He finally noticed, wobbled over and watched.

I ignored him and continued kissing Jeanette. He hiccupped loudly then swigged his beer.

The harsh morning sunlight ended our little rock-video fantasy. Jeanette awoke to unforgiving daylight about five hours later, and I summoned my brother, who was badly hungover, but he got up and gave her a ride to her car.

Over the summer, I began seeing Matt Murry around town. I'd been friends with him since Little League, but now that we were no longer in high school, we had more opportunities for adventure.

Matt was tall, with twinkling Irish eyes and deep crescent-shaped dimples. He wore a thick mustache and looked like the firefighter he later became.

He told me he had been entrusted to take care of a small house near the bottom of Sutter Street, close to the river. Andrea Hose, the mother of our mutual friend, Larry, owned the house. She had several others in Nevada and was gone frequently overseeing her properties and traveling.

I wondered how Ms. Hose had amassed a small real estate empire. According to Matt, she had been some sort of entrepreneur who had acquired several rental properties and lived off the rental income. That seemed impressive at the time—particularly for a woman in the mid-1980s. Andrea was a pioneer, no doubt showing the world and other women that success in business was not just a man's prerogative or birthright.

Matt nicknamed her house, 'The Hoser's House,' not out of any disrespect for Ms. Hose, but just because it sounded funny, using the word 'hoser' to identify the property.

A creaky wood floor covered the living room of The Hoser's House, which contained a fireplace, tiled kitchen with dark wood cabinets, wood-paneled walls, and a single bedroom. An old piano rested against the wall next to the fireplace.

There wasn't much for Matt to do. He gathered the mail and newspapers, watered now and then, mowed the lawn occasionally, but not much else, as far as I could tell. He made sure no squatters invaded or burglars stole anything; otherwise, he and friends retreated there on the weekends, drank beer and enjoyed the unsupervised private space.

We were not yet twenty-one, but Matt Murry knew how to get Budweiser. He either had a fake Nevada driver's license or knew an adult who would buy him beer.

After obtaining a twelve-pack of Bud Light one Saturday night, we sat at the wood kitchen table, drank, and pondered our futures. Matt said he had looked into joining the Air Force, spoken to a recruiter, and decided to join. "I'm goin' Air Force," he told me. He had signed enlistment papers and would report after the summer. I congratulated him. He had a plan, and he was eager to start.

After a couple Bud Lights, I sat at the piano, opened the songbook, and studied the notes. I was still able to read music on the treble clef, so I figured out a melody and practiced it. *I needed to take lessons, then I could play guitar AND keyboards.*

After a while, I gave up the piano and returned to the kitchen. Matt turned up the radio, and we resumed our discussion. We relished the freedom of The Hoser's House and our cold contraband.

Matt left for the Air Force a couple months later. I was saddened by his departure, but we both had been out of high school several years, and it was time to move on with our lives, begin careers, or at least find a good job.

He wrote letters and sent postcards from France and Germany and described his life and adventures in the Air Force. I wrote back, telling him about the goings-on around town and my progress starting a band.

While he lived at home convalescing from his broken leg, Rick didn't need to be up early to go to work, so he could stay out late whenever he wanted. He enjoyed occasionally going to the Shire Road Pub on Auburn Boulevard. It was close, and the Pub was one of the few clubs that allowed bands to play original music, though it usually wanted a couple sets of cover tunes to draw in the dance crowd. He suggested we go one evening with some friends. Matt had gotten me a cheesy fake Nevada driver's license, and I had used it successfully a few times.

We brought a couple friends, strode into the Pub, and took a table. The band's drums and amps looked enticing on the stage, little red LED lights on the amps signaling they were powered on and ready to rock.

I went to the bar, bought a couple mixed drinks for myself then returned to the table. I noticed the pretty rocker women all around— all in spandex and boots, or high heels, low-cut tops, headbands, bracelets, huge hair—standard rocker wear of the '80s.

We stepped to the edge of the stage and admired the band's gear. They looked like pros. Gibson guitars, Pearl Drums, Marshall amps—all top of the line. I was filled with envy. Five musicians had formed a band, learned forty-five songs, and now were about to entertain the crowd for the evening and get paid for it. *They were living my dream, but there was room for another guitar player and great band in this town*, I thought. I envisioned myself on stage at the Pub in my own band. Performing for a hundred strangers seemed like a prestigious achievement that put a band one signature away from a record deal and superstardom. I always assumed record company executives scouted the night clubs for talented bands, and they could be anywhere—even The Shire Road Pub on Auburn Boulevard in Sacramento. My band would be on that stage someday, I vowed.

The musicians ascended the stage, slung on guitars and started cranking out rock tunes. They sounded okay, but I was not highly impressed. I wanted to hear Van Halen's *Eruption* or *Mean Streets*, but they played mostly easy dance songs. I hoped they would at least perform a few of the more complicated pieces from groups like Judas Priest or Iron Maiden, but they stuck to easy top 40 hits, and that was understandable. They had to please the masses, so delivering familiar pop jingles was a successful strategy. Besides, almost no guitarists back then could play the intricate, complex phrases rapidly articulated by Van Halen, Randy Rhoads, Glenn Tipton, and others.

The band played none of my favorites, but we enjoyed most of their selection, asked women to dance and drank. Alcohol was cheap during the week, and ten dollars could pay for the evening.

The music ended a little after 1:00, and we lingered for a while, then a friend drove us home.

A week or two later, about 2:00 in the morning, I heard my brother and a couple of his friends pounding on the front door. They had been out drinking and decided to continue the party after the bar closed. Mom still worked graveyard and I had to be up at 6:30. I would be around saws, whirling blades, and dangerous machinery all day and needed to be well rested. I did not appreciate being awakened at two by several drunks who were bent on drinking for several more hours. They'd crank up the stereo, talk, laugh, stumble around, and make loud noise until four in the morning. The intrusion angered me, so I refused to answer the door. The knocking continued.

After ten minutes of knocking, I went to the front door and shouted, "I have to work tomorrow! Go somewhere else!"

"Open the door!"

"I can't party tonight; I have to work tomorrow!"

"Open the door!"

"I'm going back to bed! Go somewhere else! I have to work in the morning!"

I left and went back to my room.

I heard Rick mumbling about losing his house

key. He pounded on the door for a while and shouted, but I ignored him. Determined to continue the party, he climbed the fence, entered the garage through the patio door, and began banging on the garage door that led into the house. I snapped, got out of bed, put on my shorts, went to the back door, and slammed my hand against the chain lock to unlock it. As soon as I turned the door handle with my other hand, Rick pushed through, crashing his shoulder into my abdomen, driving me back, smashing into the microwave oven, making a loud clatter. He let go and started swinging, and we both stood there in the dark, throwing punches at each other.

We crashed into the living room and knocked over a table and lamp and resumed fighting in the dark. I was afraid he might unintentionally kill me in his drunken, out of control state. He could have easily picked up a lamp, a chair or something else and clobbered me in the fray, so I wanted to take the fight outside. I stumbled to the front door and had to lower my hands to unlock it. He punched me in the face as I struggled with the door handle, but I succeeded and scrambled outside. He followed.

I walked into the middle of the street, under the street lamp so I could see better and had more room. There was warm blood on my chin, throat, and chest. I had a bloody nose, but I couldn't feel any pain.

His two friends were standing nearby, watching, shocked and dumbfounded.

Rick stalked me into the street and challenged me to finish the fight. I was gasping for air and deciding what to do. I had taken two years of tae kwon do and had formidable skills with my hands and feet, but I was under a heavy psychological disadvantage—my older brother had always been able to beat me down instantly from childhood through high school. This was a couple years after high school, and we were about the same size and strength now. I might be able to take him, but he was drunk and might not feel any pain, and I didn't want either one of us hurt too badly, even though I was angered by his thoughtlessness.

We stood in the street facing each other under the nearby street lamp. I raised my right hand to inspect the blood all over the back of it. I could see my brother's eyes were glossy; he was drunk. I could easily land a hard blow on his cheek; I gasped and focused my attention on his face as he stepped toward me. I drew my right hand back a few inches, then sprung forward like a snake, thrusting all my upper body strength and speed into my punch, which landed hard on his left cheek with a loud crack, snapping his head back. The blow infuriated him, and he charged. I knew if he got a hold of me, the fight wouldn't end until police broke it up, and I didn't want any of that, so I turned and ran—sprinted like a gazelle down the street as he chased, unable to catch me.

I turned the corner and continued running barefoot and shirtless, a couple blocks to the duplex where Kathryn Farnsworth lived, the mother of my friend, Eric. Kathryn was a knockout, pretty and petite southern belle from South Carolina. I knocked loudly on the door and she opened it. The expression on her face went from sleepy to horrified, as I stood there.

“Ben…, what happened?” she gasped.

“I got into a fight with my brother.”

“Are you alright?”

“Yes, but I can’t go home. I don’t want to fight again.”

“Well come in and wash up.”

She opened the door and I walked in and went into the bathroom. After I had cleaned up, she gave me a blanket and said I could sleep in the spare room. She was clearly shaken by my appearance.

She called Eric early in the morning to let him know to pick me up at her condo. Eric drove me to my house to get some clothes and shoes. I dressed then exited quietly, Rick still sleeping in his room in his clothes.

Fortunately, after his hangover wore off, Rick realized that bringing friends home was a bad decision. He sheepishly apologized the next day, and the subject was not mentioned again. The only reminder was the large half circle of black underneath his left eye that lingered for a couple weeks. It was awkward for a while, but life eventually returned to normal.

He later moved into a house in Rancho Cordova with a couple roommates and continued surviving on his state disability check.

Soon we discovered The Island, a nightclub in Old Town Roseville that featured live bands. Unlike most other nightclubs, the Island allowed musicians to play original songs—not just popular hits playing on the radio. Rick and our friends decided to go on a Saturday night. Tim Molina, Ed Vaughn and one or two others would join us for our first trip to The Island to watch a band.

We learned a group called Diamond Blade would be playing. We had never heard of them and had no idea what to expect. All the bands we had seen previously simply played other people's music, but we wanted to hear originals.

We paid the cover charge and stood near the front door. A few minutes later, guys carrying guitar cases walked in and stood nearby. I realized, this must be the band. I saw a label on a guitar case—Gibson. Just like Aerosmith and Led Zeppelin.

Diamond Blade had two guitar players, a bassist, drummer, and lead vocalist, Jeff Keller. I was astonished when I saw all their gear. Both guitar players had full Marshall stack amps, which probably cost about $1,200 each back in the '80s. Lance Bannon played a beautiful Gibson Les Paul Sunburst, worth probably a couple thousand dollars. The other guitar player, Johnny Scarlet, played a state-of-the-art brand with EMG pickups and a Floyd Rose bridge. The drummer had a beautiful, shiny red drum kit that looked like it belonged on stage with Def Leppard or Judas Priest. The bass player had his own setup that was top-notch. They looked like complete professionals.

I expected them to be terrible, however, because I was under the mistaken impression that all the good bands were in Los Angeles. Maybe more important, they had a fat bass player, and Lance Bannon didn't even have long hair—it barely touched his shoulders—how could he play like Van Halen with short hair? Johnny Scarlet looked like a new waver, with long, curly bangs that hung over his eyes and short hair everywhere else. They had to be terrible; they looked nothing like the Scorpions, Judas Priest, Van Halen, or Iron Maiden.

After they got on stage and blasted a few songs, we were all saying, "Who are these guys? They're incredible." We watched in awe as they tore through one original after another. We had never seen a local band with so much talent.

We went back to The Island a couple weeks later and saw them again. A group of us sat at a table, drank beers, chatted, and watched another incredible show. Afterwards, I went home, but Rick went to an after-hours party somewhere and met a couple guys in the band. I saw him a few days later, and he proudly announced, "I met the singer for Diamond Blade."

"Really," I answered. "Where?"

"At the after-hours party. His name is Jeff. He's from Roseville. I got his phone number."

He looked at me triumphantly.

"How did you meet him?" I asked.

"I heard he was from Roseville, so I just walked up to him and asked if he knew some people. He knew everyone."

I listened intently.

"He knows Brandt Littleton and Pretty-Boy-Roy. I told him we should go camping, and he said let's go. We drank all night," he added with a smile.

I was astonished. Just like that, he had made friends with the lead singer of this popular local rock band.

"I met the guitar player, too," he informed me. "His name is Lance. Lance Bannon. I got his phone number, too."

Now I was jealous. I was the musician, and if anyone should meet the guitar player for Diamond Blade, it should be me, but he had met both the lead singer and the lead guitar player and was now proudly bragging.

I wanted to say, "You understand, don't you, that I should benefit directly from your new relationship with these fledgling rock stars. I'm the committed lead guitar player who has been working hard for two years, and you should include me in your activities with Jeff and Lance so they can be exposed to my guitar playing, which will somehow lead me into a great rock band." I said nothing of the kind. I expected him to recognize the importance of including me in his new circle of rising rock stars.

To my disappointment, I was not included. Rick's breakthrough friendships with Jeff and Lance were his own spoils, which he would savor and enjoy until ready to share. I couldn't blame him. He made the effort; he deserved the results. He even went partying with Johnny Scarlet a couple times, but I had not been invited. I was irked, but I'd show him. I'd start my own band, garner a following and have plenty of admiring supporters. Even so, I hoped he'd throw me a bone and invite me along sometime, so I could meet his rock-star pals, but I remained uninvited.

Over the next several months, I would learn, usually after the fact, that he'd been partying with Jeff Keller after a Diamond Blade show, or that they'd gone camping, or he'd gone four-wheeling with Lance. Being left out annoyed me, but there was nothing I could do. It felt like we were in high school again—back to our old agreement not to mix friends. I used the exclusion to inspire me to form my own band. I didn't need to tag along with my brother on his excursions. He couldn't even play a musical instrument. I'd find the right players and be on my own glorious adventure soon.

Rick and his roommates usually partied on the weekends in Rancho Cordova. They'd host a kegger occasionally, and forty or fifty people would show up. Rick told me he and his friends were hosting a Halloween party, and Jeff and Lance would attend. If I wanted to meet his Diamond Blade friends, this would be my chance.

I went to the party and Rick introduced me. Jeff was in a costume, Lance was not. Everyone was trying to cozy up to the soon-to-be rock stars. They were both friendly and cordial, but their attention was in demand. I didn't want to bother them like some eager groupie. Besides, they already knew my brother, who was an extrovert, and I was a little shy. I felt any effort on my part to make friends with them would be judged against my brother's heroic showmanship, winning their affections through his free-wheeling extroversion, and my feeble attempts at conversation about musical scales and guitars would be deemed not charming enough. But that was my own misguided assumption based on decades of growing up in Rick's shadow. I figured when the time was right, I'd chat with Jeff and Lance and get to know them. I wasn't going to press the issue like an obsessed fan.

Diamond Blade quickly became the most popular band in Sacramento and after word got out that they had been offered a record deal by Capitol Records, they became legends. They were treated like royalty whenever I saw them, always surrounded by adoring supporters. They were a juggernaut, and my brother was along for the ride.

To my chagrin, Rick seemed to continue excluding me from interaction with his Diamond Blade friends. They were his special trophies to enjoy all for himself. The childhood relic of isolating and protecting friendships seemed to resurface. If he was going to shield me from his special buddies, then I'd just continue toward my objectives alone. I didn't need his help. I knew how to play guitar and had enough talent to play in a band, I thought. Diamond Blade was soaring toward stardom, and their purpose was to increase the band's profile and popularity—not help some hapless guitar player find a band. The responsibility to locate musicians was all mine, and I fully embraced the mission.

A couple weeks later, I was in my bedroom practicing guitar in the afternoon, and I heard Rick's truck in the driveway. He was supposed to be somewhere having fun with Jeff, but showed up unexpectedly. I heard Rick's voice outside and another. It had to be Jeff Keller. I started playing a blues boogie tune another guitar player had shown me and waited for Rick to enter the room. I thought he would come in and announce he was here with Jeff, explain their plans for a fun-filled afternoon then leave. I turned up the volume and jammed on the blues tune, which sounded like something Aerosmith would play.

As I played, I heard a raspy voice in the hall sustaining a note in perfect pitch to the key I was playing. The door swung open, and in walked Jeff Keller loudly singing his own words to the blues riff I was playing. He was a rock star—long streaky light brown hair, skinny, tan. I looked at him and smiled. He sang a few more notes then stopped, smiled, and thrust out his hand to shake mine.

"That's really cool, man, I like that," Jeff said in his throaty, raspy voice

"Thank you," I said, as I shook his hand.

"Did you write that?"

"Yes," I lied.

"Man, that's a cool riff. I could put some killer vocals to that."

I almost swallowed my tongue. "I'll bet you could," I agreed.

"Play that again from the start."

Jeff tapped his foot and moved a little with the rhythm. He sang some words here and there in perfect tune and timing. After I finished, he grinned and repeated that he liked the song. Then he looked at my guitar and amp, a small Fender and a Japanese-made flying V guitar.

"You sound good. What kind of guitar is that?"

"It's just some Japanese thing. I need to get a new guitar. Maybe a Gibson."

"Keep it, man. That one sounds great."

My brother had stepped through the doorway and listened with a little smirk. I could tell he was proud of his friendship with Jeff, proud to share him a little with me, and proud that I was playing guitar well enough to capture Jeff's attention and approval. It was a perfect moment.

Jeff turned and looked at Rick, "Your brother's good on guitar, man. You guys should form a band."

Rick smiled.

Jeff continued, "I like that blues riff. Put some vocals on it. Add some blues solos, bassline, maybe cut back the distortion a little. Your amp sounds good, but you don't want too much fuzz."

"Yeah, I'll keep working on it. I need to work on tone. This distortion box is junk," I said, glowering at the small box at my feet, cabled to my guitar.

"It's fine, just dial back a little on blues tunes; keep the distortion for the hard rockers."

"What I really need is a good bass player and drummer," I announced.

"Good ones are hard to find," he said consolingly. "I got lucky. I found a band that needed a singer. They're out there; keep lookin', check with Skips, ask around, you'll find 'em."

"I'll keep lookin'."

It was time to wrap up our little conversation. Jeff concluded, "Well, we're just passing through on the way to my house, but we had to stop here to pick up a few things. You sound good, man. Keep practicin'."

"I will."

They left and closed the door, and I returned to the boogie tune I had been playing previously.

Finally, I had a real moment with Jeff Keller—one in which I was completely myself, not trying to outdo my brother or pretend to be like him, just playing my guitar in my room. Music brought us together—authentically. We connected, not as rock star and fan, but as musicians, equals.

Deep down, I knew Rick had brought Jeff to see me—away from all the fans, partiers and distractions—so we could meet as two people who shared an interest in music and talk like two friends. He knew I wanted to be involved with his Diamond Blade friends, and he was trying to include me in a way that was not forced or awkward for anyone. My brother was finally letting me into his sacred inner circle.

CITY OF ANGELS

The '80s were Reagan years. Ronald Reagan defeated Jimmy Carter in the 1980 presidential election and assumed leadership for the nation. The Cold War was still escalating, and the threat of nuclear war remained a mostly subconscious, but sometimes conscious, fear. I remember it. The loud daily missile tests at Aerojet and the overhead flights of B-52s were constant reminders of the imminent possibility of nuclear annihilation.

Politics was much different back then. The cavernous divide between the Left and Right did not exist to the extent it does today, and a handful of cultural and constitutional issues did not divide the nation into two enemy camps, each hoping their side's interpretation of the U.S. Constitution would be adopted by the Supreme Court.

Rights of gays, lesbians and others were not on the mainstream agenda in the '80s. Any sexuality other than hetero was tinged with shame, scorn and ridicule—not that it should be—that's just how it was. I was not aware of any openly gay people in town. For unexplained reasons, homosexuals lived in San Francisco; they were not anywhere in Folsom, as far as I could tell.

The news in the '80s was not dominated by partisan arguments about U.S. Supreme Court nominees, terrorist attacks, and government incompetence; there was no Fox News or MSNBC, nor any nightly cable news dissecting the latest political scandal. I recall lots of news about Egypt, Israel, the Middle East, and garden-variety reports about domestic issues—GDP, taxes, the economy, interest rates, and the stock market, among the occasional plane crash or domestic disaster.

Corruption in government occurred, but it seemed rare. A decade earlier in the early '70s, Watergate was the big scandal. I never understood it until I saw the movie, *All The President's Men,* a few years after high school and later read more about it. I figured I needed to understand this important chapter in American politics, and the movie was the best way to get up to speed.

In the mid-'80s, the Iran-Contra affair became the next great political scandal that equaled the infamy of Watergate and dominated headlines for months. Even so, the law-breaking of Iran-Contra seemed so far away and unconnected to the lives of ordinary Americans.

The operation was difficult to understand, but after a while, the basic truth came to light: our government was secretly selling missiles to Iran and using the proceeds to fund the Contras in Nicaragua. Congress had forbidden economic aid to the rebels, so our undisclosed economic support was illegal. That was earth-shaking at the time—our own military and CIA intentionally breaking the law and participating in an illegal war. It seemed possibly worse than Watergate.

The scandal lingered for months. Investigators

were determined to find out the big question: What did the president know, and when did he know it? Did he authorize the selling of arms to Iran in exchange for the release of hostages, and did he authorize the illegal diversion of funds to the Contras? Reagan said no, he didn't know about it or authorize anything and couldn't remember anything about such a complicated and elaborate scheme. That's where it was left.

Some involved in the operation were convicted of lying to Congress, but a court of appeal later reversed the convictions based on legal errors that had occurred at trial.

The Iran-Contra scandal eventually faded. Yes, there had been lying and law breaking—but it had all been for a just cause, supposedly. The scandal received much attention, but the country still did not split along partisan or ideological lines at that point.

The views of conservatives and liberals seemed limited to the op-ed section of the newspaper and William F. Buckley Jr.'s Sunday morning talk show, *Firing Line*, which I found interesting and entertaining, particularly Buckley's twitchy, quirky, professorial discourse, during which he frequently punctuated his questions and observations with a gleaming grin—as if his opponent could not possibly respond to his compelling logic. I remember the show addressing issues about the Middle East, but I did not have a good understanding of the Middle East's geo-political issues at the time. Nevertheless, I found the arguments and debates interesting.

Beyond Buckley's Sunday show, politics seemed to

fade out of my life until the next Sunday, or until a couple weeks before a presidential election, during which the presidential candidates debated and political issues received more public attention.

Legal and political issues had almost no impact on my life back in the '70s and '80s, with one possible exception. A recession occurred in the early '80s, and the effects of it may have lingered for a few years. The lagging economy may have affected my ability to find work but, more likely, my appearance prevented me from getting hired by numerous local employers. Though young adults idolized long-haired rock musicians, like Robert Plant, Jimmy Page, Eddie Van Halen, and dozens more, employers had no such esteem. Most didn't want and wouldn't hire long-haired employees—with a few exceptions, mainly in the trades and construction.

Mainstream society was culturally more conservative than it is now. There were no flexible work hours, nap rooms, or relaxed dress codes. In the business world, workers wore business attire and showed up at 8:00 or 9:00 in the morning. Construction workers started even earlier. Anyone who couldn't start on time was replaced.

I thought I should spend the week practicing and rehearsing with a band, but I needed money to buy gas, insurance, food, guitars, strings, amps, cables, speakers, clothing, concert tickets, and maybe a little alcohol on the weekend. I was sure playing in clubs eventually would become my full-time job, so I kept that in mind while I labored through the day.

Several local bands played gigs every week. They probably worked part time jobs also, but at least they were on stage doing what they loved every weekend. Why was it so difficult? Hard rock and heavy metal music were mainstream. There had to be hundreds, maybe thousands of musicians in Sacramento County. Why couldn't I find three or four? I invited drummers and guitarists to the garage now and then to jam for an hour, but finding the right mixture of talent and chemistry remained elusive.

Though I'd been striving for a couple years, my music career seemed thwarted from all sides. I just couldn't find the right musicians. They were out there, and many advertised in the periodical circulated by Skip's Music, but there were so many factors that made the undertaking a challenge. First, the expense: obtaining high-quality guitars and amps cost thousands; next, locating a practice room, coordinating schedules and paying for rehearsal space; no less important was agreeing on songs—that easily could cause a break-up; most musicians had a handful of pet favorites they wanted to play, and if you said no, they might quit.

Finally, dealing with overinflated egos could overshadow all other practical aspects and lead to divisions; there were many moving parts.

After our drummer quit Danny's band, I joined another that seemed to have promise, but it soon fell apart. The other guitar player had a drug problem, which doomed our efforts.

I'd been through a number of auditions that went nowhere, and my frustration grew. Meanwhile, Diamond Blade's popularity was soaring. Rick told me the band would fly to New York to record their first album, *Jagged Edges.* I was astonished. They made it look so easy; they just played a couple times a month, somehow attracted a record company, then signed a recording contract. The path seemed clear, but I still was not in a band and had no prospects.

After recording their debut album, Jeff Keller came back from New York and gave Rick a cassette tape of the unreleased songs. I listened dozens of times before any singles were played on the radio. It was impressive for a rock band's first release and had all the songs I'd seen the band play live at The Island dozens of times.

Jagged Edges was a huge hit, and Diamond Blade's first world tour began with the superstar band Scorpions. The little group from Sacramento had arrived on the world stage.

I decided I couldn't wait any longer to find musicians in Folsom. I would move to Los Angeles, where thousands of great players lived, find a band, and chart my own path to success. *I could do it all myself. I had plenty of talent and ambition*, I thought, and if I had to move to Los Angeles, that's what I would do.

At that point, I felt Rick had accepted me into his social circle. We both seemed to realize that holding onto childhood pretenses and differences was just silly. There was no reason we should not be complete equals and close friends. We reached that plateau, and I dropped all my misgivings about his older-brother superiority and shenanigans and fully embraced our new adult friendship. However, he was not a musician and could not fill a role in my mission to form a band.

I asked my dad if I could live with him to pursue my music career, and he agreed. I quit the cabinet shop, packed my bags, took my guitar and rode a bus all night to Los Angeles. Dad picked me up at a bus stop in the morning and never showed any lack of confidence in my dreams. He probably knew that making it big in the record business was a long shot, but he never crushed my hope. He had his own goal to be discovered as the world's greatest stage actor, so he understood my ambition.

He had moved from the Holloway House Apartments to a one-bedroom on Alexandria, just a half mile from the Ambassador Hotel, where Robert Kennedy had been assassinated in 1968. It was furnished and had a tiny kitchen and breakfast nook near the front door. My grandpa had moved in after his wife died years earlier, and the living space became cramped. He slept in a bed in the middle of the living room, and stacks of boxes at the foot of his bed formed a crude wall separating his space from the kitchen. More boxes of my grandfather's property were stacked nearby and in the far opposite corners.

All the clutter made it seem as if we were living

in a warehouse, but Dad was oblivious. What mattered was that Grandpa had not been abandoned to a retirement home. He was in his early 90s, and Dad was just fine with him occasionally sleeping all day, reading all night, covering the kitchen table with vitamin bottles, magazines, bills, health books, and sharing the limited space. Grandpa usually skipped breakfast, but joined us for dinner every night.

To escape the claustrophobia of the apartment, I used to stroll through the Ambassador Hotel in the mornings. The spacious, empty, carpeted areas on the first floor always gave me a creepy feeling, as if back in the '50s gangsters met there by the dozen to discuss business—or maybe the hotel was haunted—like the one in *The Shining.* The hotel never seemed busy in the morning, and no one ever seemed to notice as I strode by and gawked at the wall paintings and furnishings.

When I returned from my occasional journeys around the neighborhood, my dad would usually be gone, but Grandpa would be asleep on the bed in the living room or sitting at the small kitchen table. He'd been married fifty-two years, and once a week I'd find him sitting at the kitchen table, staring at a black and white picture of his wife, crying. It saddened me, but there was nothing I could do. I talked to my dad, and he told me I couldn't understand Grandpa's ongoing grief; it was just how it was, and we shouldn't try to cure or talk him out of it; he'd already tried numerous times, and it was no help.

After returning from a walk one morning, I sat at

the small kitchen table with Grandpa. The apartment smelled like rotting onions and over-ripe banana peels—a unique combination of sweet and sour that never bothered Dad.

"Are you looking for a job, Ben?" he asked.

"Yes."

"What have you found?"

"I checked with the music store. They're not hiring. I'll have to keep looking."

He smiled, as if he had me trapped. "Who's going to hire you with all that hair?"

"The music store will, but they don't have any job openings right now. I'm going to apply at a record store. I can work there with long hair."

He chuckled and continued smiling. "Have you looked anywhere else?"

"No."

He laughed, not hiding his amusement. "Have you checked the newspapers?"

"No."

"How do you expect to get a job?"

"I'm looking. I can work in a music store or record store, as soon as they're hiring."

He continued grinning smugly. "You can do all kinds of work; you should get a job and do the band on the weekend."

"I have to practice every day. It takes a lot of practice to get good on guitar."

He ignored my comment and repeated himself, "You should get a job during the week. You can practice after work and on weekends."

I was getting annoyed with his lecture. “It's hard to find a job with long hair. I'm not cutting my hair just so I can work some crappy job.”

“You're not in school anymore. You’re an adult. You're young and strong. You should have a full-time job. Do you expect your father to support you, pay all the bills?”

“No. I'll pay my share as soon as I can. I'm not afraid to work,” I said curtly.

“No employer will hire you with that hair. You should cut it. Look like a professional. You could get a good job tomorrow.”

“I'm not cutting my hair,” I said sourly, then stood up and walked into the bedroom.

I had heard enough and didn't feel required to explain and justify my career goals to my grandfather. Besides, he didn't understand. If I cut my hair short, I wouldn't have the right look for a rock band. I would have gladly worked a job that would allow long hair, but I didn't even have a car. The whole situation was a disaster. I had no money, job, or car, yet I was striving to form or join a band, which requires endless expenditures and acquisitions.

My grandfather had a valid point, but he did not understand the circumstances related to my goals. I could not just cut my hair, get another job at a fast food restaurant or retail store, and still play in a rock band. It just wouldn't work. No bands in L.A. wanted a guitar player with short hair.

After perusing local newspapers and talking with my dad, I quickly learned that all the action was on the Sunset Strip—the famous street in Hollywood cluttered with restaurants, bars, clubs, art galleries, boutiques, a few music stores and apartments—the same Sunset Strip we used to drive up every night when Dad worked at the radio station K-LOVE when I was a little kid.

The Strip was the home of legendary nightclubs like Whiskey a Go-Go, the Troubadour Club, and Gazarri's, where Van Halen, Randy Rhoads, RATT, Mötley Crüe, and Guns N' Roses had played. On the weekends, these clubs were overflowing with big-haired rockers in leather pants, spandex, boots and leather jackets. This was ground zero for heavy metal stardom in the 1980s. Bands came here to get noticed by the record companies and either sign a record contract or go home forgotten.

I started going to the clubs and watching bands, hoping I'd meet some musicians—maybe even see Van Halen or David Lee Roth having a drink—Roth was known to hang out sometimes on the Strip.

Watching musicians in these clubs made it clear that my music fantasy was even further from reality than I had already admitted. Most of the L.A. players had even more gear than Diamond Blade. Often the guitarist would not have merely a single Marshall stack towering behind him on stage, but two, and four or five expensive guitars, all top-of-the-line models. $10,000 worth of guitars and amps might be on stage for any given band. Dad dropped $400 to buy me a new Carvin 100-watt half stack, and my Washburn guitar cost $250, which I'd bought on layaway. I almost felt like an imposter with my less expensive guitar setup, but I couldn't ask Dad to buy any more gear. It just didn't seem right that he should spend a lot of money for amps, and guitars. *This was my career, and I should pay for my own gear*, though I was grateful he bought me the Carvin.

L.A. was flooded with talented guitar players. They'd played nonstop for the past ten years, so they were ahead of me, but not out of reach. Some were easily as good or better than Van Halen. I could play respectably but was probably no better than third in line for any spot in a band. I kept practicing every day, committed to becoming a 'shredder'.

After a couple months at my dad's, playing guitar half the day, checking newspaper ads for guitar players, watching bands on the weekends and making no progress, my plan felt like a fiasco. I had met no one who could help, nor connected with any musicians. I was tired of isolation, making no progress, and watching other artists while I peered from the crowd. I also missed my friends in Folsom. I thought about my options. I could always go back home, start over with another garage band. There was still time. If I failed in L.A., I'd just go back to the room my mom was keeping for me, the room with the Van Halen and Bruce Lee posters, and try again.

But I had come to L.A. to establish myself and decided not to give up without a try. I found an ad for a guitar player who sounded perfect: "Wanted, co-lead guitarist. Influences: Maiden, Priest, Ozzy, Mötley Crüe, Scorpions. Must have good gear and be willing to practice." I called the number, spoke with the drummer, and we agreed on a date and time for an audition.

A few days later, I loaded my Carvin half stack cabinet and the separate, rectangular guitar head into the trunk of my dad's Chrysler 300, and he drove me to my audition. After forty-five minutes, we found the large industrial park where the band practiced, got lost, then eventually found the correct warehouse. Dad and I began unloading my gear, and the drummer came out to greet me.

"Hi," he said warmly and extended his hand. I shook it. He grabbed a handle on my Carvin cabinet and helped me carry it into the warehouse.

"We got lost," I announced. "Missed the turn. The street loops around, and we turned on the wrong end."

"No big deal."

They had built a stage about five feet off the ground for the drums, but it was large enough for the whole band, so they could practice their show, as if performing for an audience. We placed my amp on the ground to the side, facing the stage.

"Nice amp," the drummer commented.

"Thank you."

"I haven't heard Carvin yet. Bet it sounds great."

"It does."

"You know any Iron Maiden?" he asked hopefully.

"Uh, I don't think so. I know a little Judas Priest, some Van Halen."

"Sounds good."

Dad brought my guitar in, and I started plugging

in cables and chords. Their bass player ascended the stage, plugged in, and began thumping bass lines.

This was the first time I had actually played the amp outside my dad's apartment with the volume above 1. As soon as I turned up to 5, the amp started wailing with ear-splitting feedback. I turned down the volume then slowly turned it up again, but the feedback returned. The drummer, grimacing from the feedback, walked over and examined my amp. All the EQ levers had been pushed straight up to their highest position. He lowered all the levers so they were all in the middle range of the slide, and the feedback went away. Then he looked at me like I was an idiot.

Their singer and other guitar player showed up—both skinny with long hair.

The drummer climbed the stairs and took a seat behind his drums and played some rolls and beats to warm up. The guitar player turned on his amp to the right of the drummer, slung his guitar strap over his shoulder, and began playing loud distorted chords and riffs. He stopped and began tuning the guitar at a low volume. The singer took a microphone off a stand at center stage and spoke into it.

"What do you want to play?" he asked, his question booming out of the large speakers at either end of the stage.

"How about *You Really Got Me*, the Van Halen version?" I yelled back.

He rolled his eyes. "Too easy. We're not a Van Halen copy band. How about something else?"

"How about *Livin' After Midnight*?"

The one easy Judas Priest song I knew. The singer smiled deprecatingly. Another easy song.

"How about *Green Manalishi* or *Electric Eye*?'" he countered, both more difficult Judas Priest songs.

"I don't know those."

He looked around the stage at the bass player and drummer, as if to ask, why are we here?

The drummer solved the issue, "*Livin' After Midnight*' is good. Let's do that."

"Okay."

I was silently conscious that my audition was already over. I was not on their level, but they decided to play along—and then be done with this.

The drummer cracked out the beat, and I joined with the rhythm. The singer blasted the vocals impressively from their PA system. I had never played a guitar that loud in my life, and I loved the feeling of power it gave me—all that crunching, squeaking distortion at my fingertips.

I played through the easy song adequately, nailed the short solo, then finished the remaining choruses.

"That sounded good," the drummer yelled from behind his drums. "What else?" He actually sounded impressed.

"How about some RATT?" I shouted back.

The singer shook his head, "Too raspy, can't sing like Stephen Pearcy."

"Quiet Riot?"

The singer inhaled mightily.

The drummer took control again. "That's alright.

We've played enough. We heard your amp. We got enough."

He stood up and put down his drumsticks, signaling the audition was over and walked down the stairs toward me.

I started unplugging my amp and guitar. As I was loading my guitar into the case, the drummer helped roll up chords. Then he grabbed a handle on my amp cabinet and helped me carry it back outside, just a few feet beyond the roll-up door. As soon as we were done taking my gear outside, he went back inside, closed the roll-up door, and started playing drums, leaving me alone with my amp and guitar, waiting for my dad to return.

As I waited, they started practicing, and their guitar player started wailing on lead guitar riffs, playing up and down scales, triplet blues licks and two-string bends.

My dad returned, helped me load my amp and guitar into the trunk of his Chrysler. After I was seated in the front passenger seat, he asked how my audition had gone, and I said good. It was good. They said they would call if they wanted me to join their band. We left the industrial park and began the drive back to his apartment.

They never called.

A few weeks later, I answered another ad, this one seeking a lead guitarist for an original hard rock band. This band practiced in a little wood shed on the side of a house in Pasadena, not more than a half hour from my dad's apartment. There was barely enough room, but the small shed worked. The guys in this band were much older—all in their early or mid-thirties. I was nineteen and seemed a little out of place. I asked if they wanted to play any Van Halen.

The singer smiled and answered, "No, we can't sing the backup harmonies; they're too high. No one can hit those high notes like Michael Anthony."

Then they started talking about a Van Halen concert and how Michael Anthony was busy the whole concert singing backup vocals while David Lee Roth chugged too much Jack Daniel's.

"Do you have any originals?" the older singer asked.

"Yeah, I got a couple."

"Let's hear one."

I played a few riffs that sounded like Def Leppard.

"That's not bad," the singer commented, "but it sounds like it needs another guitar. We only have one guitar in this band. Our influences are Clapton, Sabbath, Hendrix. We like Van Halen, but we can't sing their high parts."

"I'm fine with one guitar," I offered.

"Know any Hendrix?"

"No."

"That's okay. Most guitar players don't. His sound is hard to copy, but we have some originals that have a strong Hendrix influence." Then he strapped on a guitar, offered to play an original, and I listened. It was slow, with lots of echo, reverb and wah-wah pedal—a crude Hendrix imitation.

"That's pretty cool," I said.

It was clear I was not a good match with these Pasadena guys. They were Hendrix and Black Sabbath fans, and though both were founding gods in the rock and heavy metal genre, they were not the types I wanted to emulate. Hendrix and Sabbath were fifteen years earlier, back in the late '60s and early '70s; this was the mid-'80s, and the sound was a lot different now.

We jammed on a couple of their originals, and I soloed here and there, doing my best to impress them. They nodded when we were done—not bad—not the greatest—but not bad.

They cordially said they would contact me if they wanted me to come back.

They never called.

I learned Van Halen would play at the Forum in a few weeks and planned to see the concert. They were wrapping up their tour, and the Forum would be one of their last shows of the year.

Unfortunately, I would go alone, as I had no friends in L.A., but seeing Van Halen live would be its own reward. Concert tickets in Sacramento had been under $20, so I figured they would be the same in L.A. Dad gave me the $20 and said he'd drive.

The date of the concert finally arrived, and Dad drove me to the Forum in the early evening. The plan was to pick me up at midnight, where he dropped me off on the side of the road. I thanked him for the twenty, slammed the car door shut, and jogged across the road toward the enormous parking lot circling the Forum.

The vast asphalt was slowly filling with heavy metal fans, most dressed in jeans and T-shirts. Many women wore tight leather pants, or spandex with cheetah or tiger-striped patterns. Van Halen albums were blaring from car stereos; people chugged beers and swigged whiskey. The air was electric with anticipation.

I joined the masses and walked up the zigzagging ramp to the entrance to buy a ticket. When I reached the window, the cashier informed me tickets were thirty-two dollars. Panic shot through me. I didn't have enough money. I walked back down the ramp into the parking lot, hoping to locate a desperate scalper who would sell me a cheap ticket. I found one shouting, "Tickets! Tickets!" He was quickly surrounded by a dozen customers. People screamed, "How much!?" "Seventy-five!" He shouted. "I need two!" Someone screamed and thrust a handful of cash toward him. He took the payment and handed over two tickets and said he had no more.

I was stunned. There was no way I would be able to afford a ticket from a scalper.

I walked back up the ramp to the terrace that circled the Forum. I thought maybe I could sneak in one of the doors somehow. I was prepared to break and enter, sneak in, or bribe security with my lousy twenty. I walked up to a door and knocked loudly. A security guard wearing a yellow windbreaker opened the door. I offered him my twenty. He smirked and pulled the door shut.

As I was walking around the Forum searching for a way inside, three young men about my age approached. The leader was tall, with broad shoulders and narrow hips. He wore slacks and a collared dress shirt, as if he had just left work at an accounting firm. The two guys trailing him were chunky and non-athletic, decked out in rocker regalia, concert shirts, bandannas around their necks, bracelets, and torn jeans.

The tall, well-dressed frontrunner approached, smiled and asked hopefully, "You got any tickets?"

"No. I'm looking for one myself."

The pleasant expression on his face immediately vanished, and he looked me over, as if deciding whether to believe me—as if he'd mug me and take my ticket if he believed I had one. After a cold look, he turned around and started walking in the direction I had been walking, a few feet ahead of me. His two goon friends accompanied him on either side. Hundreds of people were now slowly filing into the Forum, the show would start in ten minutes.

After a few steps, the leader turned around, glared at me and said in a mean tone, "Don't follow us. Get out of here!"

"I'm not following you!" I snapped back.

Hot anger quickly spread all over me as I walked a few steps behind this jerk. He had been friendly when he thought I might have a ticket, then suddenly became mean and abusive when he learned I did not. Why did he care where I walked? He was probably a bully at school and felt good hanging around two weaklings who worshiped and obeyed him. He knew he was good looking. He probably felt pride breaking hearts and disrupting relationships.

Though I was alone, I wasn't one of his punks he could push around, and not getting into the Van Halen concert had already put me in a funk. I'd taken three years of tae kwon do, sparred hundreds of hours, won a tournament, and knew I could defend myself. He was taller and athletically built, but I was 5' 10," 175, and in great shape. I was sure he didn't know martial arts; he was too arrogant. I wiggled my arms at my side, loosening them, in case this creep told me to leave or started a fight. If he did, I was ready to launch a flurry of sidekicks, punches, and elbows.

He ignored me and continued walking with his goons, asking people if they had tickets along the terrace. I hoped he didn't get in. After a short while, I lost sight of him and never saw him again.

Minutes later, drums thundered inside the Forum, and the crowd began roaring and cheering. The distinctive guitar licks of Eddie Van Halen were soon piercing the air as the concert began. David Lee Roth howled into the microphone, greeting the fans of L.A.

I gave up any effort to get into the concert and walked back down the ramp again, passing people who were rushing toward the entrance, holding their tickets. I loitered in the parking lot for the next three hours on a patch of asphalt, listening to the muffled sounds of the concert, imagining what was happening inside the Forum.

The concert was over around 11:00, and I walked back to the spot where my dad had dropped me off and waited. Cars whooshed by for an hour as I waited under a street light, but he finally arrived.

I opened the door and sat in the passenger seat. The plastic seat covers squeaked under my weight. The familiar mixed scents of Old Spice, pipe tobacco, and bubble wrap welcomed me as I sat on the bucket seat and closed the door.

After we pulled away from the curb and chugged into the night, he asked, "How was the concert?"

"Good," I said. "It was good."

We drove to Theodore's, his favorite watering hole, and he had a couple mixed drinks while I sipped a Sprite before they closed.

I said nothing more about the concert.

Watching and auditioning for bands in L.A. made this unpleasant realization settle in: success in a rock band depended on many more things than just being a great player. The band needed financial backing and connections—unless all the band members had good jobs and could pay for roadies and all the musical gear and equipment needed for gigs, plus the expense of advertising and promoting. To get the weekend slots at the high-profile clubs on the Sunset Strip and elsewhere, bands had to submit a promo package—a demo tape with three or four songs, a glossy professional photo of the band, and a 'bio'. All that cost lots of money.

Having had no success for about six months starting or joining a band, I decided to return to Folsom. In addition to needing music-industry connections, I'd need to practice more, take some lessons, and play at a higher level. I could do it; it would just require discipline, effort, and daily rehearsal. I would just practice, study, learn, strive, and practice more until I was a highly talented player—there was no other way.

I told Dad I wanted to return to Folsom. My band ambitions were not panning out, and I needed to go back home and focus on becoming a better player. Sitting around his apartment playing guitar all day without any sort of social life or peer involvement was becoming depressing. At home in Folsom, at least I could see friends and do things when I wasn't practicing guitar. Once my playing had improved, maybe I could come back and try again someday. Dad, as usual, was fully supportive.

I packed my bags and guitar and headed back to Folsom. My amp was packaged, shipped and arrived a couple weeks later undamaged. I reoccupied my old bedroom and resolved to continue striving toward my goals, but I would need to get a job.

I could see Grandpa's smiling face telling me to

cut my hair. Maybe it was time. I tried getting a job at several places but was told no—the hair was not acceptable, so I finally cut it and was quickly hired to work in the top floor restaurant of the Macy's ladies' department in the Sunrise Mall. This little restaurant was a sort of secret, ensconced in the corner behind women's clothing. My job was busing the tables, which were usually filled during the lunch hour.

I took some guitar lessons and bought some books and a few instructional videos by legends Vinnie Moore, Paul Gilbert, and several others. In these hour -long videos, the guitarists showed all their secrets. They were like two years of expert guitar lessons crammed into a one-hour video. I watched the videos for hours and practiced in my bedroom every evening, often five or more hours a day, usually in the afternoons and evenings.

I saved money and bought another guitar, a Charvel, for nine hundred dollars. Charvel was a popular brand in the '80s, and was played by many famous guitar players. Between my Charvel and Carvin, I had enough gear to play in a local band, but opportunities were still slim. The problem was not any shortage of guitar players—everyone wanted to be the next Van Halen; the problem was finding a good bass player. Bass just wasn't as sexy and high profile as lead guitar, so if you could play bass well in the '80s, you could have your choice of rock bands.

Drummers were next in scarcity. There were many, but not many great ones. The good ones were usually in a band, so finding one would remain a challenge.

I ran into Jordan Boswell at a party somewhere, and he said if I needed a job, I could work with him and his dad roofing houses. The part-time job at Macy's barely paid enough for gas money and a couple Taco Bell lunches during the week. Jordan said I could make more money roofing houses with him and his father. I accepted his offer.

My initial responsibility was carrying forty-pound pallets of tiles on my shoulder up a ladder and delivering them to the roof, where Jordan and his dad would carry them to various parts of the roof, open them, remove the tiles, and nail them into place. I spent eight hours a day shuffling between the truck and the ladder, carrying pallets of tiles up the ladder to the roof. It was grueling labor, but I was making about twice as much as I made as a busboy and worked more hours, so I was happy for the job. Roofing was also somewhat sporadic, which I liked. We'd work a job for several days, then have a break for a week or so, then Jordan's dad would win a bid, and we'd go back to work again. I liked the rest in between jobs.

At one point, construction seemed to go into a slump, and there was no work for a month or so. A month with no income caused me concern. I needed a steady income.

Mike Cortez, a friend from high school and football teammate, worked at Snooks Candies & Ice Cream in Folsom on Sutter Street. He was only twenty-four and his hairline was receding deeply, but he was always exuberant, filled with personality, energy, and laughter, somewhat like my brother. He said he could get me a job at Snooks, and true to his word, they hired me on Mike's recommendation.

I began my new job scooping ice cream cones, making sundaes, sweeping and mopping floors, bussing tables, and washing dishes. It was minimum wage again, but at least it was reliable, convenient, and I enjoyed working with Mike.

Throughout the toil of building cabinets, bussing tables at Macy's and later scooping ice cream at Snook's, I maintained a religious, daily practice regimen. After two more years of playing scales, chords, arpeggios, studying books, videos, and experimenting, my playing had improved significantly. I couldn't claim to be the greatest; there were still many extraordinarily talented guitarists in L.A. and elsewhere, but I had enough skill to be recognized as a 'shredder', someone who could play fast and flashy with impressive precision and clarity.

Working fast food and playing guitar in my bedroom four to five hours a day seemed like not much of a future, but I was committed to achieving a career in music. I considered returning to L.A., but I'd have to give up my friends and home again. I preferred to join a band in Folsom or Sacramento, where at least I'd still have my friends, mom, and brother. *Diamond Blade had made it in Sacramento; so could I.*

I'd honed my capability and earned a chance at success, I thought.

Cream always rose to the top, supposedly.

This was *America.*

My chance would come.

A NEW DREAM

By the time I was 20, my dad realized I needed a way to make a steady living. He had nothing against my desire to become a professional musician, but it wasn't paying the bills, and he felt I should use my talents to earn a white-collar paycheck. I could always continue music on the side. I'd pursued the band fantasy for three years and made no lasting progress, other than becoming a better player. Though he never discouraged my dream for a music career, he encouraged me to pursue a parallel path in law.

On one of his trips from Los Angeles to visit my brother and me, he did a little unexpected presentation. He brought a newspaper with two full pages of job listings for paralegals in Los Angeles. After unfolding the paper, he explained paralegals were not attorneys, but they were not secretaries, either; they were somewhere in between. They did research, drafted motions, pleadings, and gathered information. This all seemed much more interesting than working in a cabinet shop or fast food counter.

He also brought an article from a magazine discussing the increased need for paralegal workers over the next decade. An accompanying graph showed that the demand for these quasi-attorneys would rise dramatically over the next ten years. The pay looked great, also. They could make $35,000 or $40,000 a year. It seemed like a fortune. Dad encouraged me to go to junior college, earn a certificate and find a job in a law firm.

I immediately accepted his recommendation and looked into the possibility of becoming a paralegal. I didn't abandon the band fantasy completely—I'd keep practicing and looking for musicians, but I'd have a new priority.

I checked with American River College and found that it had a program. Twenty-eight units and I could have a certificate. I would have to take criminal law, business law, introduction to accounting, law and society, civil procedure, legal research, and a couple others, but I figured the certificate would be good enough to get me a job, so I enrolled in the courses. I enjoyed the studies and did well, receiving mostly A's.

I earned my certificate in three semesters and was ready to join the workforce. Unfortunately, I had overlooked that the market in Sacramento was much smaller than in Los Angeles. I just assumed that a similar demand for paralegals existed in Sacramento as in Los Angeles, but I was wrong. When I started looking for work, I was disappointed to find almost nothing. If I did find a paralegal position, it invariably required a minimum of two years' experience, which I did not have—the old chicken-before-the-egg conundrum that always plagued newly qualified professionals.

I was disillusioned, and it seemed like maybe I would be trapped working fast food jobs forever. Or maybe I'd have to go back to building cabinets. No one could rent an apartment on a fast food salary, unless two or three roommates shared the rent, and that never seemed appealing. Even my friend Eric, who worked full time at the cabinet shop, still lived at home with his mom. He eventually moved out after a couple years, but most entry-level manual labor or construction jobs didn't pay enough for complete independence.

My dad, who in his spare time was a sort of amateur lawyer himself, waging battles with the IRS, FTB, Sears (over a sales tax issue), and against any traffic tickets he ever received, was taking a paralegal course at Los Angeles City College. He told me his instructor had volunteered to help anyone in the class who wanted to go to law school. He said he could get them admitted, just talk to him after class. Dad asked his instructor if he would help me, and he said he would. First, however, I would have to meet him and earn his recommendation. If I made a favorable impression, he'd pull strings at the University of West Los Angeles, a small law school in Culver City accredited by the State of California.

Becoming a lawyer now seemed like a good career goal. I had excelled in my paralegal courses; why couldn't I do the same in law school?

Dad bought me a plane ticket to Los Angeles, and a date was set. We planned to meet his paralegal instructor at his office in Century City—an upscale section not far from Santa Monica and the Pacific Ocean.

Having had so many fun times with my dad in Los Angeles, I always felt a growing excitement as soon as I got to the airport in Sacramento to begin my

400-mile flight to the City of Angels. Anticipation grew as I soared 35,000 feet above the Central Valley of California, gazing down at the endless brown, green, and yellow squares of farmland.

This time, the excitement and anticipation would be even greater, as we were taking the first step to open the door to my admission to law school, and a long, lucrative career practicing law.

After an hour, as the plane circled over the vast Pacific Ocean from the north and the wing dipped to turn inland, I saw the HOLLYWOOD sign standing prominently in the mountains, and it stirred memories of childhood visits to Los Angeles a dozen years earlier—the fairy tale summer before fifth grade that broke me when I had to leave. The nostalgia distracted me into a trance, as I gazed below at the endless squares of the traffic grid, clusters of office buildings, rows of houses, swimming pools that looked like scattered blue blobs, and freeways stretching into the distance.

From the sky, the city seemed so clean and organized. Highway 101 carves a distinct path across the mountains into the valley, and all the other freeways snake away in different directions. On descent, I searched for the towering radio station antenna on a mountain top to the left of the HOLLYWOOD sign. I spotted the antenna from the airplane window and thought about those evenings when we rode up the Sunset Strip with my dad, through all the Flower Children, up through Beverly Hills, finally reaching the station.

As the engines whined louder, a fairy-tale feeling seemed to materialize in the air, submerging me in anticipation. L.A. was the land of movie stars, rock stars, millionaires, Beverly Hills, and just about everything else—a fantasy land of limitless possibilities. Supposedly, movie stars were 'discovered' in coffee shops or restaurants by Hollywood agents. I wasn't interested in acting, but Van Halen came from Pasadena, a suburb of Los Angeles, and they were one of the biggest bands in the world. *L.A. Law* was a hit TV drama that portrayed lawyers as rich, busy partners in thriving law firms supported by a staff of secretaries, paralegals, and junior lawyers. Their problems were managing enormous caseloads, winning trials, managing difficult clients, and meeting firm expectations. *The soaring skyscrapers below must be full of L.A. lawyers*, I thought. Even notorious villains, like Charles Manson, chose to dwell in the Los Angeles area. The city had something for everyone.

The mountain landscape grew taller as the plane descended. As the ground rose closer, billboards became readable, and scenery raced by the windows faster and faster; people on the street became visible as buildings and structures rose on both sides of the plane. Gliding gently downward, the wheels finally struck the runway with a gentle thud, and the thunderous roar of tens of thousands of pounds of wind resistance raised a deafening roar. In a few moments, the wing flaps won, and the plane speed reduced, as the thunder of the engines subsided to a high-pitched whine, and the plane gently rolled and bounced down the runway. Relief settled among the passengers for a safe landing and anticipation of the wonders of the city lying ahead.

I walked off the plane and through the elevated tunnel to the boarding gate and began hearing other planes roaring for takeoff. Dozens of people were waiting to board, and others stood waiting to greet disembarking passengers. As I emerged from the tunnel into daylight, I saw my dad standing just outside the chair section of the waiting area. I gave him a hug, and seeing his familiar face made me feel safe again, like it always had. I was with my dad now, and no harm would come to me.

We approached the baggage terminal as an intercom voice droned metallically above, announcing flights, and horns, whistles and traffic sounds grew louder. Thousands of people from all over the world hurried in all directions to get their bags and begin their journey with loved ones.

I carried my shoulder bag as we walked back to my dad's car.

"I don't know about you, but I'm famished. How about a bite?" he asked, as we neared his car.

"Sounds good to me," I answered.

We drove to a seafood restaurant near the airport and ate dinner. Dad was anticipating our meeting with his paralegal instructor would be very illuminating; he had talked to him, and he seemed confident that the University of West L.A. would admit whomever he recommended. I was awed by the alleged power of this junior college teacher—how could he have so much clout?

After dinner, we went to that old movie theater in Hollywood, where a decade earlier I had been horrified by *The Deer Hunter*, and watched a movie. Then we went to my dad's favorite haunt, Theodore's, where he had been a loyal customer for twenty years.

Theodore's was a tiny bar on the Sunset Strip where aspiring actors gathered, drank and talked about their agents, auditions, and failing acting careers. They were a friendly, talkative group who always showed interest when my dad introduced me. As regulars, they saw him almost every night, so they knew tidbits about my life. When they learned I wanted to go to law school, they were impressed and joked they'd hire me to represent them once they broke into the movie business.

I had a couple mixed drinks, and Dad drank scotch and water. A pretty blonde played an acoustic guitar and sang in the corner. We listened to music and chatted for a couple hours. During a break, Dad introduced me to the guitar player. She had lots of original music and was seeking a record deal herself. She played several nights a week and hoped to get discovered, like thousands of other musicians in L.A..

At 1:30 a.m., the bar began closing, so we finished our drinks and went back to the apartment, slept until 10:00 a.m. Dad got up and made his favorite coffee, a rich, fragrant roast with ground chicory, sweetened with raw honey and cream. Then he made a hearty ground beef and vegetable omelet for breakfast.

About an hour before our meeting, Dad presented a white dress shirt and tie, informing me I couldn't meet his paralegal instructor looking like a hoodlum in a Van Halen T-shirt. I put on the shirt, then he wrapped the tie around my neck and tied it, explaining it was a double Windsor, and it looked sharp. He put on a coat and tie, and we left for our appointment.

The streets of Century City were clean, filled with Mercedes, Jaguars, Rolls-Royces, Cadillacs and other pricey cars. The nearby ocean breeze seemed to cleanse the streets of smog that lingered in downtown Los Angeles. Men in suits and leather shoes strode around with great purpose, engulfed in clouds of sweet, exotic hundred-dollar cologne. Attractive women clicked down the sidewalks in business suits and high heels. Everyone seemed busy and important, and it felt as though many high-stakes meetings were in progress in the high-rise office buildings—movie deals, record contracts, TV roles, franchise agreements. *All sorts of multi-million-dollar contracts must be in negotiation all around us,* I thought.

We were on time and were escorted by the receptionist to an office on the first floor, which was a slight disappointment. I had expected a suite on at least the 20th floor with a vast view of the sprawling metropolis below and the ocean in the distance, but we had a view of the street.

The instructor's name was Ron Olendorf. He was a tall, large man, 6' 4", 270. He had thin, curly brown receding hair with reddish tints. His locks on the sides flared, as if compensating for the receding hairline above his forehead. He was not handsome; his face was broad and lacked contour, his nose was too large, his features too blunt and fleshy, but his blue eyes sparkled with warmth and intelligence, and he had an easy, friendly demeanor. He greeted my dad and me and motioned for us to sit in the leather chairs across from his large desk.

His office looked like a lawyer's, a couple dark bookshelves filled with legal books; the law degree framed on the wall behind his large high-back leather chair; below that, his undergraduate degree. A couple colorful prints hung on an adjacent wall. A green plant crawled from its pot in the corner.

After the introductions and handshakes, we got right to business.

"So why do you want to be a lawyer?" he asked.

I figured he'd ask that. I answered, "Well, I did really well in the paralegal courses and enjoyed them. I thought criminal and business law were really interesting, and I think I'd be good at it. I seem to grasp law and legal reasoning easily."

"You can make a lot of money practicing law," he said. "I can get you into law school, but you have to understand it won't be the same as graduating from USC, UCLA or Stanford."

"Why is that?"

Ron settled comfortably in his chair, filling it entirely, "Law firms operate under the 'good old boy' network. You graduate from UCLA, you go work for a firm where a couple of the partners graduated from UCLA. Or maybe your dad was a lawyer who went to USC, and his friends hire you at their law firm. It's not just about your grades. It's who you know."

"Isn't there always room for one more good lawyer?" I asked.

"There is if you're willing to work for yourself, but there's an unspoken agreement in the 'old boy' network. They keep the spoils for themselves. Outsiders aren't welcome. They don't hire people from little private schools who don't have any money or connections. It's just the way it is, but you can find clients and build your own law practice. I made enough money last year to take off a month and go to China. Didn't need anyone's permission. I just did it."

"That sounds nice."

"It was, and I like the freedom I have working for myself. You don't get that at the big firms. I take off work whenever I want, but when you work at the high-dollar firms, you're at your desk no later than eight and leave no earlier than seven. You have monthly billable-hour quotas, and they work you to death, seventy, eighty hours a week, weekends."

"That sounds harsh."

"That's how it is."

"They don't show that part on TV," I mused.

Ron chuckled. "No, they don't. All you see on TV is the glamorous side. Most lawyers don't get the corner office on the thirty-fifth floor with two secretaries and a private wet bar. Don't expect that—unless you build your own firm."

"How do I do that?"

"I'd recommend starting with the DA's Office or the Public Defender. They'll hire graduates of West L.A. Get some trial experience. After a few years, you'll be able to attract clients."

"Do they teach you how to run an office in law school?"

"No, but you'll figure it out once you start paying the overhead, and you won't waste your time doing someone else's work. I used to have a partner who graduated from a big school, and he thought he was better than me. He used to hold meetings and refer to himself as the 'senior partner' and me as the 'junior partner'. I got tired of him always talking about 'the senior partner will do this, and the junior partner will do that,' so I quit. I told him to take a flying leap and started my own firm. I'd been practicing law ten years; I didn't need someone referring to me as the 'junior partner' and telling me what cases I'd handle."

I nodded in agreement. No need for that.

"Is the University of West L.A. a good law school?" I asked.

"It's a 'Podunk' school. It's not UCLA or Stanford, but it's a great school," he said confidently. "I went there and passed the bar exam the first time. They use all the same books as the big schools. There's no difference."

That made a lot of sense. The law would not be different at the more expensive schools.

He continued, "It's accredited by the state, but not the American Bar Association. They don't have the funds to maintain a large library and full-time professors—that's all that means. Most of the instructors at West L.A. actually practice law full-time—unlike a lot of the professors at the big schools. All they do is research and teach. It's one thing to stand in class and talk about legal theories and philosophy, and it's another thing to walk into a courtroom with a client and practice law—in front of a judge and jury."

I nodded in agreement. Dad chipped in with a short story about one of his battles in court representing himself and all the anticipation, preparation, excitement, and anxiety he experienced. He enjoyed it, but he had been a Shakespearian actor, so he loved drama, the stage, and—most of all—he loved having an audience.

Ron concluded his discourse, "So I can get you into law school, but don't expect to get hired by any of the big downtown law firms. Like I say, start with the DA's office or the Public Defender. That's how I started. Got a lot of experience there, and that's what matters most, if you want to be a trial attorney. After doing trials for five years, you can work just about anywhere."

I pondered his admonitions. "Well, I guess that I'll just have to do my best. Trial work seems interesting."

That seemed to be a good enough answer.

Ron continued talking about his career and cases and asked what sort of cases I'd like to handle. Dad added a question or comment here and there and, after half an hour, our meeting was concluded. Ron would talk to the Dean at the University of West Los Angeles School of Law and convince him I should be admitted.

After the meeting, Dad and I went out to dinner, feasted on steak and lobster, then went again to Theodore's to mingle with the aspiring actor crowd. Over the course of a couple hours, Dad finished three scotches and waters, and I downed three screwdrivers. We were in the mood to celebrate our successful meeting and my pending admission to law school.

We chatted with Dad's actor friends, and they seemed genuinely impressed and interested in my desire to become an attorney. They were proud of me, they said. Don't get into acting, they warned; it was filled with heartache and disappointment, apart from paying nothing, and I was too smart for all that. Get a real career representing actors, agents, writers—and make real money—don't follow their example. We laughed and toasted and told jokes in between meandering discussions. Suddenly filled with passion and drama, my dad, as he did from time to time, decided to recite one of his favorite Shakespeare soliloquies from Richard II. His friends went silent as his posture stiffened and his voice boomed:

> No matter where – of comfort no man speak.
> Let's talk of graves, of worms, and epitaphs,
> Make dust our paper, and with rainy eyes
> Write sorrow on the bosom of the earth.
> Let's choose executors and talk of wills.

And yet not so – for what can we bequeath
Save our deposed bodies to the ground?
Our lands, our lives, and all, are Bolingbroke's,
And nothing can we call our own but death;
And that small model of the barren earth
Which serves as paste and cover to our bones.
For God's sake let us sit upon the ground
And tell sad stories of the deaths of kings:
How some have been deposed, some slain in war,
Some haunted by the ghosts they have deposed,
Some poisoned by their wives, some sleeping killed,
All murdered – for within the hollow crown
That rounds the mortal temples of a king
Keeps Death his court, and there the antic sits,
Scoffing his state and grinning at his pomp,
Allowing him a breath, a little scene,
To monarchize, be feared, and kill with looks;
Infusing him with self and vain conceit,
As if this flesh which walls about our life
Were brass impregnable; and, humored thus,
Comes at the last, and with a little pin
Bores through his castle wall, and farewell king!
Cover your heads, and mock not flesh and blood
With solemn reverence; throw away respect,
Tradition, form, and ceremonious duty;
For you have but mistook me all this while.
I live with bread like you, feel want,
Taste grief, need friends – subjected thus,
How can you say to me, I am a king?

Dad's actor friends beamed with delight as they applauded vigorously his mesmerizing performance. They admired his commitment to Shakespeare and wondered why he had not yet been discovered by Hollywood.

We finished our drinks as the crowd thinned, and the bartender began sweeping and clearing the bar. We said goodbye and drove back to Dad's apartment, arriving around 2:00. In the underground garage, the heavy car doors crashed shut, causing a loud racket in the morning silence, and we quietly stepped to the elevator, rode to the first floor, then crept down the carpeted hall to the door.

We slept in again, then went to a buffet near the airport in the late afternoon. After a dinner of meatballs, noodles, soup and salad, Dad drove me to the departure gate. I needed no escort, but a twinge of sadness always arose when I left my dad at the airport—a remnant of the painful departure I'd experienced a dozen years earlier.

I caught a plane back to Sacramento and thought about my plans for the next day. I'd mail my application when I got home and hope to hear good news soon.

I was surprised and disappointed when, a few weeks later, I received a letter from the University of West Los Angeles advising my application had been denied. I had a brief flashback of my disappointment when I received the rejection letter from Stanford.

Ron's assurance that he could get me into law school had not come through.

I called my dad to give him the unwelcome news. He was also surprised and irritated. He seemed confident that Ron's backing would work. Dad called Ron to inquire, but he was in the middle of a three-week jury trial, the secretary explained.

Dad said he would talk to a friend of his and call me back. He spoke with Charles, who had just finished his first year of law school at West L.A.. Charles said we should go directly to the Dean to plead for my admission. Dad provided Charles' phone number and I called immediately.

After answering the phone and asking a few questions, Charles said, "Look, I know the Dean. He taught my real property class; he's a really nice guy. I think he'll let you in if you can convince him."

"How do I do that?"

"What courses did you take to get your paralegal certificate?"

"Business law, criminal law, civil procedure, accounting, philosophy, a couple others."

"Alright, let's do this—he won't expect this—I want you to be ready to give a lecture on constitutional law specifically regarding the income tax. I want you to discuss the difference between a 'direct' and 'indirect' tax and explain to him why the federal income tax is unconstitutional. You've learned all this already from your dad."

"Right. I've heard the lectures."

"Good. Give him a lecture on the Constitution. That's not taught until the third year of law school, but if you show him you understand the Constitution already and can impress him with your knowledge, I bet he'll admit you."

"Okay. I'll work on that."

"I'll set up a meeting with the Dean. Call me tomorrow evening, and I'll give you the details."

I thanked Charles for his help, hung up, and began my preparations. Dad had given me books and articles over the years discussing various theories of Constitutional law. I'd read much about the Constitution, Bill of Rights, and the taxing power of Congress. Memorizing a short speech would be easy.

I called Charles the next night, and he gave me the date and time for our meeting with the Dean.

Dad bought another plane ticket, and again I flew from Sacramento to Los Angeles. It would be a short, two-day trip, just enough to complete the meeting, then return to Folsom.

The anticipation on the flight was not as sweet and promising as the prior visit to meet Ron. Fear of rejection now threatened the dream, but this wasn't over.

Dad and I picked up Charles, a nerdish man whose polyester pants were belted high above his waist, and we drove to the law school in Culver City.

We entered the small administration building and waited for our appointment.

The University of West Los Angeles School of Law

occupied what formerly had been an elementary school, in the typical design of the ‘50s and ‘60s, with long one-story buildings, rows of classrooms. The upper half of the outer walls were consumed by windows.

We were shown to the Dean's small office. He was a lean, wiry man, in his late sixties with short, thinning gray hair and large brown eyes behind corrective lenses. He was warm and cordial.

Charles greeted him affectionately. They obviously had a strong rapport. The Dean had a copy of my college transcript and explained that although I had achieved excellent grades, I had a meager record of academic achievement, only twenty-eight units. Most students admitted to the law school had a four-year degree, or at least a two-year Associate's degree. I would need another year of full-time study to earn an Associate's degree.

“Why are you in such a hurry?” the Dean asked.

“I did really well in the paralegal courses, and I enjoyed it," I answered. “I think I have the ability to do well in law school without a degree. It seems to come to me naturally."

Charles jumped in and explained I had been exposed to legal issues my dad had been litigating and was familiar with some aspects of criminal procedure, tax, and Constitutional law. I seemed to have a good start on the legal profession.

“Can you give me an example of your understanding of any particular legal issue or any type of issue arising under the U.S. Constitution that you have studied?" the Dean inquired.

I was prepared for the pop quiz. "Well, under the U.S. Constitution, there are two types of taxes, 'direct' and 'indirect.' According to the Constitution, 'direct taxes' are required to be apportioned among the several states, not imposed directly on individual citizens, like they are now with income taxes—taken directly out of your paycheck. 'Indirect' taxes are required to be uniform. However, the income tax is neither apportioned among the several states nor uniform; it's graduated and disproportionate; therefore, the federal income tax is unconstitutional because it amounts to a 'direct tax' not apportioned among the several states, and it's not uniform, so it doesn't satisfy either of the Constitutional criteria."

"Didn't the 16th Amendment solve that problem—making direct taxes on income ok?" the Dean asked pointedly.

"That's what the IRS says, but the problem is that the 16th Amendment states, 'Congress shall have power to lay and collect taxes on incomes, from whatever *source* derived,'" I said with emphasis. "So taxable income must have a 'source'. Wages would not be taxable as income because they *are* the source. If wages are invested and the investment produces a profit, the profit may be taxed Constitutionally, but not the source."

"I'm not so sure about that," the Dean said with a wry smile, "the U.S. Supreme Court has never held that wages cannot be taxed as a source, or that the current federal income tax is unconstitutional—just the opposite—and it has repeatedly rejected tax protestor challenges to the federal government's taxing power, but you seem to have a grasp of the issues."

"Thank you."

The Dean seemed impressed with my tidbits of Constitutional law, although he clearly doubted their accuracy.

Some lawyers, researchers, and even a few scholars contend that the federal tax on wages of American citizens is unconstitutional, and they back up their argument with exhaustive analyses of the U.S. Constitution, the 16th Amendment, and U.S. Supreme Court case law. The theories are complex, but the logic is coherent and easy to follow. However, don't rely on my snippets and speculation. Consult several accountants and competent criminal defense attorneys experienced defending income tax cases before quitting state or federal taxes.

My point was not to convince the Dean, only to demonstrate an adequate understanding of legal theories that might bode well for future law school performance.

"Okay, we'll admit you, but you better do good," he said with a half-smile, as if he would pay a price if I did poorly.

I assured him I would.

Dad and I thanked Charles for his intervention and treated him to dinner before I flew back to Sacramento.

A week or so later, I received a letter from the law

school informing me I had been accepted.

I coordinated my return to Los Angeles with my dad, only this time my goal would be completion of law school. I'd bring my guitar and keep practicing, maybe hope to join a band and play on the weekends, but my main priority now would be becoming an attorney, acquiring a career and real future—unlike the dismal band fantasy.

LAW SCHOOL

Dad paid the first semester tuition in cash and gave me several hundred dollars to buy books. My grandfather gave me the keys to his 1969 Chrysler Newport and said I could use it for work and school—and whatever trifling personal pursuits I had in between. It was basically mine. I made a trip to the law school to buy the books I would need for my first-year classes: contracts, torts, criminal law. Each book was almost three inches thick, packed with cases decided over the decades and even centuries.

The first thing I noticed about class was I was, by far, the youngest student. About 90% of the pupils were in their late 30's, early 40's, or older, and most of the remaining 10% were in their late 20's. I was 21—about five years younger than anyone else.

Most law students my age in California went to school at UCLA, USC, Southwestern, Whittier, Stanford, Berkeley, Hastings and other high-profile institutions. The University of West L.A. catered to a different crowd—older students who were seeking a second career and likely already working full-time day jobs.

Classrooms were filled with a diverse swath of society: teachers, ex-cops, former legal secretaries, insurance salesmen, real estate agents, accountants, engineers, government employees—and then there was me—the 21-year-old former roofer, busboy, cabinet maker, ice cream scooper, and would-be rock star. It would be too harsh to say we were a group of indecisive misfits who could not settle on a career, but our class certainly exhibited a broad range of ethnic, cultural, social, and economic diversity. Some students pulled up to class driving a Mercedes, others drove clunkers, nondescript sedans, bicycles, or took the bus. The school showcased a hodgepodge of humanity from one extreme to the other and a sampling from all layers of social strata.

Class was three nights a week, three hours each with a short break in the middle. Having studied business and criminal law in junior college to get my paralegal certificate, I was already familiar with many of the concepts taught in the contracts and criminal law courses, so those classes seemed easy.

The law itself was not complicated, but law school instructors found a way to make the courses difficult. A few hypothetical paragraphs were provided, and the student was required to identify the legal issues arising from the facts, then apply the relevant rule of law and reach a conclusion. The most important aspect of the test was not the conclusion but identifying all the issues and discussing their resolution. Most often the solution was unclear, and both sides to a hypothetical dispute would have supporting arguments. Failing to identify the arguments of either side might mean failure.

A sample test question might contain a bizarre situation: Art tells Bob he wants to sell his house on Greenacre, fifty miles away. Bob says he wants to buy it and offers a $5,000 cash down payment. Art accepts the cash and later a $5,000 check as down payment for the house, but no written contract is signed. The memo section of the check reads 'down payment.'

Bob pours a concrete driveway on the side of the house with Art's consent. Later, Art changes his mind and tells Bob he does not want to sell his house. He returns $5,000 cash to Bob and tears up the check. Believing he would be moving, Bob quit his job and now is unemployed.

Bob becomes enraged that Art will not sell the house, calls Art and tells him he's coming over to talk, then hangs up the phone. Bob speeds across town to Art's apartment, kicks in the door and steps inside, unarmed, stands near the door, and angrily says, "Let's talk." Art stands up from the couch, removes a revolver from his pocket, and shoots Bob once, killing him.

Was there a valid contract to sell the house?

Did Art or Bob commit any crimes?

Discuss.

I was fortunate I had whatever sort of capability was required to spot the legal issues on law school exams. So many students failed.

The instructors at the University of West L.A. were mostly practicing attorneys. One, Justice Jefferson, was a highly-respected retired judge who had served on the California Court of Appeal.

Most professors showed up for class in business suits after a long day of practicing law, and they were busy, sometimes impatient people. They put a lot of effort into explaining the law and the issues referenced in the case books.

Our real property instructor, Mr. Harrison, a balding, middle-aged man with a thick beard, liked to combine property issues with contract issues, as they frequently overlapped in real life. One night during class, he presented a question involving a dispute and asked the class how an adjoining landowner, who had not been a party to the contract, could sue the other parties. How could the adjoining landowner get 'standing' to sue? He asked for volunteers. Someone raised a hand and offered an answer. "No, that's wrong," Mr. Harrison said curtly. Someone else blurted out an answer, "That's wrong, too," Mr. Harrison quickly replied. Another hand went up, another wrong answer. Now angered, he scowled at the class, searching for more volunteers. He began pacing back and forth at the front of the class, wondering out loud if anyone could figure out the correct reply. Another student volunteered a solution. "That was a ridiculous answer," he sneered, and continued pacing. Another remedy was voiced, and Harrison roared, "No! Wrong! Anyone else?" No one volunteered.

He paced around like a caged animal, glaring at the class, and lecturing us for not knowing the obvious, correct response. We should have spotted this easily, he said, and he was furious that no one did.

I was sitting in the back of the class, and having heard all the wrong answers, was sure I knew the right one. Still, I was afraid to raise my hand. If I was wrong, he would shout and tell me my answer was stupid, and I'd be humiliated. On the other hand, if I was right, I'd garner instant respect. I threw my hand up and took the chance.

"Mr. Courtney!?" he shouted back angrily.

"Can he sue as a third-party beneficiary?" I asked, loudly, then held my breath and waited for him to scream.

He blurted a profanity, affirming I had given the correct answer, then picked up a piece of chalk and slashed a diagram and stick figures on the chalkboard to illustrate his points. Everyone in the class turned around and looked at me with amazement. I was now some sort of genius, a tribal shaman who calmed the evil spirits. I felt good for successfully risking Harrison's wrath and ending the fuming replies, though he ranted for several minutes afterward.

Students were more reluctant to volunteer after that but probably studied harder and came to class better prepared. I know I never volunteered unless I was sure I knew the answer.

Ron Olendorf had warned that West L.A. was a 'Podunk' school, but the instructors had no idea. They were dead serious about class and never acknowledged any disadvantage that came with a law degree from West L.A.. They slugged it out all day in court against lawyers from big schools, and all that elite pedigree didn't matter in the heat of battle.

I was pleased I made the first-year cut but even more happy I had done well and didn't let the Dean down. I received the highest grade in my contracts class and was awarded a certificate—the American Jurisprudence Award. Unfortunately, for others, they would not continue to the second year. About half the class received failing grades and flunked out. Thousands of dollars and all that time down the drain.

Competition to make the yearly cut was increasing. Only the more dedicated, capable students were advancing, and I feared any decrease in my effort might result in failing grades, so I joined a study group and spent dozens of extra hours with several other students on the weekends, memorizing legal rules, doing practice exams, and trying to predict what to expect on the next round of test questions.

The extra effort paid off. I made the second-year Dean's list, which put me in the top 15% of my class. A third of the second-year class flunked out, including a member of my small study group. We were saddened he would not advance with us; he was smart, but he worked full time. Perhaps he did not have enough time to study and prepare for exams. He talked about the possibility of re-applying and doing the second year again, and that seemed like a horrendous burden, but it was his only option if he wanted to become a lawyer.

Though we were aware of the competition and tension among students to perform well and advance to the next year, we didn't think much about other hierarchies we'd have to face after law school—

starting at the bottom below more experienced lawyers. For now, our priorities were to learn the law and pass final exams, and that was more than enough responsibility.

If we were fortunate to graduate and pass the bar exam, we would have to start ascending the ranks, though none of us would join the 'good old boy' network on the upper floors of the downtown law firms.

CHASE POWELL & GLASS

On the wall outside one of the law school classrooms was a glass case with corkboard inside on which were tacked a dozen 3 x 5 cards with hand-written job offerings. I found a law clerk position in Los Angeles near downtown, wrote the phone number and called the next day. They asked me to come to the office for an interview.

Chase Powell & Glass was a personal injury law firm located in a one-story, L-shaped brick building near an intersection. A gas station stood on one corner, across the street a donut store, and nearby, a small market advertised groceries, beer, canned food, bread, tortillas and ice cream. Hispanic men in cowboy hats traversed the sidewalks frequently, and many business signs displayed, "Se Habla Español."

I put on a collared shirt, tie, slacks, and appeared for the interview. Tammy, a cute redhead with short hair and one of the firm's new associates, greeted me in the reception area and directed me to a tiny office in the front corner of the building.

I presented my skeletal resume, filled mostly with experience working in fast food restaurants but also listed my stints as a cabinet maker and roofer. I had no legal experience but, violating resume rules, I listed the courses I had taken to earn my paralegal certificate. I hoped the classroom topics listed in columns might substitute for real paralegal experience.

After reviewing my resume, Tammy explained a little about herself and the firm. I was surprised when she confided she probably would not stay employed there long—the pay was too low, and she would probably find another job after a year or two. I was amazed. The opportunity not only to gain experience but prove herself and earn a pay raise or bonuses seemed obvious to me—she could ascend the firm's ladder and make plenty of money eventually. How much *did she make*, I wondered?

From my perspective, she seemed already to have a good opportunity that would later blossom handsomely, but I could have been wrong; I did not know all the details. Perhaps she was underpaid. Or, maybe the firm paid her fairly and her expectations were unreasonable. Whatever the case, her resolve to find another job was unexpected.

After discussing the firm's few expectations of its law clerks, Tammy asked if I wanted the job. It paid six dollars an hour; early arrival was not required; I could bring my books to work and read in between law clerk assignments, and yes, I wanted the job. It was the perfect situation. I could leave early to make class at 6:00 and wasn't required to be in the office at 8:00, like most law office jobs. I normally rolled in around 9, and no one ever complained. Perhaps they were too busy to notice. The firm had five lawyers, and they were all in their offices in the morning when I arrived and were almost always there when I left at 5:00 for class.

A day or two after I was hired, I was visited by the

firm's founding member, George Arthur Chase. He told me to accompany him for a short drive.

Mr. Chase was in his mid-seventies and had been practicing law for about forty years. He looked twenty years younger than his age, even bore a slight resemblance to the never-aging TV host Dick Clark. He had dark hair that was gelled and combed straight back and stood about six feet tall. He always wore dress shirts, ties, and slacks, but never the suit coat—unless he had to go to court. Instead, he daily wore a blue L.A. Dodgers windbreaker and matching hat over his business attire and Vuarnet sunglasses—the dark, Jack Nicholson style. His enormous feet were covered by black or brown leather shoes that almost seemed to impede him as he walked. He had a sort of Eisenhower G-man appearance—as if he could be a third detective on the TV show, *Dragnet*. If the two plain-talking cops ever needed another partner, Mr. Chase would be perfect.

Mr. Chase was a very kind and compassionate man. Like my dad, he had served in World War II, and I was intrigued to learn he had served in "intelligence" during the war. I never learned any details, but it was clearly implied he had been involved in very risky and important undercover activity somewhere in Europe fighting against the Nazis. A picture of him in a military uniform from the '40s hung on the wall in his office, among numerous other photos, a framed diploma, law degree, and several trophy checks—enlarged copies of settlement checks obtained for personal injury clients for enormous, six-figure sums.

Whenever I was called into his office, I would always gaze at the enlarged, two-foot-wide photocopy of a settlement check payable to Chase Powell & Glass for $750,000.

He drove a light blue Lincoln Continental that was always clean and shiny. I opened the passenger door, eased onto the soft leather seat, and remained silent. He backed out of the parking space, drove out the exit, and began our drive. It was obvious to me this was a little 'get to know each other' session.

"How old are you?" Mr. Chase asked.

"Twenty-one."

"You're the same age as my son. Where are you going to law school?"

This is strange; hasn't he seen my employment application or talked to Tammy?

"University of West L.A.," I answered.

"Good school. Our new associate, Tammy, went there." I already knew this, having spoken to Tammy at the job interview.

"Where did you grow up?"

"Folsom."

"Where's that?"

"It's a little town about twenty miles east of Sacramento."

"I've heard of the prison. Why are you going to law school in Los Angeles?"

"My dad said he knew someone who could get me admitted. I thought there would be better job opportunities down here."

"What kind of law do you want to practice?"

"I'm not sure yet. Maybe criminal."

"Plenty of that here," he said with a smile.

His blue Dodgers windbreaker rustled as he steered the car.

"Is your dad a lawyer?" he asked.

"No. He's an actor, and he does voice-over for radio and TV.

"Oh, that's nice. Do you vote?"

"Yes."

"Good. Lawyers should vote."

I wondered whether he would start asking about my political beliefs, of which I had very little at the time, but he did not.

After a few minutes, we arrived at a car wash. He told me to pay inside and gave me some cash.

"I like to keep my car clean," Mr. Chase explained. "I sometimes pick up clients. I'll be asking you to get it washed once a week. Take it here."

"Okay."

"Ask Rose for the company credit card. You're authorized to use it at the car wash and gas station. And make sure you fill up the gas tank every time you get it washed."

"I will."

We completed the car wash and began our return to the office. Mr. Chase continued leading the discussion, "My son will be going to law school. He just graduated from Cal Poly. You'll meet him in a day or two. His name is George. You two should get along."

I nodded approvingly. Mr. Chase then surprised me with his next remark. "Well, you're batting a thousand in the looks department," he casually announced.

I was slightly startled by the compliment. No man, and particularly no boss, had ever complimented my looks so directly.

"Thank you."

"That matters. Everything matters. Your looks, how you dress, how you speak, how you write, what you drive, all of it matters. They don't teach these things in law school, but you learn them in life. Your looks are an asset. You should use them all you can."

I wasn't sure how to respond. I was flattered by his compliment, but not sure how I would use my looks to 'benefit my law career' in the future. I kept quiet, listening, as we wound through traffic back to the office.

Mr. Chase, seemingly satisfied with my disclosures, wrapped up our conversation with a little advice and personal history: "You can have your own big firm someday if you want, or you can be a sole practitioner. It all depends on what you want and how hard you are willing to work for it. I started this firm by myself twenty years ago. Paul and Dan started with me as law clerks. Now they're my partners with their names on the door. We're all handling a couple hundred cases or more, and we will probably need more attorneys in the future. If you're interested in handling personal injury cases after you graduate, we may have a spot for you, but if you want to practice another type of law, that is your decision. Just do well in school and pass the bar, and your future is wide open."

"Thank you."

"You're welcome."

Our discussion ended as we reentered the firm's parking lot.

My job as a law clerk for Chase Powell & Glass had been an enormous blessing. I did not get a lot of hands-on legal experience working on cases, as I was utilized mainly as a runner and errand boy, which I actually did not mind. I had lots of time each day to read the case books for class that evening and no one complained or seemed to care. I felt as though I was being paid to study, which was basically true. As long as I was ready whenever Rose instructed me to run a settlement check to the bank, take documents to court, pick up documents or things from a client, copy court records, or run Mr. Chase's Continental to the car wash, I seemed to be doing all that was expected, and the firm was satisfied with my performance.

Lucky for me, Mr. Chase had a son, George Arthur Chase II.

I met George a couple weeks later in the separate building that housed the firm's law clerks and investigators. The clerk's room was cramped with file cabinets, boxes, and a few desks and illuminated by ghoulish incandescent lighting.

As I sat at an old metal desk one day reading my

law books, George burst through the door, left it open, approached, and looked me over closely, sunlight now slicing into the otherwise dim office area.

"Hi, I'm George," he said.

We shook hands.

He was tan with somewhat of a Paul McCartney face—large cheeks and dark eyes, dark, dense eyebrows, and a full head of thick brown hair. He wore large glasses that seemed to shrink his eyes and give him the look of a scientist about to peer through a microscope or a very careful inspector of finely-made watch parts. His build was more average than athletic, but he had twice as much energy as I had.

"Where are you going to law school?" he asked.

"University of West L.A.."

"I'm applying to Whittier and a couple other schools." I thought we would begin a discussion about the relative merits of various law schools, but he abandoned the topic and asked: "Is that Chrysler yours?" referring to the '69 Chrysler Newport I received from my grandfather that was parked in the parking lot.

"Yes."

"Man, that thing's a boat!" he said, and started laughing loudly. It was a large car; people frequently called it a 'whale.'

I chuckled with him.

"How many gallons to the mile does it get?" he asked and laughed some more.

"It's a gas hog," I noted.

"You should put a flag on that thing," he said, still

fascinated by the size of my car.

"Yeah, it's pretty big."

"Do you like Klaus?" he asked.

"From the Scorpions?"

"Uh huh."

"Oh, man! That dude can wail."

"Klaus is the man!" he said with gusto. Then he mimicked the vocals from the Scorpions' hit song, *Big City Nights* and sang, "*Big titty, big-titty nights...*" and played air guitar, chirping a lead guitar lick.

I chuckled again with amusement. We had a mutual inside understanding of altered lyrics to hard rock songs.

"Gibson Les Paul, baby," he said, testing my knowledge of rock guitars.

"Can't go wrong with Gibson—Led Zeppelin, KISS, The Who..."

"Fender Stratocaster."

"Fender sounds great clean, but they sound too thin with distortion."

"Cry baby wah-wah," he continued, then mocked the sound of the guitar effect made famous by Jimi Hendrix.

"Those sound cool. I need to get one."

"You play guitar?"

"Yes."

"Sweet. The Shred Lawyer!" Then he played and chirped more air guitar, knees bent, hips thrust forward, torso leaning back, playing an imaginary guitar.

Concluding our short repartee, he said, "Rock and

roll, baby. Let's get some lunch," as if we'd been friends for years.

"Sure."

We left in his Ford Mustang and drove to the Wilshire Country Club, where we were seated at a large table covered with a brilliant white table cloth, overlooking the stretches of green fairway and trees lining the golf course.

Like his dad, George was filled with kindness and compassion. Chase Powell & Glass represented people horribly injured in car and motorcycle accidents or by dangerously defective consumer products, like defective ladders or industrial machinery. They represented family members of persons killed in airplane crashes and people injured from medical malpractice. They fought corporate and government entities to bring some measure of justice for mostly poor people. Compassion was part of their business, and George embraced the cause.

About twice a week, sometimes more, George or his dad would take me to lunch at the country club. The noon feast was a splendid treat for someone making six dollars an hour. We ate at thick oak tables prepared with heavy, shiny silverware. The waiters dashed about crisply, taking orders, delivering and refilling drinks. They'd serve a hot chicken lunch with steamed vegetables and mashed potatoes—sometimes a triple-decker club sandwich loaded with thick, chewy bacon and a heaping side of wedge fries. Other times, lasagna or a pasta dish was served and never disappointed.

I always enjoyed and appreciated the kind generosity.

I came home after work one day and discovered my grandfather lying on the floor in the hall near the kitchen. As soon as he saw me, he started calling my name. I rushed to him and asked what had happened. He had tripped on the phone cord, he said, and thought he broke his leg. He was squirming and writhing in pain. He reached toward me, and I took his hand and squeezed. He wanted to stand, but the pain was too great. I told him I was calling 911, released his hand, then picked up the nearby phone and dialed.

After providing the dispatcher the necessary information, I returned to my grandfather, kneeled to the floor, and held his hand again. "Paramedics are on their way," I told him. He continued writhing and gasping in pain. I squeezed his hand and assured him he'd be okay. Help was on the way, just hang in there, Grandpa, hang in there!

Within ten minutes, paramedics arrived and took over. They hovered over my grandpa, asked him questions, took his blood pressure, then carefully placed him on a board, strapped him down, and carried him out of the apartment. I asked where they were taking him, and they gave me the name of the hospital.

A half hour later, my dad arrived, and I told him what had happened. He winced and gasped at the startling news. I told him where the paramedics had taken Grandpa, and we left for the hospital.

My grandfather had, indeed, broken his leg. The fracture was high on the femur, near the hip. It must have been agonizing. Unfortunately, when the bone broke, it released a festering cancer that quickly spread and, within a couple weeks, my grandfather passed away at the age of ninety-four.

Dad made arrangements to fly Grandpa's remains to Chicago to be buried next to his wife. That had been his wish. I was saddened; my grandfather had been in excellent health before the fall, and I thought he might live to 100. No one knew he had cancer in his bones.

My brother and I accompanied Dad to Chicago, met our six cousins, attended the funeral, then took a brief tour of Chicago a day or two later. We returned to California, taking different flights, as he was flying to Sacramento, and I was flying to Los Angeles. It was good to see Rick, even if only briefly for the grim occasion.

Dad was aggrieved by his father's sudden passing but comforted by his religion, which taught that my grandfather was now in Heaven, rejoined with his beloved wife, and my dad, mom, brother, and I would all join them someday. Crying and wallowing in pain and misery was just dumb, as far as Dad was concerned. God had taken his father, and there was no philosophical or moral ground to question God's judgment. When it was our time, there was no delay, no appeal, no postponement. Dad accepted what he believed to be God's judgment and did not remain immobilized by grief and misery.

Occasionally, the afternoons at Chase Powell & Glass were boring. George and I would sit at the desks in the clerk's room, talk, and amuse ourselves. One afternoon, I wrote a short *Twilight Zone* character description. Doing my best Rod Serling impression, I stood up, squinted at him, stiffened my upper lip, and said: "Paul Glass... an overworked, underpaid attorney in a small personal injury law firm, clinging to life like a patient in the intensive care unit. Hollow-eyed and underweight, Mr. Glass measures his days not by hours, but by cups of coffee. His mornings are spent in solitude, groping through endless stacks of paper to build a case against a rich corporate defendant. His afternoons are consumed on the phone desperately attempting to convince smug insurance company representatives to offer his injured clients a meager settlement. His soul creaks daily under the growing weight of a lifetime of disappointment and unmet expectations, but he still has faith. Someday he hopes to land the 'big fish'—a fat, flopping tuna that will change his future, relieve him from his daily drudgery, and secure his financial future. Mr. Paul Glass wants to make a name for himself and become a force to be reckoned with, but before he gets his wish, he'll first have to file a motion in... *The Twilight Zone...*"

I tilted my head, wrinkled my forehead, and squinted at George.

He burst out laughing, "Dude, that was awesome!"

"Thanks," I smiled, returning to my chair.

"I'll do one. I'll do one."

He wrote furiously for a few minutes, then finished. He stood up and read his character description, imitating Rod Serling. I giggled when he started. He described another attorney at Chase Powell & Glass, "sulking in the doldrums of another bleak afternoon" and pondering the threats of a "cold, heartless opponent." It was good, and I liked it. I laughed and clapped when he was done, and we each did another. It broke the monotony and provided entertainment.

I had been a law clerk for Chase Powell & Glass for almost two years when a secretary called on the intercom one afternoon and informed me Mr. Chase would like to see me. I immediately rose and headed for his office in the adjacent building.

Mr. Chase was at his large desk. I sat in the comfortable leather client chair across from him.

"I need you to deliver some documents to Scott Baker," he began. "We settled the case yesterday for ten million dollars."

My eyes bulged.

Mr. Chase continued. "Two years ago, I hired Fiona to work full-time on the case. That was her sole responsibility—the Baker case. She researched county records, located maps, found important documents, and helped build the case. That's the sort of commitment required in these types of cases. Hard work. No shortcuts."

"What happened?" I asked.

"Scott went off the road on a corner that had no sign. There used to be a warning posted about the curve, but some kids shot a bunch of bullet holes through it. The county took down the sign and never replaced it. By the time he realized there was a curve, it was too late. The car flipped over, and he was ejected. He broke his neck. If there had been a sign warning of the dangerous turn, he probably would not have crashed."

"That's terrible," I mumbled.

"Very tragic. Two years ago, Scott was a normal 21-year-old kid. Thanks to the county's negligence, now he's a quadriplegic, paralyzed from the neck down for the rest of his life."

"I can't imagine."

"He needs a copy of these documents," Mr. Chase said, sliding an envelope toward me. "I told his mother you would deliver them this afternoon. She'll be there when you arrive; they're both expecting you around three. Here's the address." Then he handed me a separate sheet of paper with the address and gave me directions to the location.

I took the envelope and address, left Mr. Chase's office, and thought about my assignment. Something struck me as odd. Why wouldn't Mr. Chase deliver these documents himself? Why would he choose me to deliver them? I had never met the client or worked on the case, and it seemed strange that I would be given this personal assignment to meet not only the client, but also his mother.

At 2:15 p.m., I left to deliver the envelope to Scott Baker. I drove across town, found the location, parked. I was wearing a long-sleeved shirt, tie, slacks, and loafers.

I took an elevator up a few flights to Scott's floor and found his hospital room. When I walked in, his mom was standing near his left shoulder. The bed was raised at a forty-five-degree angle, and Scott was lying there wide awake, watching me as I entered his room. He had curly red hair, a full red beard, and deep blue eyes. His face was lightly freckled, and he looked thin, but not emaciated. I strode forward with the envelope.

"Hi, Mr. Chase sent me to deliver this," I said, waving the envelope and extending my hand to Scott's mother.

"Ben."

"Thank you, Ben" she said, and shook my hand. "Carol."

"Nice to meet you, Carol."

Carol was an attractive middle-aged woman whose face could not hide the pain and heartbreak of her son's injury.

"This is my son, Scott," Carol said.

"Hi, Scott," I said, and looked directly at him.

"Hi," he said softly.

I held up the envelope and remarked, "This is just

the legal paperwork dismissing the case now that it has settled."

Carol looked at the envelope and nodded.

"There shouldn't be anything else to do." I handed Carol the envelope.

A grain of panic now sprouted somewhere in my psyche. Mr. Chase had told me to deliver the envelope, but he had not told me what to do next, and now I was standing next to the bed of a 23-year-old man, only one year older than I was, who would never again walk or use his arms, and I could not simply turn around and leave. All of my prior concern about how to act and what to say to a quadriplegic now vanished.

I looked directly at Scott and asked, "Have you met Fiona? She worked really hard on your case."

Scott nodded.

Carol said, "Yes, we met her several times. She was very helpful."

I looked at Scott and said, "That's all she did. Mr. Chase hired her specifically to work on your case and no others."

"She was nice," Scott murmured.

"We're very thankful for her and Mr. Chase," Carol said.

"Did you have to give a deposition?" I asked.

"Yes."

"The lawyers came here," Carol explained.

"How did that go?" I asked.

"I just told 'em what happened," Scott answered.

Maintaining eye contact with me, Scott suddenly asked with interest, "What do you do?"

"I'm a law clerk in Mr. Chase's firm. I'm also going to law school. I'm in my second year."

A little smile appeared on Scott's face. He looked just like kids I had grown up with or had competed against in high school. He could've been on one of the wrestling or football teams. As he lay there, the thought that he could not use his arms or legs was incomprehensible. I felt guilty for standing there with perfect legs and a strong back. His little smile communicated something. It seemed to say, "If you and I had gone to high school together, we would have been friends."

I smiled back, as if to say psychically, "I agree, Scott. I see that little mischief in your eyes. We would've been friends."

"Are you going to work in Mr. Chase's firm after law school?" Carol asked.

"Maybe. I'm not sure."

I wasn't sure what else to say, but it seemed too early to end the conversation. "How's the food here?"

"Not bad," Scott said, his little smile remaining.

He continued gazing at me somewhat oddly. It was as if he had not seen anyone his own age in two years, only doctors, nurses and hospital staff.

"Where do you live?" Scott asked.

"Down off Wilshire Boulevard, around Third Street. I didn't grow up here, though. I grew up in Northern California.

"Do you like it here?"

"It's okay. I don't like the traffic, but there are lots of things to do here."

Scott smiled a little broader.

"Where in Northern California?" Carol asked.

"Folsom. Little town about twenty-five miles east of Sacramento."

"It's beautiful up north," Carol added.

"Yes, it is. Folsom's between the ocean and Lake Tahoe. It's nice to be close to both," I said.

"Oh, Lake Tahoe is gorgeous."

There was not much else to say, so before the conversation dwindled into uncomfortable awkwardness, I announced I had to leave. "Well, I have to get back to work. Do you have any questions or anything you want me to tell Mr. Chase?"

I looked back and forth between Scott and Carol for a response.

"Just thank you," Carol replied.

"Okay. It was nice meeting you, Scott. I'm sorry about your accident."

"Thank you," he said, and blinked slowly. With a half-smile he added, "It was an accident."

The pained look returned to Carol as I said goodbye and walked away. She thanked me and I strode away, still feeling somewhat conscious that merely walking almost seemed like gloating.

I was saddened by Scott's horrific injury, but now I understood why Mr. Chase had sent me to deliver the envelope. He wanted me to see the deeply human side of personal injury cases. Behind all the motions, pleadings, wrangling, and court oration was a human being whose life, in many cases, was dramatically and irrevocably changed. There was no way to communicate the human stakes involved; I had to experience it for myself.

I'm glad Mr. Chase sent me to meet Scott.

I'm sure he would have been a great friend.

AN UNEXPECTED RETURN

During the summer break after my second year of law school, I spoke to Rick on the phone, and he told me I should come back, and we would start a band. He'd fully recovered from his broken leg, found a job welding, and was making good money. He said he would buy a bass guitar, learn how to play, and he'd even sing. We would just need to find a drummer, but that would be easy. He knew the perfect person.

For the first time in my life, I sensed that he actually missed me. We had become best friends as adults, but my career aspirations had taken me to southern California. I assumed I would graduate from law school and begin a career practicing law in L.A. and see my brother a couple times a year. He worked with welding torches, and I analyzed cases in law books. We would not have concurrent careers in the same field.

I missed him, but I had to make sacrifices to pursue my dreams. Moving to L.A. and leaving behind friends had been the most difficult, but I had to take the opportunities that were provided.

His sincere request that I move back to Folsom, however, moved me at a deep level. This was not some frivolous request to ride my motorcycle or borrow ten bucks; this was my brother saying, in his own way, 'come back, I miss you. Let's start a band.'

I felt this was my chance not only to play in a band again, but to reunite with my brother. He had welcomed me into his social circle much more as an adult than before, and I enjoyed being part of it.

The decision was easy. I told him I would call Lincoln Law School in Sacramento, and if they would accept me as a third-year transfer student, I would come back.

Lincoln was another 'Podunk' school, a small, state-accredited school that carried none of the prestige of Stanford, USC, UCLA, Harvard, or any other big university, but it taught law, and tuition cost about ten percent of what the big institutions charged. I didn't buy into Ron Olendorf's warning that my career opportunities would be sharply limited by going to a small, unknown law school. There was no reason why any professional doors should be closed after graduating and passing the bar exam. *I'd have cleared all the academic and professional hurdles and would be as qualified as anyone*, I thought. I wouldn't accept any elitist barriers to my success.

Besides, nepotism and favoritism didn't truly exist in my mind. This was America, not some Third World country with a rigid caste system. Commitment, persistence and ambition were rewarded. Employers recognized talent and creativity, and honest, hard-working people were given a chance to succeed. Anyone who passed the bar exam was officially qualified to practice in any state court or law firm. Some former Lincoln students had become superior court judges in Sacramento, where they presided over trials conducted by lawyers from supposedly better schools. Any attorneys who felt superior to the judge kept that to themselves while in court. Gauging from the respect they displayed, they might as well have been in the U.S. Supreme Court.

I contacted Lincoln, and they would gladly accept a transfer student who had already completed two years and made the Dean's List.

I said goodbye to George and a couple friends from law school. I was heading home to finish law school in northern California. They were sad and surprised to see me go, but they didn't understand the deeply-rooted dynamics with my brother that compelled my return home.

The small law school occupied a small two-story building on J Street adjacent to a shopping center. There was a large classroom on the ground floor and two smaller classrooms on the second. A parking lot wrapped around the side and back, enough for maybe twelve cars. Most students had to park in the nearby space for the grocery store or somewhere on J Street. It was maybe a tenth the size of my prior law school in Los Angeles, but it taught the same curriculum, provided a law degree, and opened the door to a career practicing law.

The building felt old and converted, as if it had previously been a furniture store or perhaps a suite of doctors' offices, but if going to Lincoln could make you a judge, it was as good as any school in the state, as far as I was concerned.

I briefly looked into attending McGeorge Law School, Sacramento's gem, but the cost and admission requirements were out of my reach. McGeorge cost about $20,000 a year back then and required a college degree. I couldn't wait another three years to get a college degree and couldn't afford tuition, so it was Lincoln or nothing.

McGeorge was ABA-accredited, and the campus was composed of enormous, ornate brick buildings, shaded by tall trees, and featured a large circular auditorium with tiers of seats surrounding a lectern on the floor. The school's special pride was Associate Justice Anthony Kennedy, who had taught a course in Constitutional law before President Ronald Reagan appointed him to the U.S. Supreme Court.

I told my dad I intended to move back home to Folsom and complete my law school education in Sacramento. He didn't question my decision and was fully supportive. As long as I was continuing my legal education and working toward a future career as an attorney, I could have moved to the South Pole, and he would have supported me.

Returning to the room at my mom's that she always kept for me, I settled back into life in Folsom. Friends I hadn't seen in two years were glad to see me, and I was quickly reabsorbed into my prior social circles, playing guitars in living rooms, losing petty cash in poker games, going to concerts and nightclubs with my brother and our friends. It was great to be home.

Ray Larousse had married and had two children, so his time was committed to raising his family. I dropped by to visit, and we spent an hour catching up.

Rick informed me he had bought a bass guitar and

amp, and I told him to bring it over, and we would play one Saturday afternoon. He showed up, unloaded his bass and amp, and set it up in the garage. I plugged in my guitar and played some riffs. He started making noise on the bass.

"Gimme that thing," I told him, as I removed my guitar and placed it on a stand.

He didn't know how to play or understand music theory, so I decided to teach him a blues pattern. He handed me the bass.

"You need to learn basic blues patterns," I announced. "I'll show you one to get you started. We'll start in the key of A. Start here on the fifth fret and play these four notes. Then jump up a string and play the same pattern. Then slide up two frets, play the same pattern, slide back down and play it again, then one more time, where you started. It's the same pattern in three different places."

I fretted the notes. He watched carefully, then I handed the bass back to him. I pointed at the bass neck as he struggled to play the notes in proper sequence, but after a few minutes, he caught on.

"That's it; that's it! You got it! Now keep playing that while I solo."

He plucked and thumped the strings with some difficulty but persisted, and I played over and around his off-time thumping. We jammed for about a half hour and he was glowing with enthusiasm when we finished.

"This is fun! I can't wait to learn more!" he declared and thumped a few more notes.

I later bought him some instructional video tapes to teach himself as I had done with lead guitar. We watched one, and I took the bass and played the licks and patterns slowly, showing him the notes one by one. He made amazing progress. A month later, he was able to play blues bass patterns smoothly and was ready to learn some new rock songs. He found an experienced bass player who lived close and agreed to give him lessons. Soon he was booming along to a dozen or so songs sufficient for us to play house parties and, later, club gigs. I was impressed with how fast he learned and how much potential he had on the instrument.

Rick found Marty Prowinski, a drummer who lived in the countryside of Cool, California, and we could practice in his garage. Marty was absolutely phenomenal. He kept perfect time, unlike most drummers, and blasted thundering drum rolls expertly across the toms. He was easily good enough to go on tour with Def Leppard, Scorpions, Judas Priest, or any other '80s era hard rock band, and we were lucky to have found him.

After one practice, we all agreed we were a band. We called the band 'Skinner', but after a while, I didn't like the sound of it or its grisly imagery, so I suggested we change the name to 'Citizen Kane,' after the famous movie masterpiece by Orson Wells. Rick loved it, and Marty had no objection, so that became our new name. I wondered whether we might get sued for copyright infringement but figured the record company executives and lawyers would advise us to change the name before we recorded an album if there were any risk of a lawsuit, if we ever got that far.

I left my heavy amp in Marty's garage, which made practice much easier. I could just show up with my guitar, plug in and play. Loading and unloading the amp added fifteen minutes of heaving, pushing, pulling and cussing to move the blocky, unwieldy thing, so it was nice to eliminate that drudgery.

Rick played bass and sang lead vocals. Marty sang high harmony backup vocals, and I played guitar, doing my best to play Van Halen and Dokken solos, which I played pretty close to note for note. We practiced a couple times a week, and no neighbors ever complained. The only drawback was the drive. It took forty-five minutes of snaking through the bends and turns of Salmon Falls Road to get to practice (which always reminded me of Driver's Ed. with Mr. Marlette), then another forty-five minutes to get home. But we were sounding good. I had enormous freedom as the sole guitar player to add whatever licks and fills I chose and didn't have to hear complaints of a second guitar player that I was taking too many solos or playing too loud.

We didn't sound as full and complex as a band with two guitars, but plenty of great bands had only one guitar—Rush, ZZ Top, Triumph, Van Halen, and as far as I was concerned, our band could be added to the list.

We cranked up loud for practice and all the swelling and booming tones pumped us up as if we were about to begin a concert for a full arena.

I ran into Mike Cortez, my old classmate and former co-employee at Snook's Candies and Ice Cream, and he invited me to the three-bedroom house on School Street he shared with roommates. Mike was now in college, and on the weekends, his rental house was a hive of partying, poker, and good times. They had a gathering every month or two, and thirty or forty people showed up; most of them I knew from school.

Mike was an aspiring guitarist, and once a week or so during the summer, I'd bring my small practice amp to his house, set up in his living room, and play along to Diamond Blade's *Jagged Edges* album. I showed Mike how to play a few songs off the CD, and we'd crank up loud and play along with Diamond Blade blaring from the speakers—our own little live concert. Searing, high-pitched guitar leads squealed throughout the evening as I mimicked the solos on the record and added my own.

After a year or so, Mike moved to La Riviera Drive in Sacramento and invited my band to play at a party. We could have the whole living room and all the beer we could drink. I said fine, we'd be happy to play.

After we had agreed, Rick had some impressive news: "Jeff's going to the party."

"Really?" I asked incredulously.

"He wants to hear us, so I gave him the address."

"He'll get mobbed."

"He'll be fine. He'll have a couple friends with him."

"That's awesome."

"He said he'll get there around ten—hang out for a little while."

I was inspired to hear that Jeff Keller—Diamond Blade's world-famous lead singer, would come to the party to hear our band. I couldn't wait.

The Saturday of our gig arrived, and we loaded our guitars, amps and speakers and drove to Mike's house, arriving in the late afternoon. Mike had cleared all of the furniture out of the living room to make space for the band. We placed the drums against the wall next to the kitchen and occupied about half the living room with our gear and speakers.

"I'm stoked, brother!" Mike exclaimed, as he greeted me near our amps.

"Thanks for letting us play, man. I can't wait!" I told him.

He smiled and patted my shoulder. Mike was touchy-feely.

"Sweet. Look at those drums and that ax!" he said, pointing to my guitar and swigging a beer. He admired my guitar and our equipment for a few moments. Our amps, speakers, mic stands, drums, and guitars looked impressive.

"Want a beer?" he offered.

"Sure," I answered.

He stepped to the keg in the kitchen, poured a beer, came back and handed it to me. We toasted and talked while the house slowly filled with partiers. I knew about half the people who showed up. By 9:00, about sixty people filled the kitchen, garage, and living room, admiring the guitars, amps, and drums.

An electric anticipation hung in the air.

Rick and Marty were mingling among the crowd. I was hoping to see Jeff Keller, but he had not yet entered.

Finally, it was time to play. It was warm, and I was wearing a tank top. I slung my guitar over my shoulder, turned up the volume, struck a blaring power cord, and let it ring as if I were on stage at Woodstock or Day on the Green. Everyone started raising beers, cheering, whistling and hooting. It was *almost* like watching Diamond Blade at The Island five years earlier. Lots of friends were watching, and they couldn't wait to hear our band.

My power chord rang with deafening resonance as Marty thumped his bass drum and played rolls across the toms, then crashed and drummed the symbols making them swell in unison to the ringing power chord. Rick thumped out some heavy bass notes and Marty counted off the beat, clacking his drum sticks. We began playing a crunching original tune. Roaring bass, drums, and guitar filled every corner of the house, and a cramped crowd of twenty gathered in front of us to watch and listen.

Halfway through our first song, I played a blistering solo no one had ever heard, as this was our original music, the first time it had been played for an audience. I shredded through the E pentatonic minor scale, descending, ascending, bending notes, sustaining powerful vibrato, bending two strings with the double-stop technique, then releasing back to the tonic note. The guitar players and musicians in L.A.

would have to admit, it sounded pretty good. I did not sound like a novice anymore.

We finished our first song, and the whole house cheered. They loved our music, and they loved us. We played some popular hard rock songs everyone would know, a couple from Van Halen, Dokken, The Cult, Scorpions, then a couple more originals and took a break.

Friends and strangers stepped forward to congratulate us and shake our hands.

After half an hour break, we played another set and received the same reaction of cheers and applause. We stopped around eleven. If we played much longer, the cops were sure to show up, but we had played two sets, and that was good enough for Mike. He enjoyed every moment and thanked us profusely after we were done.

I never saw Jeff Keller at the party, but Rick told me the next day that he had parked a block away, sat in his car, and listened to us. He was impressed and liked our originals, but he had not wanted to come inside and cause a distraction. This was our band's time to shine, and Jeff did not want to spoil that. I would have preferred he did spoil it, but that was his decision.

In the coming months, we played little dives in Roseville and Lincoln and backyard parties. I was pleased to be making progress on both a legal and music career.

Months later, Rick showed up Christmas Eve with a twelve-string acoustic guitar. I was shocked to see him walk in the front door carrying the instrument. It must have cost at least a couple hundred dollars, but he was proud and excited to give it to me. He stepped inside and handed me the guitar with a grin. "Do you like it?"

"I love it," I said. "Thank you."

"Play it."

I sat down and strummed a chord. It was badly out of tune. I adjusted the strings tediously for ten minutes and after finally eliminating all the sharp and flat tones and getting it tuned, I began strumming a song. The twelve-string omitted a deep, full resonance of double octaves, as if two players were playing the same notes an octave apart. I picked melodic sequences and strummed chords, filling the living room with pangs of resonant acoustic guitar. Rick smiled and watched, pleased with his gift. I would use the twelve-string for a couple songs at gigs, I told him. It would be perfect. He was delighted I was happy with his gift and would use it with our band.

His present meant a lot to me. It wasn't just that he had spent a lot of money; I appreciated that, but the guitar showed his admiration and faith, probably the first time ever he had gone out of his way to acknowledge my talent in a symbolic way.

I felt closer to my brother than I ever had.

Fortune shined on me again, as I soon found a job as a law clerk for Don Parks, a solo personal injury practitioner in Sacramento. His office was located in a one-story '70s style office building in midtown Sacramento. The entrance from K Street had a yellowish iron gate beyond which were large glass windows of the front offices. Once inside, the long, carpeted hallway continued directly to a double-door exit sixty feet away. Offices lined the hallway on either side. A tall tree outside kept the entrance in shade most of the day.

Don's office was in the corner by the front entrance. Unlike Mr. Chase's office in L.A., there were no enlarged copies of huge settlement checks framed on the wall; no pictures of Don in military uniform during World War II; no law degree or undergraduate degree on the wall behind the desk. Architectural drawings were tacked to the walls, some blueprints, and a single landscape painting. Rising above the stacks of papers and files on his desk were two large framed pictures of Don's daughters, one 15, the other 17. The floor was covered with stacks of boxes, rolled up charts, a couple hand trucks, and several briefcases. Tendrils of cigarette smoke rose slowly all day from a large, square ashtray on the corner of the desk.

I met him only briefly on my first day of work. He was a bearded Caucasian man in his late fifties whose ties were always loose, and he always seemed distracted and preoccupied, as if he had just received news the bank had foreclosed on his house. He sat in his office muttering into a phone or dictating to his secretary, Lori. He disappeared from the office and reappeared unpredictably.

Lori typed all the legal pleadings and motions, and a file clerk sorted and filed paper all day. The only associate attorney, Andrew, dictated legal pleadings and motions into a handheld tape recorder. Like Don, he could not type or operate a computer.

There was a noticeable difference in mood and appearance between this small law firm and Chase Powell & Glass. The interior of Chase Powell & Glass was clean, organized, and decorated with paintings, framed prints, plants, vases of flowers, and unobstructed hallways. Each lawyer had a couple client chairs across from the desk for comfortable, private meetings, and the offices were clutter-free.

My office at Don's had a couple bookcases and a desk, no client chairs, nothing on the walls, and stacks of boxes near the entrance. The other employees worked in plain, undecorated spaces, cramped with banker's boxes, and files. The entire interior smelled like fresh paint. It was as if the law firm had just moved in and had not finished unpacking, or was moving and had lots of work remaining. Three offices were completely empty.

At Chase Powell & Glass, the tapping of keyboards could be heard all along the hallways, as legal secretaries churned out briefs, pleadings, letters, and legal documents; attorneys spoke in professional, businesslike telephone conversations throughout the day, a laugh and chuckle here and there. Secretaries strode about in a hurry making photocopies, getting coffee, retrieving mail from the receptionist, shuttling paper and office supplies; they answered phones with a detached, professional tone. The place hummed with productivity and urgency from 8:00 a.m. until at least 6:00 p.m.

Don's suite of half-complete, half-occupied offices was dreary, quiet, almost creepy. He could be heard droning on the phone in his smoke-filled office during the mornings, but rarely did any laughter, humor, surprise, or emotion emanate from his headquarters. Lori spent a lot of time in his office taking notes, locating documents, answering questions, and assisting him. After a couple hours in the morning helping Don, she'd go to her desk across the hall and spend the rest of the day at the computer, typing and producing letters and legal documents.

I worked mainly under the direction of the junior associate, Andrew, who was friendly and eager to utilize me to lighten his caseload. I wouldn't be getting anyone's car washed here or running checks to the bank; I'd be cloistered in an office behind a computer monitor, drafting legal documents, doing legal research, and searching a thick file for information. That was good for Andrew and good for me. I received real legal experience, and Andrew had a clerk to do his job.

Andrew was a stocky, burly man with thick dark hair and a matching bushy mustache. He looked like someone who never exercised and gorged on pizza and cheeseburgers daily. He had more of a dockworker look than attorney, but he was really smart, and he was showing me the ropes for civil litigation.

On my first day of work, he gave me a thick file and told me to write a response to a motion to dismiss. Our client had delayed bringing the case to trial, and now the other side was asking the court to dismiss it due to the long delay. I was just thrown into the emergency task without any training, but I cracked the books, did the research, and drafted a response in a week or so. I'd found a couple legal excuses that might save our case and presented my response to Andrew. He reviewed my work, said I did a good job, added a couple minor edits, then printed a final copy to file.

When the date for the hearing arrived, I put on a dress shirt and tie and made the two-hour drive with Andrew to court. He had a beat-up old car, and we left early to make the 9:00 a.m. hearing, rattling down the freeway in the cold. We arrived at the courthouse in Martinez, California, and found the department, a large wood-paneled cavern with a jury box and elevated judge's bench.

The somber chamber quietly filled with attorneys, who waited for the judge to take the bench. He finally entered, silver-haired, wearing a black robe. The whispering and paper shuffling went silent as the magistrate ascended to his chair.

After listening to attorneys argue several other cases, ours was called. Andrew rose and walked to the podium. I watched intently. Andrew repeated the defenses I had made in our written brief, and the judge listened patiently and asked a couple questions. Then he called the other side. The opposing attorney took the podium and pleaded for the judge to dismiss the case. Our client had simply delayed too long, and our proposed excuses were inadequate, he argued. The judge gave no indication how he intended to rule. He remained inscrutable and said we would receive his decision in a few days.

After we left, I noticed Andrew was sweating profusely, as drops beaded down the sides of his temples. He asked what I thought, and I said I believed the judge agreed with our position. The case would not be dismissed. Andrew looked at me with concern and wiped away sweat with his hand. He hoped I was right.

A week later, we received the judge's ruling in the mail. The motion to dismiss our case was denied. We had saved our client's case from dismissal and probably a malpractice case against Don. Andrew came into my office, handed me the judge's ruling, and congratulated me on my work. He said he would take me to lunch to celebrate.

We went to an all-you-can-eat pizza buffet down the road and relived our court triumph, satisfied that our thorough and professional research and articulate in-court arguments had prevailed. I felt like I had hit a home run on my first at-bat in the big leagues. If this was all there was to practicing law, I was going to be a superstar.

Soon I began going to lunch frequently with Andrew, as I had previously with George, but there were no country club lunches at my new job. Our main lunch spot was an old Shakey's Pizza that served a buffet lunch with a salad bar for about five bucks.

After a few weeks, during one of our pizza feasts, Andrew felt comfortable enough to make some very private disclosures. As we sat at a table, he explained, "The trick to legal writing is to plagiarize. Don't reinvent the wheel. Use the research someone else has already done; put that into your motion, then argue the facts, but don't spend a lot of time trying to put together a summary of the law. Witkin has already done that. Use his summaries."

I looked at him with some disbelief. Witkin was the name of a publisher that provided exhaustive summaries of every topic of California law.

Andrew continued, "You think I spend a lot of time doing legal research? We're a contingency law firm. Research is for defense lawyers who get paid by the hour. We get paid nothing for ten hours of legal research. Time is money. You have to utilize your time very carefully in contingency cases, or they'll eat you alive." He swigged a draft beer from a mug, then continued, with just a hint of condescension. "I'll show you some motions I've done, and you'll see what I mean. You can see that I just copied right out of the form books."

"Don't you have to read some of the case law?" I asked.

"Very little. You need to find the controlling case and read that and understand how it applies, but you don't need to read the next ten cases and summarize them for the Court. That's a waste of time. That's why Witkin is so good. He identifies the controlling case law, so you don't have to spend hours to find it."

"That makes sense."

"You won't see Don doing any legal research. He's the general who meets with clients, thinks out case strategy, and negotiates cases, but he doesn't spend a lot of time in the law library. He hired me for that, and I've learned how to do it efficiently."

"I'll start doing that."

"Use my motions as templates. You'll catch on," he said, and chewed more pizza. Then, between bites, he confided, "I've been with Don two years. I almost didn't get licensed to practice law."

"Why?"

"During the State Bar's background check, they found out I got convicted for selling meat illegally. It was only a misdemeanor, but I got it cleared up after I submitted the paperwork showing the conviction had been expunged. It held up my application for almost a year."

He looked at me, waiting for my response.

"Selling meat? What was that all about?" I asked.

"Well, I wasn't in a store. I found a supplier, and I'd load up my trunk with frozen steaks and go door to door, but someone turned me in."

I'd never heard of knocking on doors to sell steaks. Who would buy sirloin from someone knocking on the front door? Apparently, lots of people.

Andrew continued recounting his triumphs selling beef. He felt unjustly charged by the District Attorney's office. He had simply been engaged in commerce, providing a product that was demanded by the market. He was no more than an agent of the cattle rancher, delivering goods to the customer. He resented the government regulation and intervention between buyer and seller, and he never seemed concerned that the beef was safe to eat and in compliance with safety standards. If the steak had thawed and sat in a warehouse for a couple days, so be it. The buyer should be able to tell good meat from bad, and if there was a problem, he would work it out, but the government really had no business charging him for brokering merchandise demanded by hungry consumers.

"I made a lot of money selling meat," he announced wistfully. "I only had to work a few hours a day, sometimes only a couple weeks out of the month." It seemed he missed his job selling steaks out of the trunk of his car and wanted to return to it. "I'd consider going back to it if I had some help," he said, hinting that maybe I'd like to get into the steak-selling business. "I'd make three or four thousand dollars in a week and spend it all in Tahoe over the weekend. Sometimes I'd come home with more money if I had a good night at the poker tables. I'm thinking about getting back into it. Lots of money to be made. Just have to be careful. Get regular customers. I got careless and sold to strangers, but I won't make that mistake again. If I go back to it, I'll let you know, if you're interested."

"I don't know. I probably wouldn't be interested," I said.

He ignored my deflection. "You should think about

it. You could make a lot of money," he said, and then went back to devouring pizza and swigging beer.

Over the ensuing weeks, it became clear that gambling was Andrew's passion, or maybe an addiction. Once every couple months, he would not show up for work for a day or two, and when he finally did, he would explain that he received some money from Don and had been playing in a lowball tournament all weekend, won a few thousand dollars, and was taking a couple days off work, now that he could afford it. A couple times, his luck had failed, and he lost thousands. When he finally came back to work after a big loss, he would be grim and surly all day, wouldn't want to get lunch, and I wouldn't want to be around him.

It seemed working as an attorney was merely a way to facilitate his gambling addiction. It was very strange, as all the other attorneys I had previously encountered were fully committed to functioning in their highest capacities as lawyers, not merely striving for a quick personal injury settlement to pay for a weekend of gambling. They certainly were not interested in selling frozen steaks out of the trunks of their cars, but anything that furthered Andrew's gambling seemed acceptable.

I decided I would not participate with any of Andrew's meat-selling schemes. I was not going to law school to sell steaks door-to-door after work.

After about six months, Lori informed me that Andrew had quit. She did not explain why, but he had not been at the office for several days, and I assumed he had been hungover following a gambling binge. I saw him a couple days later leaving Don's office, and he told me to come outside. He explained that he quit because Don owed him a substantial amount of unpaid wages. He had just concluded negotiations for monthly payments of back earnings to avoid a lawsuit. Andrew was now looking for clients to build his own practice and suggested that I contact him, if I ever stopped working for Don. He warned I would be next to experience financial disappointment.

Unfortunately, Andrew was right. A few months later, Don's law practice was scandalously faltering and about to fail. I arrived one morning to find a large moving truck in the rear parking lot and movers loading his office furniture. Lori told me Don had been evicted, but he had rented an apartment about a mile away and was relocating there. She gave me the address and told me to report the next day, and we would start reorganizing.

When I arrived, I found the apartment crammed full of desks, bookcases, computers and file cabinets. I felt sorry for Don and didn't understand how he could have fallen on such hard times. I had previously worked in a busy, thriving personal injury firm in Los Angeles that received enormous settlement checks every week, but in the course of a year at Don's, I heard of one or two cases settling. At Chase Powell & Glass, I was routinely given settlement checks to run to the bank and would deposit checks for tens of thousands of dollars, sometimes $80,000 or $90,000, sometimes more. A personal injury law firm seemed to be a cash cow, but Don seemed to be settling almost no cases and going out of business.

No one asked about the new office arrangements, but it was obvious Don was having problems. He still seemed to have dozens or hundreds of cases, and everyone seemed to remain busy all day, but the mood was gloomy. I received a paycheck for over $400 that bounced, and that made the reality clear. Don was bankrupt. His problem was now my problem and caused alarm. My check was made good about a week later, but the next one bounced, and I knew this was the end. Months earlier, Andrew had quit and threatened to sue Don over back earnings, and now everyone else was experiencing the same disappointment.

I didn't want to quit, but I couldn't continue under a cloud of financial uncertainty and continuing disruptions. I felt bad leaving Don floundering, but living at my mom's, I was expected to pay a small amount of rent and personal expenses—gas, insurance, food, clothing. I needed a steady, reliable income, and picking up the broken pieces of a law practice and making it profitable was far beyond my ability.

I had saved one case from dismissal, but I could not save Don's entire practice.

CORPORATE AMERICA

Lincoln Law School had a three-ring binder in the administration office with job postings for law clerks and attorneys. My timing was perfect; a local Sacramento law firm had just placed an ad for a law clerk, and I applied. I called, set an appointment, and arrived a day later to meet a balding, narrow-faced, skinny man, who seemed always to exhibit a hollow-eyed look of surprise and a halting, unconfident bearing. I somehow had expected someone with a full head of thick gray hair, baritone, and direct, self-assured manner, but Allen seemed more like a shifty accountant with the voice and wormy, evasive behavior of a teenager with lots of secrets.

It wasn't much of a job interview. Allen didn't even ask about my experience and background. He looked over my resume, asked if I would be able to work while attending school, if I could type, and when I answered yes, he offered me the job. I was very fortunate. The pay was ten dollars an hour, almost three times the minimum wage, and they would accommodate my law school schedule. I'd have my own office and work under the direction of the general liability attorneys, gathering information, doing research, writing briefs and motions.

This was the "in-house" firm for TIER1 Insurance. TIER1 was an enormous insurance company that wrote policies for general liability and Workers' Compensation and made hundreds of millions of dollars every quarter.

About ten lawyers, each with his or her own secretary, staffed the insurance defense squad. Now I would be on the other side of the lawsuit—the defense side—the side with all the money and resources. Chase Powell & Glass had represented injured clients, but TIER1's in-house firm represented companies sued by injured plaintiffs, and their job was to protect the assets of their corporate clients.

Half the third floor of a three-story, red brick building was occupied by TIER1's lawyers. I was now at or near the top of the legal hierarchy. I felt a little smug that I'd overcome Ron Olendorf's warning that I'd never work in an elite law firm. *Here I was at the in-house firm for an American corporate giant—just where I belonged*, I thought.

The offices reflected the usual levels of social rank—large window offices for the attorneys overlooking the freeway and cityscape, identical cubicles, desks, and computers for the secretaries. Down one hall, a row of cubicles was reserved for law clerks. The entrance displayed tall, heavy, double wood doors and a full-time receptionist. Two large conference rooms provided space for depositions, meetings, birthday parties, storage; a photocopy room housed two large copiers, file cabinets, and shelves filled with office supplies; a law library with books from floor to ceiling stored all the necessary resources for comprehensive legal research, and domestic necessities were met with a lunchroom, cabinets, table, refrigerator, microwave, and a gym downstairs.

Two weeks earlier, I was reporting to work in a two-bedroom apartment, cramped, cluttered, and disorganized, and now I was here, in the well-lit, high-ceilinged, spacious office suites for TIER1's in-house counsel in Sacramento, California. What a difference.

I was exhilarated to start my new job. I'd bet none of the attorneys here wanted to sell steaks out of the trunks of their cars after work.

The best part of my new occupation was lunch. Every day at noon, female secretaries and an attorney or two would show up in the lunchroom, remove Tupperware from the refrigerator, and start heating the containers in the microwave. At least two or three secretaries routinely ate in the lunchroom, sometimes more.

They were all friendly and talkative, sometimes complaining, but always hilarious. After a month or two of lunch with the secretaries, we all seemed to be at ease and relaxed around each other. Soon the topics turned from missed deadlines and court appearances to more personal subjects. They gradually felt comfortable enough to start cracking jokes about sex or making innuendos. Some of the comments or questions would be considered clearly inappropriate by today's standards, perhaps even sexual harassment, but no one ever complained.

There were two attorneys the secretaries seemed particularly comfortable ribbing and teasing. One was Kent, a jolly-faced, rotund man with receding gray hair that ringed his head like a monk's, and Hank, a polished, mustached, debonair sort who was soap opera handsome and had a picture of himself in his office. The secretaries teased him so much about his self-portrait that he took it down and put it into his desk drawer, but it remained there in case he ever got the courage to put it back on the wall.

Kent was an early riser who used to get to his office at 5:00 in the morning and work in the quiet for three hours, until others started arriving. By noon, he had already put in seven hours, so after a short lunch, he would go home around 2:00 or 3:00. He didn't like ties and wore them only when he had to appear in court. He looked almost out of place in a tie; they always seemed too long, as they flowed, like a country road over a gentle hill that was his abdomen and dangled below his belt buckle. He seemed to linger around the lunchroom from time to time, waiting for the right moment to make a suggestive comment or witty remark. He especially liked the secretaries' occasional off-color quips. His face would turn from white to red as he howled and squinted with laughter, a large moon-pie smile stretched across his face revealing a clownish visage with a large gap between his front teeth.

Hank, too, loved the teasing. The secretaries would find his weak spot, then pounce all over it. He laughed along at his own expense. Everyone enjoyed the risqué banter and participated, and the women always led the charge.

One secretary had caught my eye, Victoria. She was ballerina thin, green-eyed with a sort of oval little girl face, pointed nose, curled brown bangs, and a pouty lower lip. She had long eyelashes and a mischievous smile. After a couple months of lunchroom banter, I asked her to get a bite after work, and she agreed. She was getting divorced, and she had become very friendly and flirtatious. I took her to dinner one Friday after work, and when a lady selling roses walked by our table, I bought her one. With that, our relationship officially started.

Within a couple weeks of starting my new job, Kent called me into his office and closed the door. I sat in one of the faux leather client chairs across from his desk, and he settled into his chair.

“There are going to be some changes around here soon,” he said seriously. “You may have noticed that Allen is not in the office very much. In fact, he left again today before 1 o'clock. That’s because he’s a moron. He’s never tried a case in his life, and he has no clue.”

I ignored the insult.

“Why is he the boss, then?” I asked.

“He used to work in Claims. They liked him and made him managing attorney when they opened this office. I don’t know how they ever thought that was a good idea, he has no trial experience and no business being the managing attorney. Claims is really upset with him because he won't take any cases to trial. He settles everything, and they don't like it. They've already complained to the Regional Manager. He'll probably be getting fired.”

Then Kent did his signature desk move: he placed both arms on the armrests of his chair, pressed as if he were going to stand, rose a few inches, then shifted his body thirty degrees, and plopped back down, as if he were a child playing in a high chair. The seat squeaked and exhaled air as his heft flattened the cushioning. Sometimes, he'd tuck a foot under his bulk and lean on the arm rail to one side, like a child about to listen to a story. Once resettled, he continued, "I've done nine jury trials. Hank's done seven. Why an attorney who has never done a single jury trial would manage an office of trial attorneys makes no sense, and I think TIER1 finally realizes that." He raised his eyebrows for emphasis.

"That does seem odd," I remarked.

"When you work for an insurance defense firm, you basically have two clients: the client who bought the insurance, and the Claims Department. Claims spends a lot of time investigating these cases, and they want to be involved with the litigation and any settlement. They've already done a thorough assessment, and they have an idea what the case is worth and what it should settle for, and it pisses them off when attorneys settle a case they think should go to trial." He gazed at me casually from his reclining position. "You need to know that."

"I appreciate that. I'll keep that in mind."

"We're going to start taking cases to trial; are you interested in trial work?"

"I'd love to do trials. Seems like fun," I said.

"They're fun if you prepare," he said with a pedagogic tone. "If you're not prepared, they're a nightmare. The basic rule is this: for every one day in court, you need two days of preparation—at a minimum. So, if you're in trial one week, you need at least two weeks of full-time trial prep, assuming all the discovery is done and the case is ready for trial."

"Sounds like a lot of work."

"It is, but there's no substitute for preparation. I enjoy every bit of it. Never much enjoyed research and writing but give me a courtroom, a jury... performance!" he howled, waiving his arm like a bad actor. "You'll get a lot of trial experience here. All the depositions need to be summarized and indexed, all the discovery needs to be organized, motions in limine have to be filed, trial briefs—it's impossible to over-prepare."

"I'd love to help."

"Great. You'll enjoy it."

Then he returned to his original topic, "Now, back to Claims. Sometimes the client is eager to settle, and in that situation, Claims may agree if the settlement is reasonable. However, if Claims thinks the settlement demand is unreasonable and wants to take the case to trial, you need to talk to them and get their input before settling. The client usually wants to settle, but the settlement has to be justified based on what can be proven at trial. Allen wasn't doing that. He wasn't including Claims in the settlement process, and he was settling cases just to avoid going to trial. He's afraid to try cases. Unfortunately, he's alienated Claims, and you don't want that. He settled too many cases for too much money, and Claims is not happy."

I pondered all this.

"Seems odd that they would hire someone with no trial experience to manage the office," I said.

"Well, he had good connections, but that's all changing. I just wanted to let you know so you don't make the same mistakes if you get hired after you become an attorney."

"I'll make sure I don't."

Then he did his signature desk move again—rising a bit, then turning and dropping back into his seat, and changing topics abruptly as if wanting to unburden himself. "Man! I love not having clients anymore," he said, with relief. "That's what's great about working here. Claims deals with the clients; we just handle the litigation."

I thought about Scott Baker, the quadriplegic client I had met in L.A. Good thing his attorneys were not too busy or bothered to have a human being for a client.

Then Kent continued, somewhat apologetically, "Don't get me wrong. I did plaintiffs' work for eight years and represented hundreds of clients. I enjoyed my work and produced great results; it's just nice not to have all the complaints and headaches anymore. I can focus on practicing law, not dealing with clients and all their problems. Personal injury clients can take up a lot of your time and be a real pain in the ass."

"Don't you have to meet with company owners or corporate presidents now and then?" I asked, curiously.

"Oh, sure, but far less often than clients in

personal injury cases. The policy holders in our cases deal mostly with Claims; they're comfortable with the Claims representative because that's their first contact after the lawsuit is filed. If we keep Claims happy, Claims keeps the client happy, and that makes practicing law so much more enjoyable."

I nodded in understanding.

Satisfied with his disclosure, Kent stood and opened the door, signaling the end of our discussion, and I returned to my cubicle.

During my initial months at TIER1, Rick's friendship with Diamond Blade lead singer, Jeff Keller, continued to flourish. Diamond Blade had been on tour for months, but Jeff came home periodically on break and usually saw my brother.

One night, Rick called and said he was at Jeff's house. I hadn't seen Jeff or Diamond Blade for almost a year. He asked me to come over, gave directions, and I arrived an hour later.

Jeff was living in a recently-built rental home that was filled with expensive new furnishings. After I arrived, I walked into the room where Jeff and my brother were listening to music. Jeff was on the floor, his back against a bed, a large stereo to his right. Rick was in a chair in the corner. Jeff reached over and turned off the stereo as I stepped forward and extended my hand.

"Hey, Jeff," I said with a smile.

He shook my hand and answered with a smile, "Hey, Ben, how you doin', man?"

"Good. Thanks."

"How's school?"

"Good. Two more semesters."

"That's great, man, awesome. Rick says you guys have been playin' some gigs."

"Yeah, we've been playing little parties, clubs; it's a lot of fun."

"That's great. You guys should make a demo tape."

"I'd love to. We'll have to work on that."

Rick then turned the conversation, "Let him hear the rough tracks from your new album."

"Oh, yeah, I'll play a couple," Jeff said, as he reached to the stereo and pushed the rewind button. "I'm really happy with our new songs; we worked really hard on these; we got it just right," he said with raspy pride.

We spent a half hour listening to Diamond Blade's new songs. Jeff talked about parts he had written and sections he liked the best. I told him it all sounded great and couldn't wait for the new CD. He explained their next album was scheduled for release after they finished their current tour and told us a few short stories about encounters with other famous bands and rock stars. By then he had met many.

He was excited about the release of their new album. There would be another world tour, and they would join the greatest names in hard rock music at the largest cities and venues.

After an hour or so of visiting, I congratulated him again, thanked him for letting me hear his unreleased music, and went home.

My brother's call to visit him and Jeff was further confirmation I was now welcome in his inner sanctum. I was proud he invited me and pleased to see Jeff again. Touring with Diamond Blade, Jeff was living my former dream, but things were different now. I was in a good position to rise high in the ranks of an elite corporate law firm.

I was satisfied that two career paths lay ahead: one as a high-paid attorney for TIER1, the other as a lead guitarist in a band with my brother.

The possibilities seemed endless.

CROSSROADS

Class at Lincoln had been much like class at West L.A.—three nights a week, three hours per class, now and then a surly instructor. We had about a hundred pages of reading per class and discussed the case facts, legal rules, and, most important, the application of the rule—that's where cases were won or lost. Like the teachers at West L.A., the professors at Lincoln were all practicing attorneys and still fascinated by law.

At the end of the third year, about 20% of the class flunked out. I was once again relieved I made the cut. There was *no way* I would be told I was not eligible to obtain my law degree—not after three years of continuous study, attendance, exam preparation, stress, worry and enduring the periodic petulance of impatient law professors.

I could not fathom the disappointment of the students who received failing grades after three years of law school. That must have been devastating beyond comprehension.

I buckled down for my fourth year, joined another study group and put in extra hours on the weekends debating legal theories, dissecting prior exams, writing practice essays, recounting rules of law and their endless exceptions and arguing about what to expect on the final exam. It was somewhat like becoming a better guitar player: no shortcuts, just hard work, analysis, memorization, repetition, commitment, practice and persistence.

The hard work paid off. I passed all final exams.

Shockingly, five or six students failed finals our fourth year and did not graduate. Unthinkable.

Following successful completion of my fourth year, I graduated with all the usual pomp and circumstance. Former presidential candidate George McGovern was our commencement speaker and, after the ceremony, my mom, dad, brother and some classmates celebrated at a nearby restaurant. I still faced the last hurdle before becoming a lawyer, however: the California Bar Exam.

The bar exam intimidated and terrified most students. The test took three days, six hours per day and covered thirteen topics of substantive law. There was no way to fake it through the ordeal except possibly cheating somehow, but even that would not likely help. Day one presented six essay questions, three in the morning, three in the afternoon. Unless you knew the questions in advance, cheating would be almost impossible.

The next day was multiple choice questions, 100 in the morning and 100 in the afternoon. If you didn't know the law in detail, you wouldn't be able to analyze the facts on the spot and select the best possible answer.

The last day was the performance test. Some law was provided along with a simulated memo from an attorney with instructions to evaluate the data and provide advice and recommendations. It truly measured a student's ability to digest complicated information quickly, analyze and organize it, then write a responsive and coherent evaluation.

The worst part of the bar exam was waiting for the results. The three-day tribulation was administered in July, but the results were not mailed until November, around Thanksgiving, four months of tension-filled waiting. I had taken a full-time two-month bar review course, so I felt prepared. It was administered at McGeorge School of Law in Sacramento in a cavernous conference hall ringed by seats, resembling a small amphitheater.

During the preparation course, instructors told us that if we received a thin envelope from the State Bar around Thanksgiving, it meant we had passed the exam. It took only a single page to say congratulations, you passed, but if you failed, the bar generously included forms to fill out and return to take the test again, thus the thick envelope.

Four months later, the day after Thanksgiving, an envelope arrived from the State Bar. I felt it, and it was *thin.* Excitement and adrenaline shot through me. This was a good sign. This was a really good sign. I ripped open the envelope and pulled out a single page, read the first word and went into a state of jubilation and euphoria: "Congratulations…".

I had passed the bar exam on my first try, unlike more than 50% who had taken it. I would be sworn in by the State Bar as an attorney licensed to practice law in the State of California the following December.

I called my dad and told him the good news. He was elated and announced that he would come up in a week to celebrate. Meanwhile, my mom, brother and a few friends and I went out to dinner and drinks to celebrate.

I strode proudly into work the next Monday and brought my congratulations letter. Everyone happily applauded and delighted in my new status. Kent and Hank shook my hand, as did the other attorneys and welcomed me to the club. I was now an official member of the attorney tribe.

More good news soon arrived. Hank was handling a food poisoning case, and he needed full-time help. A fast food worker sick with Hepatitis A had gone to work and was suspected of contaminating the salad bar and infecting numerous customers. About a hundred people became ill with Hepatitis A, and an elderly woman had died. The State of California conducted an epidemiological study to locate the source of the outbreak and concluded a fast food hamburger franchise was the source. TIER1 provided the insurance policy to the franchise, and our in-house law firm was defending the lawsuit.

This was a big, potentially multimillion-dollar case, and it required an enormous amount of time and resources. Hank was assigned to work on this case and no others. Now that I was soon to be sworn in as an attorney, I was offered a full-time contract position to work as Hank's assistant. I would be paid $20 an hour, which was pretty good money, and I would have access to a company car and reimbursed expenses.

Hank was gone a lot, taking depositions, and I was busy doing legal research and working on a motion for partial summary adjudication. The plaintiffs were arguing that the fast food franchise owner had acted maliciously by not requiring employees to wear plastic gloves. The infected plaintiffs wanted not just compensation for their illness, but punitive damages against the franchise owner—monetary fines awarded to punish the defendant for despicable, outrageous conduct.

Our first big fight was over the plaintiffs' entitlement to damages. We'd hoped the judge would agree that, although possibly negligent, our client owner had demonstrated no wicked or intentional conduct that would justify punishment. If we could get the punitive damage allegations dismissed, that would be an enormous relief to our client, as his insurance policy did not cover intentional acts and would not pay a judgment for punitive damages, which might be in the millions.

Hank called me into his office to discuss the motion. His self-portrait remained in the desk drawer. A picture of his girlfriend and kids was on his desk.

I sat, and he began, "I don't think there's much chance we'll win a motion for partial summary adjudication on the plaintiff's punitive damages allegations, but we have to try. I've talked it over with the Regional Manager, and he agrees. If we don't at least try, the client might claim malpractice later."

"I think we have a shot at winning," I said.

"Why do you think that?" he asked, his eyes fixed on me like a hungry predator.

"They're claiming that the restaurant owner exhibited a malicious and callous disregard for the plaintiffs' rights because the food workers were not required to wear plastic gloves, but there's no evidence of malice or any intentional misconduct. It's negligence, at worst."

Hank smiled skeptically, "Oh, I'm not so sure of that. A lady died from eating our client's food. That's pretty bad."

"Yes, but there was no intentional misconduct."

"The employees were intentionally not instructed to wear gloves," Hank countered.

"Yes, but not with any intention of causing customers to become infected with Hepatitis A."

"According to their expert that was a foreseeable outcome."

"It's still negligence. There's no proof anyone was instructed not to wear gloves to infect customers with Hepatitis A."

"They're going to argue intent may be inferred from the callousness and gross negligence of not requiring food handlers to wear gloves."

"I don't think that's enough for punitive damages," I maintained. "The acts must be despicable and done with the intention of causing the result, or a conscious disregard of the plaintiffs' rights and safety."

"That's where they'll get us," Hank said. "We consciously disregarded the risk of infecting customers with Hepatitis A."

"No one knew the worker was infected. How could we have consciously disregarded a risk that no one knew about?" I asked. "You can be infected with

Hepatitis A but not symptomatic for a few days."

Hank interlaced his fingers behind his neck, leaned back, stared at the ceiling and thought for a few moments, then commented slowly and deliberately, "They're going to argue that we knew of the risk of infection and disregarded it; it doesn't matter that we did not know that a specific employee was infected at a given time. We knew that allowing food handlers to prepare food without using plastic gloves created the risk of infection."

"The risk was extremely remote," I replied. "Our client was only required to exercise 'reasonable care'. I think he did."

"I wouldn't bank on it," Hank replied. "Any time the jury is asked to hold someone accountable for a death, they take a very close look at the facts, and here we have an 85-year-old lady who just went into a restaurant for lunch and came out infected with Hepatitis A. The jury won't like that, and they might decide to hold our client responsible for punitive damages. You'll see the facts differently after you have some trial experience," he said condescendingly. "Juries are unpredictable, but I doubt they'll be sympathetic in this case. They eat fast food, too."

I ignored his appeal to experience.

"I still think we can beat it," I said.

"Good. Get to work on the motion. I'll be gone all week taking depositions, but I'd like to see a rough draft by the end of the month, if possible."

"No problem."

"Great."

Our meeting was over, and I returned to my office to continue work on the motion to dismiss the plaintiffs' punitive damage allegations.

The band was now gathering a following, and we were starting to make money—as much as $250 or $300 for a gig, which wasn't bad for three guys. We had a good turnout every time we played, and the club owners liked us because we filled the bar. We were getting offers to play parties, clubs, and events.

Rick knew a sound technician who helped us make a demo tape. We picked our four best songs and spent an afternoon recording with the sound engineer. He took the recordings home, mixed the tracks, then presented us with a couple cassette tapes the next time we saw him. The recording was not CD or record quality, but it was much better than a tape recording of practice.

My brother said he brought the demo tape with him on one of his excursions with Jeff Keller recently, and they had sat and listened to all the songs. He said Jeff liked it, and he particularly liked one song I had written, which I knew he would, as it was perfect for Jeff Keller's raspy but powerful vocals. The verses were clean, picked, electric guitar in a smooth descending melody, and the chorus switched to crunchy, distorted guitar, establishing a dynamic contrast between verse and chorus. "Jeff really liked this one," Rick said. I was euphoric. I knew I could write good songs. Then he revealed unbelievable news. Jeff was going to help our band get noticed! I was thunderstruck. Nothing was guaranteed, but he'd do what he could. This was the coolest thing ever—maybe better than passing the bar exam. Incredible! Unbelievable!

The plan was to keep playing, keep writing originals, and make a new demo after we had a few more great songs. At that point, Jeff would pull strings to get our demo heard by a record company representative. I knew this was all real. Rick had become best friends with Jeff over the past six years, and this was not condescending babble or a heap of false promises. Jeff was a solid, stand-up guy, and if he said he was going to help our band, he was going to help our band.

I thought this whole law school thing may have been all for nothing. After all, if Jeff Keller would be helping our band get noticed by a record company, we would probably sign a record contract, have a hit song or two, and go on a world tour, as I had envisioned for so many years. If my career went that direction, I wouldn't be practicing law for at least a decade, maybe not ever, and that would be fine.

I was at a very exciting crossroads.

A week or so after my discussion with Kent, Allen was fired, and we were told that a new managing attorney would be hired. A full month went by before the new boss arrived, but he showed up one day and introduced himself to everyone in the office. His name was Zack Claussen. He had worked in an insurance defense firm in Los Angeles for ten years, had trial experience, and was committed to repairing the office's relationship with Claims and taking cases to trial. He was a fit man of medium height, neat brown hair, and trim mustache. His jaws were squarish and muscular, hinting at his Germanic heritage. He looked businesslike, efficient, and professional.

A couple weeks later, Hank summoned me to a meeting in Zack's office. He wanted to discuss the food poisoning case and the status of the summary judgment motion.

When I entered, Kent was seated on a small sofa nearby, a managing attorney's perk, and I sat next to Hank in the client chairs across from Zack.

Zack began, "All right. I've talked to Claims and the Regional Manager about this case, and the client is extremely concerned. As you all know, there is no coverage under the policy for punitive damages, so if the client gets hit with a big verdict, he pays out of his own pocket. I've invited Kent to give his thoughts. We need to think this through. What's the status of the motion?"

Hank crossed his legs, steepled his fingers and answered, "It's in progress, but to be candid, I'm not optimistic. To win the motion, we have to show no triable issue of material fact, but I think the plaintiff will be able to make a successful argument that our client's failure to require employees to wear plastic gloves while preparing food constituted willful, malicious and despicable conduct, warranting punitive damages. After all, a woman died from eating our client's contaminated food."

"So, you think there is a triable issue of material fact."

"Most likely, yes."

From behind us, Kent volunteered his assessment, "I agree. I think it's good that you're doing the motion, but I strongly doubt that the judge will grant it. I think there are several issues of material fact regarding the glove issue, and I don't see the judge granting the motion."

Zack looked at me directly and asked, "What's your opinion?"

"Well, according to all the research I've done, punitive damages may be awarded only when the conduct is malicious, willful or in conscious disregard of the plaintiffs' rights and safety. Mere negligence is insufficient, and I think that's all that the facts show in our case. The fact that gloves may be more effective in preventing food contamination does not mean our client exhibited willful or malicious conduct by not requiring employees to wear them. Our client did not even know that an employee was infected with Hepatitis A, so he could not possibly have consciously disregarded a risk that he did not know existed. On top of that, our client was never instructed or informed by the Health Department that food handlers were required to wear gloves, so I don't see how the plaintiffs will be able to establish a material issue of fact regarding intent. There's just no evidence of any malicious intent and no evidence our client did anything with the purpose of infecting anyone. They may be able to prove negligence, but punitive damages require a higher level of proof, and the facts just aren't there."

Zack considered my argument, "That has to be our angle."

Hank responded, "I agree, that's our angle, but I doubt the judge will agree. If our client had required food handlers to wear gloves, these people would not have been infected with Hepatitis A, and one woman would not have died. I think our client had a duty to foresee the more remote risks associated with preparing and serving food. I'm not sure the judge will agree that just because no one told our client to make sure employees wear gloves, he should be let off the hook."

"I agree," Kent announced earnestly.

"He won't be 'let off the hook'," Zack observed. "At the very least, the jury will find negligence, possibly strict liability, but the policy covers that. We know the jury's going to find negligence; there's no way around it. The epidemiological report establishes the source of the outbreak, and we'll look stupid fighting it. We should probably stipulate to liability and limit the trial to damages. Keep a lot of unpleasant evidence out of the trial that way."

"I agree," Hank nodded.

"You agree, Kent?" Zack asked, looking over

Hank's head.

"Yes. Eliminate the issue of liability. The jury doesn't need to hear about all the risks of foodborne illness and the hazards of food workers not wearing plastic gloves."

"It's going to come in anyway under the punitive damages theory," Hank noted.

"Motion in limine to keep as much of it out as possible," Kent replied.

"Do they have an expert?" Zack asked.

"Yes. Some clown," Hank answered. "I forget his name. He's not an epidemiologist; he's an M.D. with a general practice."

Kent hollered from behind us, "I'd move to exclude his testimony with a motion in limine, sounds like he's not qualified."

Hank replied over his shoulder, "I'll be looking into that."

"Do we have an expert yet?" Zack asked Hank.

"Yes. I've received authorization to hire Dr. McMillan. He's an epidemiologist and professor at U.C. Davis. Impeccable resume and academic background."

"What was his fee?"

"Twenty-five hundred a day for trial."

"That's reasonable," Zack mused. "What does he say about the state's epidemiological study?"

"He agrees. The state did a thorough job investigating the outbreak. He found no basis to challenge the report's conclusions. Everyone who got infected ate at our restaurant within the time frame for exposure."

"Just like I thought. We have no defense to liability."

"That's how it appears so far."

"What about this glove issue; what does Dr. McMillan say about that?"

"He says that gloves are effective—as long as they're properly used."

"Well, since the restaurant workers didn't wear gloves, I don't see how that's relevant," Zack questioned.

Hank clarified, "Well, what he means is that gloves are no guarantee that food workers will not transmit a virus while working with food. The more important aspect is washing hands frequently, particularly after using the restroom."

"Right. So you don't get a crap sandwich," Zack said deadpan.

Kent laughed behind us on the sofa, "I didn't see that on the menu," he said with a goofy smile.

Hank agreed, "That's basically what it boils down to."

Zack continued, "As I understand it, the Hepatitis A virus is excreted with the feces and transferred by hand contact."

"Well, it's even worse than that," Hank explained, "transmission occurs via the 'fecal-oral' route, meaning someone gets fecal matter on their hands, transfers it to food, then someone else eats the food and ingests the virus. And the person can be infected and contagious and not know it."

"Great. We better hire a jury consultant to see what sort of exposure we're facing at trial."

"I've already received authorization," Hank noted.

"Good. Let's try to get this case settled," Zack said. "Claims actually would prefer settlement to trial. We don't want to pay for serving customers toilet sandwiches. That'll be disastrous."

"I agree," Hank said.

Zack wrapped up the discussion, "See if you can stipulate to liability with the plaintiffs' attorney and limit the trial to damages. That'll save everyone a ton of time and money. He might be interested."

"I'll be seeing him tomorrow. I'll run it by him."

"Great. Okay, for now, the best we can do is file the motion to eliminate the punitive damages issue. If it goes to the jury and the client gets hit, he can always appeal, maybe get the judgment reversed or reduced. I'd like to see a copy of the motion before it gets filed."

"I'll make sure you have a copy," Hank assured him.

Zack looked at me and instructed, "Make sure you check local rules for law and motion procedure. They sometimes have some specific requirements and fees. We don't want to get hometowned by some Bozo for not paying a fee or filing a form."

"I'll check," I responded.

Our meeting ended, and I returned to my office to continue working on the motion for partial summary adjudication.

I worked full-time on the motion for another two

months and finally submitted a forty-page draft to Hank and Zack. Hank made a few minor edits and said it was ready to file. Zack reviewed it and gave his approval, and I began assembling all the evidence and exhibits that would accompany the motion, about three hundred pages of documentation.

After Carrie added a neat table of contents and authorities and exhibits were tabbed and organized, I mailed a copy to the plaintiffs' attorney and the original to the court.

After the other side filed their opposition to our motion, we'd get the last word with a reply brief then wait for a decision from the court, which would likely take several months.

Under the freeway near Watt Avenue, The Cattle Club was a dark, grimy, low-ceilinged rectangular cave-like structure, but it was one of the few places in Sacramento that allowed bands to play original music. I submitted our demo tape, and they agreed to book our band, Citizen Kane, for a Thursday night. The catch was the band was required to sell tickets for the show. If the band didn't sell enough tickets and bring enough paying customers, the club wouldn't schedule us again.

Our gig was a sort of debut on the Sacramento club scene. Previously we had played tiny bars in Roseville and Lincoln and house parties, but now we were playing a more mainstream club—one with gigantic black speakers flanking both sides of the large stage and plenty of space for the drums and guitar amps.

We arrived around 6:00. The place was empty, but we loaded our gear onto the stage, set up the drums, plugged in our amps, and did a sound check. By 6:45, we were ready to play. People started trickling in, and at 7:00, there were probably 20 people scattered among the tables and seats. We waited a little while longer to allow a few more people to arrive, then took the stage.

We cranked through three originals before taking a short break to address the crowd, which had now swelled to about 75. Rick shouted into the microphone, and the crowd cheered.

Our band was gaining momentum. It was palpable. Crowds liked our originals; Rick's vocals sounded better and better, strong and filled with passion. We didn't sound like a garage band anymore; we sounded like experienced rock musicians on their way up the ladder to stardom.

Rick and I were excited about Jeff Keller's offer to help. His influence might fling open the door to a record contract, world tour, and soaring fame.

We were getting close to something big. I could feel it.

I had been confined to the office during my term

as Hank's assistant, doing legal research and working on the partial summary adjudication motion, but a court hearing was coming up in July in Eureka, and an attorney needed to be present. Eureka was a 6-hour drive, and the attorney handling the case did not want to do a 12-hour, round-trip for a 10-minute court hearing, so he offered me the opportunity. This was simply a case management conference in which the attorneys discussed with the judge scheduling a trial date and deadlines for discovery and motions. I could have handled it with a phone call.

I was glad to have the assignment, however, even though it required a 6-hour drive north. I was happy to get out of the office for a couple days and actually appear in court, wearing a suit and tie as an attorney at law—fulfillment of the long-percolating lawyer fantasy.

The case management conference was scheduled for a Friday in July at 1:30 in the afternoon. If I left at 5:30, I would arrive around 11:30, enough time to get some lunch, find the court, and attend the hearing.

Our motion for partial summary adjudication had been undecided by the court for about four months, and we were anxiously checking the mail every day for a ruling. Before the day arrived for my departure north to Eureka, an envelope from the court finally arrived. I came back from lunch one afternoon and was walking down the hall to my office when Carrie came running toward me in her dress and high heels, waving a document.

"We got the ruling! We got the ruling," she said

breathlessly. “We won!” She handed me the fifteen-page document.

I looked at the front page across from the legal caption and read the words, “ORDER GRANTING DEFENDANT’S MOTION FOR PARTIAL SUMMARY ADJUDICATION ON PLAINTIFFS’ PUNITIVE DAMAGES CLAIM.”

I gasped, “We won…”

Carrie was smiling.

“Does Hank know?” I asked.

“No, he’s in depositions. I haven't been able to reach him on the phone, but I'll keep trying.”

“This is great news!” I said.

“Congratulations!”

“Thank you!”

“Hank’s gonna be so happy,” Carrie gushed.

“I’ll bet. I have to go read this!”

“Zack knows; I already told him,” she hollered at my back.

“Great; thanks!” I yelled back, as I dashed to my office to read the court's ruling.

I was halfway done when Kent poked his head into my office and said warmly, “Congratulations, Ben. I heard about the ruling. I’d like to read it when you're done.”

“Thank you. I'll make you a copy.”

I was exhilarated. More than six months ago we plotted an objective, did the research, filed a motion, and achieved our goal. Our client would be ecstatic. Claims would be euphoric.

An important rite of passage had been achieved. I

had been vindicated. None of the other attorneys had any confidence that the motion would be granted, but I always thought it was possible. Why had they doubted the clear, simple, unavoidable logic that pointed in our favor? It had seemed obvious to me, but they had made it so complicated.

Zack called me into his office later that afternoon. He had a copy of the ruling on his desk. I sat in a client chair.

"Congratulations," he said sincerely.

"Thank you."

"I didn't think the judge would grant the motion, but your argument convinced him."

"It always seemed cut and dried to me."

"It's good you're able to perceive issues with such clarity. That will be a great benefit in the future."

"Thank you."

"I think this result is due partly to your native intelligence, but an enormous amount of work and research went into the motion; that cannot be overlooked. We out-worked 'em. With more effort, they might have been able to defeat our motion," he said, now detracting from my victory. "But we're dealing with a small plaintiff firm. He probably didn't spend more than ten hours on his opposition. You worked on the case for months. He couldn't or wouldn't put in the time required to address our motion fully, and he paid the price."

"I doubt more work would have produced a different result," I said.

"You may be right. I don't want to take away from

your success. I just didn't see a lot of effort from the plaintiffs' attorney. Looks like his law clerk did all the work. At any rate, you did a great job," he said, with a smile. "Claims will be happy."

"Thank you."

I left and returned to my office.

Strange that my victory would be characterized as a success only because the other side had not worked hard enough, but I let it go. I supposed this was not the time to gloat. I had already heard the lectures about my lack of experience making my judgment and opinion suspect. Jury trial skill was now the new criterion that separated attorneys on the hierarchy, and I had none.

When the startling news was discussed around the office, I made sure everyone knew how much work I had done on the motion. Something told me not to get too cocky, but I wanted credit for my work. I was the *only* one who thought we had a chance of winning from the start—not Hank or Kent, or even Zack, but it seemed I might be stepping out of line if I openly claimed victory. It was Hank's case, and the unspoken message in the air was *Hank* deserved credit for any favorable outcome. I was just a helper who worked under his sage guidance, even though he had not shared my confidence in our prospects for prevailing. But I had researched, written, and won the motion, and the other attorneys knew it.

A week later, it was time for my trip to Eureka. I rose at five, showered briefly, took a cup of coffee for the road, and left for my 6-hour drive to court.

It was a dull, dreary drive up Interstate 5, dry empty fields on both sides of the freeway.

As I travelled up the straight freeway in the morning twilight, my thoughts drifted back twenty years. . .

CHRISTMAS

My first memories were when we lived in Thousand Oaks, a suburb of Los Angeles, California. We lived in a three-bedroom, two-bath house with a huge backyard. We were straight middle class, though I had no knowledge of any different classes at the time.

I thought about the first Christmas I remembered. Rick woke me in the quiet darkness of Christmas morning and told me Santa Claus had just filled our stockings, and he had watched him do it. He urged me to get up and go with him to see Santa in our living room before he went back up the chimney.

I left the warmth of my bed and crept down the hall behind my brother. Like two burglars in shadows, we inched down the hall toward the living room; he whispered at me to be quiet; we didn't want to scare away Santa Claus—although why Santa Claus would flee at the sight of children was not explained. We skulked around the corner into the living room—slowly, quietly—expecting to see the white-haired, red-suited gift-giver, but no one was there. The tree lights were sparkling brilliantly in the dark, amid gold garlands, tinsel, and shining bulbs. Some magical essence of Santa Claus appeared to remain near the fireplace amid the colorful twinkling orbs. Our Christmas tree had shed dozens of needles onto the floor, and the room was filled with the pine's sweet fragrance.

Rick crept toward the fireplace, where our stockings were now bulging. He peeked into the fireplace, then informed me Santa was gone. Then he pointed to the half-eaten cookie lying on a coffee table nearby and the glass of milk we had left out, which was now only half full. The proof was undeniable: Santa had been there, eaten part of the cookie, drank half the milk, filled our stockings, then vanished back up the chimney. Rick had received the special privilege of actually witnessing the legend in the flesh. I had missed the thrill of a lifetime; maybe next year.

Without waiting for my disappointment or questions, he removed the stockings from the fireplace mantel, handed mine to me, and we started unpacking them. I removed a plastic box with a clear cover containing a small toy car—the kind that travels on orange plastic tracks in circles and in figure eights. What a magnificent toy—just like the kind shown on TV—and now I had my own. For a little kid, it was like holding the Hope Diamond and knowing it was mine to keep. Excitement, exhilaration, and infinite gratitude to Santa Claus.

We explored our stockings and found more gifts, chocolate and candy canes, examined them briefly then returned them to the mantel and went back to bed. It was about 3:00 in the morning.

A couple hours later, we woke our parents and dashed back into the living room to open presents. It was still dark. Mom and Dad wearily rose from the darkness of their room and joined us in the living room. We tore open presents, then pretended to be surprised by the contents of our stockings.

It was a wonderful, special, memorable time that was simultaneously occurring in houses all across America.

SUPER HEROS

We had one of those thick, square televisions, with maybe a twenty-inch screen that rested on short wooden legs. It was about two-thirds the size of a dishwasher and ponderously heavy.

One of my early favorite TV shows was *Batman*, starring Adam West. I remember not understanding a lot of the dialogue and story line, but I understood that Batman was good, and he fought and defeated the bad guys.

Dad made a little wood "Bata-rang," a crescent shaped thing with a scalloped side. He drilled a hole through one end and tied a rope through it. He painted it silver, so it resembled Batman's. Mom gave me one of her garments that served as a cape, and she bought a little dark blue ski mask to match. My rain boots completed the ensemble, and with my Bata-rang, I'd venture into the backyard in my mask, flowing cape, and rain boots, toss the device over the back fence until it hooked, then climb up a step or two, just like Batman and Robin climbed up tall buildings. I *was* Batman.

Halloween was another wondrous time of make believe and excitement. Buckets full of free candy from neighbors, and we got to dress up in a costume. Seemed preposterous, but it was true. Rick had been the first to trick-or-treat a year or two earlier, and when he came back with a plastic Jack-o'-lantern full of candy, he was not required to share any of it with me. That was *his*; he had dressed up like a pirate, gone house to house and filled his plastic pumpkin with candy, and it was all his to hoard and enjoy. It didn't seem fair. He had more candy than he could eat in a week, and he got to keep it all for himself. Not even a lousy sucker or Tootsie Roll for me? There were no explanations about private property, return on investment, personal responsibility, or anything else. I'd just have to wait until next year when I'd be allowed to go trick-or-treating and get my own pumpkin full of candy.

When my turn finally arrived, I was a fan of Spiderman. To my surprise and delight, Mom told me I could be Spiderman for Halloween. I was astonished. Where would I get the Spiderman outfit? Easy, she explained, they sold them at the drugstore. I would look just like Spiderman on TV, she assured me. She'd take me to the drugstore, and we'd buy one.

I was exhilarated as I envisioned myself in my Spiderman suit, shooting webs from my palms and swinging from the rooftops. We went to the store and, sure enough, there it was on a shelf, the unmistakable image of Spiderman. There it is! Mom took the box and paid for it. I couldn't wait to get home and put on my very own Spiderman suit.

I filled my plastic pumpkin with candy on Halloween, then returned home and marveled at my bounty, which I'd dumped onto my bedroom floor. This time, the candy was all *mine*, and I didn't have to share any with my brother. I didn't understand the pagan origins of Halloween or why modern kids dressed in costumes and went door-to-door every October to collect candy. It was a wonderful, magical time during which imagination soared with visions of goblins, flying witches, black cats, and buckets full of free candy, and that was good enough.

MISCHIEF

Dad had built a small, wooden playhouse in the backyard next to the fence. It was simply four walls, a roof, and two hinged doors. Perhaps eight small children could fit inside.

We had a bat, some baseballs, and a couple little gloves. Rick and I would play catch and hit baseballs in the backyard.

One day Rick brought one of the kids from the neighborhood into the yard, and he wanted to hit baseballs. He was a scrawny, hollow-eyed, tired-looking little kid of about 9. I felt privileged to play with an older kid and quickly agreed.

I gathered up several baseballs and prepared to pitch. Somehow, the little stranger convinced me that he needed to be close to hit the ball. It would be easier if I lobbed it underhanded to him to smack over the fence. He stood about six feet away and told me to lob the ball high. Then he took a baseball and demonstrated what he meant. I lofted the ball slowly into the air, and as I looked up to watch, I was suddenly clobbered and felt great pressure and pain. That little psycho had stepped forward quickly and swung the bat, landing solidly across my throat.

The shock and pain sent me crying and running back into the house. I told my Mom the kid had hit me with the bat. She examined me, then came outside and investigated. The little liar told her it had been an accident, and he would be more careful. Mom told us not to stand so close and to be careful. After a while, I seemed to recover from my injury and wanted to play again.

The other kid was ready. I made sure there was plenty of space between us this time, probably fifteen feet. There was no way he could rush in and hit me with the bat after I threw the ball.

He stood with the bat ready to swing, and I pitched another baseball. He stepped forward, swung mightily, and smacked the ball back at me in a line drive. It crashed into my throat, directly where he had previously walloped me. Intense pressure and pain once again flared. Somehow, this little psychopath hit me in the throat again! I screamed in pain and ran away crying into the house. I was outraged that this little savage was intentionally hurting me. I told my Mom that he had hit me again, and now she was pissed. She stormed outside and told the little thug to go home and took the bat from him. She came inside, examined me to make sure my injury wasn't serious, then told me to lie down and the pain would go away.

I never saw that little felon again. He probably went home and killed the neighbor's cat.

We had an old red car, a Ford Falcon. It seemed old even back then. It was parked across the street in front of our house. I was maybe four and had not yet started school. I was searching for entertainment in the late morning and decided to look inside the car. I walked outside, crossed our front yard, and approached the Falcon. There was no activity on the street or anywhere in the neighborhood.

When I pulled the door handle, I was delighted that it opened. I climbed into the front seat and closed the door. Sitting there I held the steering wheel but could barely see out of the windshield. My feet dangled over the seat, far from the brake and gas pedal. The dash had several large cracks revealing porous yellow padding and a thin layer of dust, yielding the distinctive odor of dried, aging foam.

I turned knobs and pushed buttons on the dashboard. Mom passed by the little kitchen window sixty feet away.

After I had touched everything on the dashboard and examined all the dials and pushed all the radio buttons, the only thing left to do was pull the gear lever attached to the column of the steering wheel. I knew this lever had to be shifted for the car to move. I pulled it and heard a clunk. The car started rolling. I had traveled no more than five feet and was gaining speed when suddenly Mom somehow appeared at the driver's door and yanked it open. She held the door with one hand and reached inside to hold the steering wheel with the other. The car was now rolling too fast for her to stop it, so she ran alongside, steering with one arm.

I scooted over a little, expecting her to jump behind the wheel, but she couldn't get inside. I was not at all scared. I looked both ways before pulling the lever, and no cars were coming in either direction. This was just a slow ride across the road. Mom was terrified.

She ran with the car for probably thirty feet until it bumped against the curb and stopped. She pulled me out and asked if I was okay. I didn't understand, at the time, why Mom was so afraid and concerned. I thought I would be in trouble for playing inside the car, but I was not. Mom was happy and relieved that my little ride had not ended in disaster.

The car doors were always locked in the future.

THE WICKED LADY

Morning traffic was getting heavier as I made progress on the long drive to Eureka. Everything looked the same on both sides of the freeway, long stretches of flat, empty fields. I pulled off the freeway, bought a cup of coffee, stretched a little, then returned to the road and continued recounting my earliest memories.

When I was five or six, we visited my Mom's friend across town now and then. We must have gone during school time, as the kids of this home were almost never there.

One day, Mom dropped me off for the afternoon. An unfamiliar lady was there this visit. She was probably in her late forties, with big blond hair and dark brown eyes. She probably had been a head-turner twenty years earlier but smoking, alcohol, medications, and heartbreak had taken a toll on her face.

Mom brought me inside the house, chatted with her friend for a bit, and met the other lady. After a brief, friendly conversation, Mom left.

My host went outside to resume yard work, and I wandered into the kitchen and was just aimlessly browsing when the quiet stranger silently appeared and stood in the entrance. She watched as I fiddled and fidgeted in the kitchen, touching chairs and exploring my surroundings. Her gaze was unsettling. I noticed her dark brown eyes fixed on me. Was I doing something wrong? No one told me to stay out of the kitchen. Why was she staring coldly? I was used to adults being friendly and smiling, but not this lady. Her face was expressionless. Why didn't she say anything? I kept expecting her demeanor to change and become friendly, like most adults I encountered, especially anyone who knew my mom. After a long, awkward silence, she finally spoke.

"Would you like a glass of milk?" she said with the faintest smile.

"Okay."

"There's some powdered milk under the sink," she said, her dark eyes now glowering down on me.

Powdered milk? Hmm. At that point, I'd never heard of it. I had heard of chocolate powder that was mixed with milk to make chocolate milk, but not powdered milk.

"There's a glass in the cupboard," she said, pointing. "Just mix it with water."

I stood on my toes and reached for a glass. Thinking there might be real milk in the refrigerator, I stepped toward it and pulled the door open a few inches. She pushed it shut.

"It's under the sink," she said, pointing.

Hmm. Weird. Powdered milk?—under the sink?

I opened the cupboard and removed a green box. I poured some of the powder into the glass, and the strange lady vanished.

I could not read well, so I did not know what the box said. I filled the glass with water. Hmm. Green milk? Just doesn't seem right. I sniffed my 'powdered milk'. Didn't smell anything like milk. For probably the first time in my life, I experienced intuition. *Something's not right here*, a voice told me. *This 'powdered milk' doesn't look or smell right. Think I'll skip the milk for now.* I left the foamy green drink on the kitchen counter and wandered off.

An hour or so later when Mom returned to pick me up, she came inside, and her friend reappeared, along with the powdered milk lady. We were near the kitchen when the friend discovered the green drink and asked what I had done. I tried to explain that the lady had told me to make myself the toxic potion, but it didn't seem right, so I didn't drink it. The poisoner denied any such suggestion and pretended to be shocked and horrified, gasping and clutching herself. My defense was lost in all the fake concern and surprise. *Well, making milk from a box was a bad idea*, I thought to myself. Thankfully, I had enough skepticism not to drink the venomous mixture.

Mom was horrified and lectured me on the way home, but I didn't understand. Mixing 'dry milk' with water was not my idea, and she could not, or would not, believe that the adult woman had tried to poison me.

I did not feel scarred or traumatized, just puzzled. Why would that strange woman do such a thing?

I'm just lucky I had enough sense not to drink green milk.

THE HAUNTED HOUSE

I was maybe halfway through my drive to Eureka when thoughts of my first trip to Disneyland materialized. This occurred about the same time as my mom's divorce from my dad and the start of her new relationship with my stepdad.

Dallas was a tall, plain-looking, soft-spoken salesman from Arkansas. He was a good stepfather, but his business ventures repeatedly struggled. He invested first in a bar, then a restaurant, both of which failed within a year. He sold real estate and cars in between business investments, but he was kind to my brother and me and never caused us any stress or harm. Keeping his commitment to my mom was another question.

We went to the Magic Kingdom one weekend for our first Disneyland experience. I spent most of the day walking and being carried by Dallas, as I was too small to ride most of the rides by myself. It was a safety rule, but I didn't understand why height mattered. I could hang onto the crossbar as well as anyone. Why wouldn't they just let me in? It seemed atrociously unfair that I was prevented from enjoying the fun rides, but I just had to live with it.

Rick was enraptured on one ride after another and, like all children, could not get enough of the Disneyland fun and magic.

Toward the end of the day, it was time to venture into the catacombs of the creepy haunted house. Rick was eager to take the ride. There was a discussion whether he should go by himself. He was only about eight but insisted he could go alone. His confidence convinced my mom and Dallas, so they gave him a little yellow "E-ticket" (all the best rides required an E -ticket), and he dashed off for the line. In a few minutes, he disappeared through the entrance.

Ten minutes later, he emerged, euphoric and excited. Dallas checked with my brother.

"Was it fun, Ricky?" he drawled.

"Yes!" my brother shouted.

"You wuzn't scared, wuz ya, Ricky?"

"No. That was fun!"

"I thought so."

"I saw the ghosts!"

"You did?"

"Yeah, they were neato!"

"Neato," Dallas echoed.

"Can I ride it again?"

Dallas looked at my mom.

"Why don't we all ride it this time?" Mom suggested.

"Yeah!" my brother shouted. He couldn't get on the ride again fast enough.

I hadn't been on any rides except maybe the twirling teacups, and I certainly didn't want my first 'big kid' ride to be this scary haunted house.

"I'm scared. I don't want to go. I'm afraid of the ghosts," I told my mom.

"The ghosts aren't real."

"I'm afraid."

"It's just a ride, the ghosts aren't real."

I kept protesting that I didn't want to see any ghosts; Mom kept telling me they were fake, and it was a fun ride. My brother had fun, and I would, too.

Rick was clamoring to go again, and I was holding up the group. Dallas tried to console me. "I'll ride with you, Ben. Them ghosts don't scare me. They won't hurt you. Okay?"

"I don't want to go," I complained.

Mom decided we would all ride together, and I would accompany Dallas, who was six-two, and appeared to be a formidable opponent for any human, but not a ghost, as far as I was concerned.

The decision was made. My mom and brother would ride together, and I would ride with Dallas, and this would be fun because the ghosts were not real.

We inched forward in line until finally we reached the ticket terminal. Dallas asked the attendant if I could ride with him. The gate-keeper looked at me and considered the question seriously; he agreed, but cautioned not to let me sit at the edge of the seat, because I might fall out; Dallas affirmed he would keep his arm around me, and we would both hold the bar enclosing us in our seat. With that agreement, we surrendered our E-tickets and were admitted.

We walked through the entrance and the solid foundation of asphalt and concrete was replaced by the cushioning of soft carpet in the dim interior. We shuffled forward into the 8-sided gallery and waited. The walls were darkly paneled, and crouching gargoyles holding long candles in each hand were mounted on the points of the octagon a few feet above our heads. On each panel of the angular room was mounted a painting depicting a person or two in a seemingly normal pose. Oddly striped wall paper covered the upper half of the walls.

Eerie, discordant organ tones played as people filed into the slowly filling chamber. A low, spine-chilling voice spoke, as if through the walls and ceiling, welcoming us on our adventure. The sound seemed to be everywhere—disembodied and occupying the room: "Kindly step all the way in, please, and make room for everyone. There's no turning back now." Dallas pointed as the ceiling began grinding upward slowly, and the walls grew longer. I watched horrified as the gargoyles rose slowly. The room seemed alive, growing taller, and we were simultaneously sinking into the dark bowels of this ominous abode.

The ghost host continued: "Is this haunted room actually stretching? Or is it your imagination?" He asked with sinister delight, then chuckled. As the paintings grew longer, the previously hidden portion was exposed. One revealed an alligator with a gaping mouth below a woman on a tightrope holding a parasol. Another showed a man in striped boxers standing on a barrel of dynamite with a lit fuse. A third displayed a man with folded arms sitting on the shoulders of another, who was on the shoulders of a third, who was submerged to the waist in quick sand. The paintings depicting disaster seemed to foretell our fate. The narrator concluded, speaking slowly and deliberately: "And consider this dismaying observation. This chamber has *no doors* and *no windows*, which offers you this chilling challenge; to find a way out!" He then laughed maniacally.

"I'm scared! I'm scared!" I shouted.

Dallas picked me up and held me in his arms as the ceiling continued to drift upward, and the menacing voice concluded its warnings. Thunder roared and flashing bolts of lightning burst above, revealing a skeleton dangling from a rope at the top of the ceiling. A final inhuman scream pierced the gallery before silence, then hidden side doors opened.

I clung to Dallas as he carried me forward toward the row of strange, rotund vessels creaking forward in a single file line. They resembled large, high-backed chairs with rounded roofs, large enough to accommodate two passengers. My mom and brother boarded a car, and Dallas and I stepped into the one behind them. A horizontal bar lowered in front of us and Dallas put an arm around me. I clutched the crossbar, and we started our rickety journey.

Our carriage twisted and jostled forward, slowly descending into the haunted underbelly of this living house. Gloomy organ music droned in the darkness. Dallas did his best to help me enjoy the ride. His arm was sheltering me, as I gripped the cross-rail, but the sight of a candelabra floating in a hall startled me.

Ghostly human figures dressed in 19th Century clothing sat at large dinner tables, ballroom-danced, played musical instruments and howled and shrieked through the air. Dallas huddled against me protectively, but I kept my eyes closed for most of the ride.

It was all too much. I was not able to overcome my fear of ghosts simply because Mom and Dallas said they were not real. To me, the experience was very real and very scary, and I did not enjoy it.

We finally completed the ordeal and ascended into the exit area. Rick was exuberant. Two trips through the haunted house would be something to brag about to the kids in school. Mom wanted to know if I enjoyed the ride.

"Was he scared?" she asked Dallas.

"Yes," he answered.

Rick heard this and seized the opportunity to make himself the hero and me the coward. "You were scared; ha ha. I wasn't scared. I rode it twice."

"Stop it, Ricky," Mom said. "You're eight; your brother's only five. He won't be scared next time."

I sulked.

Dallas consoled me. "That's okay, Ben, when we come back next time, you'll be older, and you won't be scared."

"When will that be?" I asked.

"I don't know," he said, "maybe a year or two. Probably two years."

"Two years?"

That was almost half my life; it seemed like I was being punished for being scared.

I mulled over the situation. Rick had spent the day in rapturous joy riding many of the rides at Disneyland, and my cowardice had wrecked the fun. A steely determination sprouted in my core. I would make this right somehow. I would not let my brother triumph over me. Otherwise, I would have to live with his gloating forever. No, that was not acceptable. Things would not be right until I rode through the shrieking, wailing dungeon, walked out and smiled in his face, and said let's do it again.

I had another year or two to overcome my terror. Until then, Rick could tease and torment me with reminders of my failure and celebrate his superior courage. Beyond that, he would use his heroism as a sort of argument-ending tranquilizer. Anytime he felt the need to shut me up or put me in my place, all he had to say was, "You were scared of the ghosts! Ha ha! I wasn't! I had fun! You're a baby!" He was the prime rib, and I was a slice of baloney—an insurmountable difference in quality—proven by my fear of ghosts at Disneyland.

The shame eventually wore off, and the teasing stopped, but I knew the matter was not settled. We'd go to Disneyland again someday, and I'd have the chance to redeem myself.

A couple years later, we were both visiting our dad, and Rick began beseeching him to take us to Disneyland. He lived an hour from Anaheim, where the Magic Kingdom was located. Rick always knew important logistics of this sort and was ready to rattle them off to support his requests.

Dad agreed to take us on the weekend, and my brother was euphoric. I was also excited and desperately wanted a chance to prove I wasn't the coward he gleefully reassured everyone I was.

"Ben won't ride the haunted house; he was scared last time," Rick announced triumphantly.

"Why were you scared, Ben?" my dad asked.

"I don't know. It was scary."

Rick smiled and laughed. "He was scared; he's afraid."

"There's no reason to be afraid, Ben," my dad calmly declared in his deep, rich baritone, "It's just a ride."

I gazed blankly, unconvinced.

Dad continued, "The ghosts aren't real. They're like the ghosts you see on TV; they're made up, using cameras, editing, light and so on. It's all an illusion."

Then Dad went into a long explanation about how special effects are created in movies to make things appear to happen that do not really happen. They could film one scene and separately film another and put them both together to make two scenes look like one, but it was just a trick to create the illusion—a big word to use for a little kid, but Dad had a vast vocabulary and never spoke down to us.

He concluded, "I'm telling you the pictures and the ghosts are not real. They can't hurt you. Okay?"

"Okay."

I pondered Dad's explanation. I had to beat the ghosts, or I would be teased, tormented, and ridiculed by my brother forever.

Our journey was planned. The next day, we would go to Disneyland, and I would face down the ghosts. My brother was happily anticipating my fear and failure and his resulting exhilaration. *We'll see*, I thought, *we'll just see how things go this time.*

On the drive to Disneyland, Rick turned around from the front seat and looked at me.

"You're scared," he said with a wicked smile.

"No, I'm not."

"Yes, you are. You're a baby."

"Shut up."

He then started twinkling his fingers at me and making ascending and descending howling sounds, mimicking ghosts.

Dad, in has implacable manner, quelled the teasing, "Richard, stop teasing your brother."

He poked his tongue out at me, then turned around and started whistling merrily.

We finally arrived, parked, and began the long walk to the entrance. Rick was hopping around like he just drank a triple espresso.

"Can we ride the pirate's ride first, Dad?"

"That's fine, Richard."

"Yay!"

Rick danced with enthusiasm as we approached the Magic Kingdom.

I was filled with anticipation and dread that fear would get the better of me. We forged on, and soon we were inside, among thousands of people drifting here and there, Minnie and Mickey Mouse strolling about, greeting people.

We rode the Pirates of the Caribbean first, and that was a good start. All those drunk and cheerful pirates seated at tables drinking and chasing women.

The pirate skeletons, amid the various piles of treasure, were also good forerunners for the haunted house. They all looked very real, but they did not scare me; it was very exciting.

We finished the pirate ride, and now it was time for the showdown—the haunted house. Rick smiled at me knowingly, "Can we ride the haunted house ride now, Dad?"

"Sure. Let's go."

My brother seemed to know exactly where to go, so he led the way. Soon I saw the forbidding structure that had terrified me a couple years earlier. Fear shot through me, but I plodded forward. *The ghosts aren't real*, I told myself.

We stood in the roped-off line, and Rick was twirling, fidgeting, and smiling with excitement. We weren't even on the ride, but the anticipation was apparently just as fun.

Finally, we reached the entrance. I was now clearly tall enough. I handed my E-ticket to the attendant and stepped through the turnstile, which croaked as I pushed through. The three of us entered the paneled foyer where I had been terrified on my last visit. Rick gave me one last smile before the doors closed behind us.

We stood in the dark waiting for the eerie voice. The creepy host began oozing from the walls, as the drama started again.

I watched as the paintings stretched skyward. The rising walls now seemed mechanical, not supernatural. Houses didn't suddenly grow taller.

Somehow, a couple years made a difference in my perceptions.

I made it through the taunting introduction unafraid then walked through the side doors toward the carriages. As I walked, I peered at the glowing pictures on the wall and could see the fingerprints of human technology all over them. There were just a couple images, one on top of the other, and with a change in lighting, they appeared to switch. It was all man-made special effects—just like Dad had told me.

I could feel all my pent-up fears from years earlier leaving my body, like air from a balloon with the knot untied.

I rode the ride and enjoyed it this time. All the ghosts, which previously had terrified me, now dazzled and delighted me.

I finally understood Rick's exuberance for the ride.

I also knew I would never again be afraid to journey through the haunted house, and when I stepped off the ride and smiled at my brother, he knew it, too.

All his power to make me ashamed of my fear vanished like a ghost in the haunted house.

SACRED SOIL

The rolling hills dotted with oak trees reminded me of Newbury Park, where I met John. He was a typical little kid from Southern California, with dark curly hair, freckles, and blue eyes. He could have been one of the kids on the famous Life cereal TV commercial. We became good friends and spent a lot of time together after school, exploring the fields nearby and riding our bicycles.

Across from the condo complex was a small strip mall, and behind that, rolling hills, trails, scattered trees, and a stream. We spent afternoons exploring the wild behind the stores. There was no fear of kidnapping or crime back then. We'd see other kids exploring, so it seemed like we were all on one big playground.

One afternoon, while we were searching for lizards, someone found a brown, hard shell briefcase on the rocky slopes behind a building. It was locked and resembled a little piece of airline luggage. Rick was with us, and he seized the find for himself. We were all extremely curious to know what was inside. Rick took it to the condo and showed it to Dallas. He seemed concerned and asked us questions. We explained how we had found it, and he said we should take it back and leave it. The owner may be trying to find it.

Before leaving, Rick located a screwdriver and quietly slipped it into his pocket. John and I accompanied him back to the empty asphalt above the rocky slope where we had found the mysterious luggage. We put the case on the ground, and Rick poked and pried for probably ten minutes until finally a 'pop' was heard, and one of the locks was broken. A few more minutes of prying and cranking and the other lock popped and the container was opened.

We were hoping to find it full of money or maybe something else of value, but it was full of plastic folders containing papers none of us could read. There was no money. A stack of business cards spilled onto the ground, a few pens and a couple other office gadgets, but nothing of use or value to us. We put the broken vault back where we had found it, and left a few items on the asphalt.

After a day or two, we went back, and the case was gone, along with all the spilled contents.

The sudden disappearance left me with an unsettled feeling.

Next to the condominium complex was a large vacant lot about the size of a football field. We were exploring the empty lot one day when John announced we should build an underground fort. We found a patch of dirt not covered by rocks and bushes, and John said it would be a good place to start digging. All we had to do was dig a hole, cover it with boards, then shovel dirt to camouflage the fort. Sounded like a great idea to me.

John brought a couple shovels from his condo, and we started digging. We dug for a couple hours and made a hole about knee-deep and six feet across. That wasn't deep enough, so we agreed to come back the next day and dig some more.

We resumed our work the following afternoon and dug until the hole was about waist deep. It looked like a little bomb crater. I wanted it deeper, so we could stand in it, but John insisted it was deep enough. We gathered wood and boards lying nearby and formed a crude roof. Then we shoveled loose dirt onto the boards until it looked like loose soil, except for a small opening.

We were pleased with our work. We sat in the darkness of our fort, happy that we were unseen by the world. It had taken two afternoons of hard digging and shoveling, but it was done.

The next day, I met John at his condo, which was closer to the fort than mine, and we headed back to our underground hideout. As we entered the field, we were surprised to see several kids in the area. They were all two or three years older, so there was some cause for concern.

We plodded through the field. When we arrived, at least three kids were lingering in the area. They had scraped the dirt off the roof and removed some of the wood. I was shocked and angered.

“This is our fort,” John told them.

An older, taller blond kid snapped, “It’s not your fort, you don’t own the land.”

"We built it," John replied.

"So?"

I was now pondering this older kid's point. We did not own the land, but neither did he. Where did he get the right to destroy our fort? We had labored to dig the hole and cover it. They had no right to damage our creation, from my point of view.

One of the older kids rode his bicycle across the roof of the fort.

The older blonde kid continued, "We're gonna wreck your fort. It's dangerous."

"It's not dangerous," John protested.

"Yes, it is. If a car ran over it, the roof would cave in and you'd be crushed."

I was wondering how could a car possibly get into this rocky, brush-covered field. There was no road. Impossible.

The blonde aggressor kicked more dirt off the roof and glared at us. The confrontation was now escalating. I was not prepared to fight, so I remained quiet and observed. John retreated from the conversation and we backed away.

The conquerors then seemed disinterested in all the work necessary to wreck the fort and instead just lingered, waiting for some other distraction. After a while, they walked away and appeared to be interested in something else in the field.

John and I returned the wood that had been removed and pushed dirt back on top of it. I climbed inside to inspect, and all the areas that were allowing light to enter along the edges had returned, so we had more shoveling to do.

I hadn't been inside very long when I heard John shout my name. That kid was going to ride his bike over the roof again. I waited, then heard rumbling and creaking of the wood. I heard laughing and shouting. The land merchants had returned.

John shouted, "Ben! Don’t come out! Don't come out!"

I was afraid and didn't want to stay inside while the kid rode across the roof. I slowly poked my head out of the opening and turned around to see a stranger holding a bow and arrow pointed directly between my eyes. I ducked back inside, terrified. I heard laughing and taunting from outside. The bike continued to rumble above, and I hunkered on the dirt bottom.

Eventually, John shouted that the interlopers were gone and I could come out. I wanted to make sure I did not hear any voices before I ventured through the opening. When it seemed sufficiently quiet, I crept slowly from my shelter and dashed out of the field, hoping never to see the bullies again.

We both abandoned the fort and never returned to reclaim it.

SUMMER CAMP

One summer, Mom informed us that during the days, we would be going to this 'camp' in the mornings, where we would do fun things all day, then come home in the afternoon. The babysitters were not available to take care of us all day during the week, so this daycare camp would be our new daytime residence.

I was highly resistant to the idea. I didn't want to go to some dumb camp; I wanted to stay home and have fun in the neighborhood with my friend, John.

On the first day of camp, a little VW bus picked up my brother and me around 7:00 in the morning and drove us away. I was grumpy and suspicious as we boarded the small shuttle, but Rick assured me this was our ride.

We picked up a couple other kids on the way and finally arrived at an old, small, abandoned school. One of the camp counselors paired me with some other little kid who was my age and told us we should stay together, play together, and be friends, as everyone else was older and already paired up.

I had the choice to make a new friend or be completely alone. I chose friends. He reciprocated. We both seemed to realize that each other was all we had in this strange new camp world.

Meanwhile, Rick, who was naturally outgoing, was talking, laughing, and playing among the older kids, apparently enjoying himself and not missing home at all. I wanted to go home, but would do my best to get through this.

The leader of the camp was a short, hairy, gnomish-looking man who always gathered the camp in a group, told us to be quiet, then explained exactly what the plan was for the next 8 hours. One day we might go to a park and barbecue hot dogs; another, we might go to a museum. A school bus was used to take us places.

A few times, we went to the movies, which seemed like a hassle, keeping all the kids together. We saw *Planet of the Apes*, which was terrifying. The mean, talking apes throwing nets over humans and hauling them away to ramshackle prisons was petrifying.

Fridays, we always went to Zooma Beach, which was somewhere north of L.A.. The leader would start this weird tribal chant whenever he talked about going there. He'd wave his arms up and down and bellow, "Zoo-ma... Zooo-ma!... Zoooo-ma!!... Zoooo-ma!!!" He encouraged everyone to chant with him, and fifty kids would join. I didn't understand why he would erupt with such contrived gusto every time he mentioned Zooma Beach. I guess he thought this was how to stir up enthusiasm, but I just thought he looked dumb, like some kind of pretend chief baying at his tribe. But he was a good camp leader. He always lectured us carefully about safety, staying together, coming back to the bus on time, not wandering off, and was conscientious with our care.

I looked forward to Friday and Zooma Beach. It was an all-day trip; it would take a couple hours to get there, a few hours of fun in the ocean and sand, then a couple hours to drive back home. We were told to pack a large lunch and bring towels and swimsuits.

Friday arrived and Rick and I were picked up for camp. I found my assigned friend, and we boarded the school bus. The kids filled the seats, and there were several adults, including a very pretty dark-haired woman, who bore a strong resemblance to Cher. She was gorgeous, but in a mystical, witchy way.

We finally arrived, and our destination seemed to live up to all the hype. It was a beautiful stretch of beach, abutting the vastness of the Pacific Ocean. A salty aroma permeated the air, mingled with scents of sour, dry seaweed, lying in bunches on the shoreline. Sea gulls squawked and hovered, and waves crashed and foamed onto the shore. The cool breeze and endless crashing, splashing waves foaming toward shore was a new, hypnotic experience.

The camp custodians brought along some toys and things for us to play with—hula hoops, frisbees, beach balls, footballs, volleyballs. We had all we needed for a wonderful day at the beach.

We spread our towels on a spot, then went to a bathroom to change into our swimsuits and headed for the ocean. The receding tide exposed little crabs digging and clawing through the sand, emitting tiny bubbles. We were pelted by a fine, cool mist as waves crash in the surf, while we dug for crabs and ran along the shore. Frisbees and footballs were being tossed around, and kids were struggling to keep the hula hoops circulating around their hips. A couple small radios crackled pop music into the gusty sea air. This was pure 1970's.

We ate our soggy lunches and roamed about the beach. Someone pointed out that there was a snack bar. Word quickly got around that one of the older kids, Doug, had ten dollars, and he was now at the snack bar buying everything.

Ten dollars? I was awestruck. I had a quarter. Doug could buy something like twenty ice cream sandwiches and a few hot dogs with all that money. His parents must have been millionaires. How could they afford to give him ten dollars for a day at the beach? I was jealous. A group of kids was so impressed that they dashed to the snack bar to watch Doug make his purchases. My friend and I followed.

We arrived and some kids were already there, loitering and peeking through the door, watching Doug spend his fortune. He was probably twelve years old, the largest kid in our group. He stood inside, surveying the overhead menu boards. After a while, he emerged with his hands full, carrying a small cardboard box containing two large hot dogs covered with relish and a couple ice cream sandwiches. The kids were yelling at him, "How much did that cost, Doug? Do you have any money left? Can we have a quarter?" He told them no and strode away with his magnificent bounty. I watched him amble past. My friend and I could smell the hotdogs, and we both salivated as Doug sauntered away.

We calculated he had at least eight dollars left. If we could only talk him into giving us a few crummy quarters, we could buy one of those mouth-watering hot dogs, but it wasn't going to happen. We accepted the fact that we were not going to get any of Doug's money and returned to our towels.

Soon, it was time to return to the bus for the trip home. For some reason, I was one of the first kids back to the bus. I boarded and found a seat about halfway back. I noticed the gorgeous, witchy woman was about three seats behind me. Across from her was another counselor. We were the only three on the bus. The Cher doppelganger was probably in her twenties. I was about six, maybe seven, and there was not much for me to say.

I took my seat and waited for the other kids to arrive. Not long after settling in my seat, I heard the witchy woman behind me moving, making the leather squeak. "Don't turn around," she said, "I have to take off my bathing suit and put my clothes on."

I was shocked but remained still, my eyes looking forward. She apparently was going to be partially nude just a few seats behind me.

She was talking out loud as she changed, and she announced she would put on a T-shirt, then change tops underneath. I heard clothes rustling and the seat squeaking. This seemed to go on for a couple minutes, and I wondered why she was struggling. Then I heard what sounded like a belt clinking and fabric chafing. After more moments of clothes chafing, leather squeaking, a zipper zipping, and a belt clanking, I couldn't resist. I turned around and glimpsed briefly. She was standing up, pants still unzipped, corners dangling, exposing a view that immediately seemed forbidden. I made eye contact then quickly turned around.

She said, "It's okay, I have my bathing suit on underneath."

I was thrilled, embarrassed and puzzled. Why didn't she just tell me to get off the bus while she changed? Her permissiveness intrigued me; she seemed to enjoy the little performance.

Whatever her reasons or motivation, I'm glad the uninhibited camp counselor let me stay on the bus.

NEVADA

After living in Newbury Park for a year, Mom told us we would be moving. Dallas had bought a bar in Reno, Nevada. I was sad. I had enjoyed so much fun with my new young friend, John, exploring the fields and rolling hills surrounding Newbury Park, riding our bicycles, building forts, and getting into other mischief. I did not want to move, but there was nothing I could do.

I enjoyed what time I had left with John, and before we left the condominium for the last time, Mom said I should call him, say goodbye, and get his phone number if I wanted to talk to him again. I called and told him I had to move. He was surprised and tentative, and I could tell he did not know what to say. I took his phone number and said I would call someday. We agreed we would stay friends, and he would look forward to me calling.

I started third grade in Reno, Nevada. New classroom, new teacher, new kids. I did not want to adapt to my new school. I wanted my old friend back.

Once again, we lived in a two-story condominium, although this one was different. The condos were joined in long blocks, front doors in a row. Large square patches of grass were scattered among the complex, interlaced with sidewalks and streets.

Our new town near Reno was surrounded by brush-covered flatlands and several barren mountain ridges in the distance. It was much colder than southern California; it snowed in the winter and we sweltered in summer.

Early in the school year, Mom instructed me to report after school every day to an old lady who lived in a nearby condominium. She babysat six or seven kids, and I would be one of her new wards. Once again, I felt discrimination. Rick was exempted from the requirement, and I thought that was unfair. He was allowed to roam free after school, and I had to sit in the living room of a babysitter and watch cartoons.

The lady was sweet and friendly, and her condo smelled like cherry suckers and Tootsie Rolls, but I didn't like the restriction on my after-school freedom, until one day a beautiful little blue-eyed-blonde girl was in the living room when I showed up. She looked a little like Cindy, the youngest daughter on the television show, *The Brady Bunch*. I was suddenly jolted with unfamiliar feelings—a core-melting, disoriented sensation, heart racing, floating out of my shoes.

I sat on the couch and pretended not to notice the pretty little blonde. Boys supposedly disliked girls, but I liked this one. She turned around and stared for a few moments. I glanced and continued watching cartoons.

The TV was loud and the room was filled with the funny sounds and voices of cartoon characters. Three or four other kids were on the floor watching the TV, suckers in their mouths. No one introduced me to the girl, and I didn't know what to say. I heard the babysitter call her Kelly, so at least I knew her name.

She went back to watching cartoons, and I sat on the couch in my otherworldly state.

The next day, I looked forward to seeing Kelly again, but she wasn't there. I was disappointed but figured I would see her the next day, but she never returned. After a week of her absence, I concluded her single appearance had been a one-time event.

I saw her at school a few times, but after the end of the year, I never saw her again.

Visible from the condominium complex in the distance was Rattlesnake Mountain. It looked like a small volcano jutting up from the surrounding flatlands. The mountain presented an irresistible challenge, and Rick and I agreed we should conquer it. We asked Mom for permission to hike to the top of the mountain, and she consented.

One Saturday morning, we dressed warmly, filled a canteen with water, attached our buck knives to our belts, stuffed a bag of trail mix into our jacket pockets and began the half-hour-long walk to Rattlesnake Mountain.

We trekked along a four-lane street that led to the mountain, crossed the final intersecting street, and entered the field. We eventually reached the base and noticed the large rocks, as if ejected by a volcanic eruption. The chunks became smaller farther up the slope, turning to gravel, then finally soft dirt.

Water erosion had carved a wide, rocky crevice. It looked as if a giant scoop of earth had been removed from the side of the mountain. The brushless gap appeared to provide a path to the summit. Thick bushes covered the mountain everywhere else, except the upper region, which was somewhat flat and mostly dirt and boulders.

We stood and studied our challenge. The mountain now seemed much larger than it had from the condominium. We concluded it would take a half hour to complete our goal.

Now that we were far away from people and traffic, silence became eerie. Rick and I were out in the wild, completely independent and vulnerable, but we had knives and each other. The quiet and morning stillness brought a ghost-town feeling, as we lingered and studied our surroundings.

We decided to hike straight up the crevice, as that appeared to be the most direct path to the top. I shrugged off the cloying eeriness and followed my brother as he led the way. After climbing a couple hundred feet, he turned around, put a vertical finger to his lips, then pointed up the mountain directly ahead of us. I looked and saw two little kids about seventy-five feet away climbing in our path. Where had they come from? Why hadn't we seen them? They just suddenly appeared in brightly colored jackets, red and blue. Rick stepped toward me. "Don't follow them," he whispered. "Let's go this way, around the side," he said, pointing to the right, then stepped away and *vanished* into the bushes.

I stopped and thought, *why should I not follow them? They don't own the mountain.* Going through the bushes around the side would take a lot longer. Besides, I was concerned about encountering rattlesnakes in the thick brush, even though I had my buck knife. I decided to disregard my brother's advice and continued up the craggy fissure.

I took no more than two or three steps when I heard a loud thud, then a second. I looked up and saw a rock, the size of a couch pillow, tumbling directly toward me, about thirty feet away. I reflexively turned and ran down the slope as fast as I could. I sprinted to the bottom, miraculously not falling. As I strode across the chunky gravel, I heard a loud smacking sound behind me, then silence. I slowed on the rocks, turned around, and the big stone was gone. It had apparently broken into pieces, because I could not find it.

Those little hoodlums. They pushed that boulder intentionally and might have killed me. If I saw them, I was going to start swinging until blood or teeth were hitting the ground.

I started back up the mountain and looked for the two little demons, but they were gone. I followed the path Rick had taken through the brush to the side, but he was nowhere to be found—nothing but dirt, rocks and brush everywhere. With every step, I inhaled the sweet, spicy aroma of desert sage and sundried bark. I took my buck knife out of its sheath and began hiking through the thick shrubbery.

I looped around the side, careful with each step, wary of snakes and the stranger kids. Eventually, I arrived at the top, where I found Rick, gazing at the magnificent view all around.

"Where did you go?" he asked.

"Those kids pushed a big rock at me. I ran back down to the bottom."

"I told you not to follow them."

"Did you see where they went?" I asked.

"No."

I walked all over the top looking for them, but they had mysteriously disappeared. I could see down all the sides, and there was no trace of their bright red and blue jackets anywhere.

We stood and enjoyed the panoramic view and caressing breeze. We saw our condominium complex in the distance; it looked like a miniature Christmas village set up on a table.

After a few drinks of water from our canteen and some trail mix, we lingered for a while, soaking up the conquest of the mountain then decided to return home.

We trudged through the brush down the mountain, retracing our steps. I continued looking for the two little fiends but never saw them.

An hour later we were home.

We had conquered Rattlesnake Mountain and never went back.

As spring rolled around, there was this little

blonde kid who occasionally wore a blue Cub Scout shirt with little colorful badges sewn on the pockets. Around his neck was a yellow neckerchief, and he wore a blue hat. We became friends. His name was Raymond.

The wallpaper in Raymond's bedroom was covered with rockets and astronauts soaring in outer space and landing on far away planets. Model airplanes and toys covered his dresser and hung from the ceiling, bringing to life the little fantasy chamber. I spent the night at his house and marveled at the possibilities of space travel depicted on his walls. In the morning, his parents made us a wonderful breakfast of waffles, bacon, eggs, and orange juice.

I told Raymond I wanted to play Little League baseball, but my mom had checked, and there were no leagues for 8-year-old kids in Reno. He said he played on a team in nearby Sparks, and he would check with his coaches and see if they would let me play. A few days later, he told me his coaches had said yes, and soon I was playing baseball with my new friend. I rode with him after school to practice a couple times a week, and Mom drove me to the games.

After baseball season ended and summer began, we moved to Oregon. Dallas's bar had failed, and he was buying a restaurant with his brother. I was sad again. This was now the second friend I had to leave.

Mom drove me to Raymond's house to say goodbye the day we left. He and his parents were expecting us and came outside when we arrived. Mom and I got out of the car and greeted them in the driveway. She chatted briefly with Raymond's parents. They were pleasant but quietly sad that their son was losing a friend.

I stepped close to Raymond, told him I was glad he talked to his coach, and I had a lot of fun playing baseball with him. Raymond's blue eyes sparkled as he smiled and said he did, too, and was also glad we were friends. We shook hands, and he wished me well in Oregon. He was sincere, but I could sense his sadness. He probably felt mine.

I waved goodbye to his parents, walked back to the car, and sat in the front seat. Mom said goodbye, got back into the car, started it, and began driving away. I waved one last time to the trio standing in the driveway as we drove away.

I did not take Raymond's phone number.

OREGON

After I said goodbye to Raymond, my mom, brother, and I made the long drive to Oregon and finally arrived after an overnight stay in a motel. Dallas was already there, overseeing his new restaurant business.

We moved into a three-bedroom, two-bath house on thirteen acres, half of which was a large pasture with a sloping valley, another quarter section of forest and pine trees, and another quarter of flat grassy pasture. More than fifty sheep roamed the pasture and came back to the barn to eat and lie in the shade. When my brother and I approached the sheep, thinking they could be petted like dogs, they rose terrified and bolted away, stampeding into the pasture, flicking up dirt and dust in their wake. I never understood why they were so frightened. After a while, we discovered a couple that would allow us to pet them, and the fear among the rest of the herd seemed to dwindle.

I quickly found an odd tree fort in the nearby forest. It looked like a green, triangular UFO parked in the trees. It hovered fifteen feet off the ground; a ladder leaned against it. The pine trees were not suitable for tree houses, as the trunks grew vertically and branches laterally, leaving no space for a fort. The builders of this fort found three trees six or seven feet apart, forming an equilateral triangle and simply nailed boards to the trunks to form a triangle, then constructed the remainder of the frame. It was the best they could do with the trees available.

I explored the fort and concluded I would not spend much time there, as the ceiling was too low to sit without crouching forward uncomfortably.

Our new home was in a rural suburb of Salem, mostly large patches of green farmland interspersed with large sections of pine trees and fruit orchards.

As an incentive and inducement to accept our new home and life far away from everything we left behind in Nevada, Dallas bought Rick and me Shetland ponies. He showed us how to saddle and unsaddle them, attach the bits and reins, mount and dismount. He told us to brush their backs gently after riding and pick rocks out of their hooves.

After learning the basics, we rode all over the thirteen-acre parcel until we had explored every foot and knew the location of every trail, rock, and tree.

I soon learned my pony did not necessarily enjoy taking me for rides whenever I chose. One afternoon, I had ridden through the forest section of our property into the grassy rectangle a few hundred feet from the house. This area was half the size of a football field, and patches of tall, thorny weeds called "tansy" grew on the edges of the forest section. I was in the tall grass about a hundred feet from the tansy when my mount suddenly jolted into a run and galloped toward the forest. I hollered at him to stop and pulled the reins, but he ignored me and galloped faster. He was heading directly toward an apple tree, and I could see he was going to run directly under the branches, which would strike me at mid-chest and knock me out of the saddle. I had no choice; I put both hands on the saddle horn and pushed forward and sideways, diving off the saddle and flying through the air like a hawk swooping on a mouse. I ripped through the tall tansy and crashed into the dirt. Needle pricks from the tansy stung all over my arms, chest and legs, and large red rashes covered my elbows from the collision with the ground. I lay there for a while with the wind knocked out of me while my pony galloped away.

I walked back to the house, sore and stinging, and told Dallas what happened. He told me the pony could sense that I did not yet know how to control him. If a horse knew you were afraid or lacked confidence, it would do whatever it wanted, including dashing away to get you off its back.

I was surprised to learn the animal had that much intelligence and sensitivity, but I believed Dallas. I had to convince the pony I was not afraid and that I was in control.

I fed him carrots, brushed his back, carefully pried rocks out of his hooves, petted his neck and head, and talked to him to convince him I was his friend. I was no 'horse whisperer', but I eventually persuaded him I was not afraid, and he never again sprinted away or tried to buck me.

Rick and I explored the fields, dirt roads, streams and lakes. One of our favorite weekend activities was making the half-hour walk to a private pond to go fishing. Fruit and nut orchards flanked our path, separated by an occasional house with a raised front porch.

We carried our fishing poles and tackle boxes along two-lane roads that led to a dense raspberry orchard. A dirt path cut through the fruit grove, leading to a small lake. From shore, a narrow ramp led to a floating, twenty-foot wooden dock, gray with age and wear. The dock put us a little closer to the fish, and we cast our lines from the edge, reeled in bluegill and perch for a couple hours, then returned home with our catch, snatching raspberries on our way.

Along the boundary of our property stood an electric fence. One afternoon while exploring the forest, Rick discovered a small chainsaw on a wood stump twenty feet on the other side of the barrier. He wanted that chainsaw, but the threat of electric shock was intimidating.

By tapping at the fence with his fingertips, he discovered that a couple wires running across the top carried electric current, but the remainder appeared neutral. The shock was mild but uncomfortable, and he encouraged me to test for myself. I tapped the upper wire and felt the buzzing sensation.

Rick climbed up the fence post, carefully swung his legs over the top wires and dropped to the other side. He dashed to the chainsaw, picked it up, and ran back to the fence, where he handed it over to one of his friends, then carefully climbed the post and dropped back onto our property. We all quickly ran away with the stolen machine.

After we were a safe distance from the location of the theft, Rick hid the chainsaw under some bushes and announced we could not start it for a few days, as the noise would alert the neighbor. We agreed to wait, then before school, we would start it and cut down a tree.

We picked a day and gathered with some kids in the morning for the pretense of walking to school, then retrieved the hidden plunder and searched for a suitable tree to cut down. We located a pine that was perhaps forty feet tall. Rick figured the small saw should be able to cut through the adolescent tree. He pulled the cord to start the engine, but it took numerous attempts. Finally, after injecting gasoline into the starter chamber with the choke button, the machine sputtered to a smoky start, and it whined loudly. I was sure the neighbors would hear the blaring, call the police, and they would show up in moments and arrest us all.

Rick told us to stand back as he raised the saw and began cutting. He sliced horizontally through the tree, and the small whizzing blades chewed into the trunk, spitting lines of white pulp horizontally. He seemed to cut easily for the first three inches, then the high-pitched whine lowered to a groan as the saw struggled to cut deeper. About halfway through the tree, the motor groaned to a stop and smoke poured from the engine. Rick pulled and yanked the handle to loosen the blade, but it was stuck under the tree's weight. The pine had seemingly saved itself by clamping down on the blade, stopping the rotating chain. He struggled mightily to withdraw the trapped blade, but it was immovable, like the sword from the legend of King Arthur.

We left for school, and the evidence of the theft was now securely locked under the weight of the almost-fallen pine tree. We pledged never to say a word about the incident and would deny knowledge if ever confronted. It would just have to remain stuck there for eternity, or until someone else found a way to remove it.

I felt relieved. Cutting down the tree seemed such a pointless exercise of raw power. This young beautiful pine had done nothing to any of us, and we had attempted to cut it down merely to watch it fall. Fortunately, my brother's ignorance of tree-felling methods doomed his effort.

REDWOODS

The hours of driving were uneventful until I finally encountered a patch of ancient redwood trees. I had entered Humboldt Redwoods State Park. Suddenly, I was dwarfed in an enormous, sprawling forest. I was so astonished, I had to stop.

I found a place to pull over and parked, stepped out and looked up at these majestic, sky bound entities, swaying gently hundreds of feet above me. I had never seen redwood trees. Some were twenty or twenty-five feet wide—gargantuan compared to regular pine trees. I walked under the quiet branches of these magnificent giants and marveled not only at their massive size, but the unprecedented feeling I experienced. They emanated a mysterious energy that seemed to connect and engulf everything in the forest. I was literally surrounded by endless tons of life sprouting from the ground and growing hundreds and hundreds of feet into the air, but I did not feel separated from the trees. It was as if my inner being was now part of this gigantic community of protective creatures that lovingly covered and embraced everything under their perfumed shadows.

As I lingered in awe at the base of these immense, towering hulks, I became intoxicated with their sweet aroma that scented the area. I was overcome with a strange feeling, an out-of-body experience in which my physical presence was dissolved in relation to these soaring titans. All my physical strength and capabilities seemed trivial and vanishing compared to the vast, overpowering strength and sturdiness of the trees. My consciousness was somehow absorbed by the mammoth trunks and overhanging branches in this otherworldly feeling of connection.

After basking in the greatness of the redwoods for a while, I got back into my car, still somewhat light-headed and dreamy, and continued to my destination.

When I finally located the hotel in Eureka, I drove into the parking lot and parked. It was about 12:30, and my court hearing wasn't until 1:30, so I had plenty of time to get dressed and ready for court. Lunch would have to wait, I decided.

As I carried my overnight bag and suit from the parking lot toward the hotel, a young man in hotel-employee clothing approached and said, "Hi, are you Mr. Courtney?"

"Yes," I answered.

He extended his hand, and I shook it. He told me his name and welcomed me to the hotel. *Now that was unusual*, I thought. *I've stayed in hotels, and the employees don't usually greet people in the parking lot and give them a warm welcome.* Maybe he was just a very friendly hotel employee.

I continued toward the hotel two-hundred feet away. It was a two-story half-timbered building that seemed to match the mountainous surroundings.

I walked through the entrance toward the reception desk. A couple people were standing in line. As I waited, the female employee behind the reception desk, Sarah, looked up and scowled at me briefly. I wondered, *was I in the wrong line? Did I track mud into the hotel? Why did she look at me so coldly*? Sarah looked down and busied herself with the other customer as I waited with some impatience.

After maybe five minutes, it was my turn to check in, and I walked forward to the counter. Sarah was a pretty, dark haired lady, probably in her mid-thirties, with a sort of farm-girl look, full cheeks, but not fat, big blue eyes, sweet, innocent looking.

"Are you Mr. Courtney?" she asked.

"Yes."

Twice now a hotel employee had asked if I was Mr. Courtney. *Why is everyone here trying to identify me*? She looked down grimly, grabbed a piece of paper off the countertop and said, "There's a message for you. You need to call this number," and handed me the piece of paper. "Let's go to an office upstairs where you can have some privacy."

I thought the message would be from the law office, giving me last minute instructions about the hearing. *Didn't they trust me to handle this? It was just a routine case management conference; I didn't need any last-minute instructions about what to say or how to act. I'd been a lawyer more than six months; didn't they realize I could think for myself and handle this easy court hearing*?

Sarah came from behind the reception counter, motioned for me to follow her, and we walked toward a staircase at the far end of the building. We ascended the stairs, then turned and walked toward a corner office. On the way, I unfolded the paper and looked at the number. It was my home phone number. *That's weird,* I thought. *My mom worked graveyard and slept during the day. Why would I need to call home at 12:30 in the afternoon when she is sleeping*?

An uneasy feeling now oozed from my core. Sarah opened the door to the corner office and stepped back so I could enter. She pointed at the phone on a desk and told me I could have a seat in the chair and call. *What on earth was happening that I needed to have a seat in this tiny office and call home*? The office had enough space for one person only, and a sense of panic was now developing in my chest, as Sarah carefully and quietly stood outside, waiting for me to call. Her tentative, cheerless manner standing by the door now told me something was very wrong.

My heart suddenly began pounding, and my breathing became shallow as my throat shrunk to the size of a straw.

I punched the numbers on the phone and waited for an answer. After a few rings, Mom answered.

"Hello?" she said, in a wounded, heartbroken voice.

"Mom, what's going on? I just got to the hotel, and they told me to call home."

She paused a few moments then began sobbing. "Ben…your brother's dead," she sobbed and began crying.

"What!? I don't believe it," I growled into the phone.

She sobbed and cried some more in the most broken, crushed tone I'd ever heard. "He was killed in a car accident last night. His car hit a tree. The Highway Patrol called me. I've been drinking Scotch all morning."

The world tilted sharply, and my vision went out of focus, unable to see any detail, just vague imagery. My heart was now pounding as if I were running the 100 meters in the Olympics. "*Don't tell me that. Don't tell me that*!" I shouted. The shocking, horrible news clobbered me as if kicked in the stomach by an angry bull. All my strength, reason, and resistance evaporated, and I burst into streaming tears.

"There must be a mistake! There must be a mistake!" I said, tears gushing down my face.

Sarah came into the office and stood beside me, holding my shoulders.

"You need to come home," my mom sobbed. "Your father's on his way up."

"I'll get you a flight back to Sacramento," Sarah interjected. "I've already talked to your office, and they called the court and informed the judge of the situation. The judge will excuse you from the hearing."

"Come home," my mom sobbed.

I was now crying uncontrollably. "Okay," I sobbed back.

She hung up, then I went into severe shock, shivering violently, uncontrollably. Sarah became alarmed and said I needed to get under some blankets to get warm. She escorted me to a nearby room and told me to lie on the bed. She came back a few minutes later and covered me with a thick blanket, but I continued shivering violently, sobbing and crying in shock and disbelief.

Sarah hugged and held me and began crying also.

"I don't believe it, I don't believe it," I kept chanting through my clattering teeth, shivering mightily. The devastation was complete and consuming, a bottomless agony that saturated every cell in my body with oozing, immobilizing grief.

After five minutes of intense crying, Sarah came close to my face, tears rolling down her cheeks and said, "Ben, is there anything I can do? Anything?"

I looked in her eyes and softly said, "No."

She put her head on my chest and arms around me. I hugged her back. We lay sobbing on the bed for about fifteen minutes, then she got up and said she would arrange a flight to Sacramento that afternoon. She left, and I remained on the bed under the blanket, still shivering and devastated.

A half hour later, Sarah returned and told me the flight had been booked. I could leave my car at the hotel overnight and send someone to pick it up later. She would drive me to the airport for my afternoon flight. I thanked her and waited for our departure to the airport.

When it was time to leave, Sarah came back and took me to a car. A bellhop carried my overnight bag and loaded it in the trunk. There was not much to say on the way to the airport. We arrived, and Sarah told me she was so sorry for my loss, gave me a hug, and left me at the terminal. I thanked her for being so kind through this horrible time. I couldn't imagine having to deliver news like this to someone.

The wait seemed forever to board the small commuter plane for the flight back to Sacramento. Finally, passengers began boarding, and I took a seat midway in the plane. Tears continued rolling quietly out of the corners of my eyes during the entire flight home. For some reason, I didn't want strangers to see me crying, but the emotions were too powerful. I was in more control than I had been in the hotel room with Sarah, but several passengers noticed my grief.

The flight back was tumultuous, accentuating the agony. The plane seemed to be on a gigantic rubber band, bouncing up and down, tilting and dipping left and right, seemingly out of control for most of the flight.

We finally landed in Sacramento, and I stepped out into the sweltering July heat and walked down the stairs to the tarmac. My dad and Victoria greeted me at the terminal. I hugged my dad tightly, and we both cried mightily. We all sobbed as we headed back to the car. This was without question the worst day of my life and my dad's.

We arrived at Mom's in the early evening. She was sitting at the kitchen table with a friend from work, Maggie. She was bleary-eyed and plastered, having been drinking scotch all day. I stepped into the house and broke into gushing tears again and hugged my mom. She hugged me so tightly that strands of her hair fell into my mouth, choking me. I gagged and tried to get away, but she held firm. She finally let go, and I caught my breath and continued crying and sobbing and telling her I didn't believe this; there must be a mistake.

She said the Highway Patrol Officer had called in the morning and asked if she was alone. She asked him why, and he kept repeating, are you alone? Is someone there with you? Mom wanted to know why he was calling, and he finally said that unfortunately, her son had been in a car accident the previous night, and he had not survived. Mom shouted profanities and hung up. He called back, and she hung up on him again. He called back a while later, and Mom picked up and listened. The officer said he was very sorry, but it was his duty to inform her of this news, and she should not be alone. He said she could pick up my brother's wallet and some personal effects at the CHP station the next day.

Concerned and grieving friends started showing up, Ed Vaughn, and soon Eric Farnsworth, Tim Molina and numerous others. Throughout the evening, people dropped by to express their grief, shock, and condolences. The phone had been ringing every ten minutes, so Mom took it off the hook, and the house became a shrinking cocoon of shock and deep, dark agony.

I cracked open a beer and drank for the next several hours.

Everyone wanted to know what happened. We were not yet sure, but when we later received copies of the CHP reports, we learned the details. Rick had been at a bar drinking with a co-worker and another guy. They left the bar at about 9:30, the same time I had called from Victoria's trying to reach him, the same time I felt a strange uneasiness when his girlfriend told me he was not home. For unknown reasons, Rick had not driven his own truck to the bar. When they left the tavern, he sat in the middle.

They came down the hill and were about a mile from Placerville when the driver lost control, skidded off the road, hit a tree, and the truck flipped over. The cab crushed halfway down, but Rick was not physically injured. He had been pinned inside the cabin awkwardly with his chin against his chest, suffocating. The other two men were uninjured.

The driver was later charged with manslaughter, convicted, and sentenced to two years in state prison.

I grieved with friends throughout the evening. No one had much to say, other than they could not believe it and were shocked and profoundly saddened. Rick was everybody's best friend; how could he possibly be gone? By 11:00 or so, our visitors had left, but Mom remained with Maggie in the living room.

By 11:30, I decided to go to bed. After crawling under the sheets, I drifted into an uneasy, alcohol-induced sleep.

PARTINGS

I went with Mom, Dad and Victoria to the California Highway Patrol office to pick up my brother's belongings and get a copy of the police report. After we showed ID, we were handed a small brown envelope containing Rick's wallet, keys, and a few scraps of paper. The wallet had six dollars in it; there was a little change. We decided not to spend his money but keep it for unknown reasons, as if spending his last six dollars and change would be disrespectful.

We learned from the police report that the driver had no driver's license and no insurance. We could sue him and win millions of dollars for killing my brother negligently, but we would never collect a penny. He had no assets and would never be able to pay what he rightfully owed for his negligence—unless he won the lottery someday.

We later talked to a lawyer who said it was possible to sue the manufacturer of the truck for a design defect, as the cab of the truck should not have collapsed, but it was a 1968 GM, and it met safety guidelines when it was made. Proving the truck had been defective in 1968 under then-existing design standards would be difficult. Besides, GM didn't drive the truck off the road and hit a tree.

We decided not to file a lawsuit against GM; they were not the true culprit, nor was the county somehow liable for building a defective road in the middle of too many trees. No, the true culprit had no license or insurance and would soon be going to prison for manslaughter.

I hated him for a few years, but the odium eventually dissolved. I knew he did not intend to kill my brother—it had simply been a tragic accident, but his carelessness was so profoundly costly.

I no longer hate him.

A Highway Patrol Officer advised us that Rick's body had been transported to the Chapel of the Pines Mortuary, and we could view it if we chose. To resolve all doubts, we had to view the body.

We called the mortuary, got their address, and set a time for the viewing. We arrived in the afternoon and parked in the nearby parking lot. Mom and Dad got out of the car immediately and walked toward the building. Victoria joined them, but I remained in the car, not yet ready.

After waiting about ten minutes, I gathered all my willpower, got out of the car, and walked toward the rear entry, where we had been told to go. I entered the quiet, dim building, and someone directed me to a large room at the end of a carpeted hall. I walked down the hallway, entered the room, and saw Mom and Dad standing near a table where my brother was lying covered by a white sheet up to his neck. The uncontrollable tears came back as I approached the makeshift funeral.

I saw his rusty red hair contrasted by the white sheet as I neared. As I walked, I felt as though I were pressing through clear gel that slowed my movements and weighted my limbs. Step by step the true horror grew into focus, as I finally came within a couple feet of the table, and there he was, lying on his back, mouth slightly open, chin up, appearing as if he were sleeping on my bed after an afternoon Thanksgiving feast. He looked alive, but he was motionless. I stood and stared in disbelief, hoping he would move or speak, but he remained still as a statue. Mom and Dad were sobbing and mumbling. A few chairs had been provided. Victoria and I sat and gazed in disbelief at this obscene, disgraceful, despicable sight of my twenty-nine-year-old brother lying dead on a table, ten feet away.

I grimly accepted the reality that my brother was dead. I had seen it for myself. After lingering in misery and disbelief for a half hour or so, we had seen enough and left. There had been no mistake.

Friends continued calling and periodically dropping by the house to show their support. They were shocked, grief-stricken and baffled that this horrible tragedy was real. We put out word of the time and location of the funeral and continued dissolving in misery.

A dozen or so bouquets of flowers arrived in the first week after his death, and many dozens of condolence cards trickled in through the mail over the next several weeks.

Robert Blevins sent a card with several beautiful, handwritten passages with the memorable line, "Rick was a rose among daisies." Mom was moved by the sentiment and gave it to me to read. I was also touched. It was filled with warm personal insights and heartfelt sadness. Like hundreds of people, Robert had known my brother for many years growing up, liked and admired him, and he was affected by the tragedy.

Mark Channing, who had been a great friend I had known since Babe Ruth baseball, offered his friendship unconditionally. If I needed to meet for a drink, that would be fine, or we could dash to Tahoe for the weekend, win or lose big, and forget about the world. He didn't care; he was there to support a friend however he could, in for whatever was on the agenda.

More than 350 people signed the guestbook at the funeral services a couple days later. People I knew came into the chapel, sad and subdued, shook my hand or hugged me, expressed their sorrow and disbelief, then plodded to the casket at the other end of the room. The sweet aroma of flowers, usually wonderful and signaling joy and expectation—like before a prom or wedding—now smelled sickeningly sweet, choking in my nostrils and throat. In the casket, flanked by flowers, my brother was lying in a red shirt, black vest, and blue jeans. I couldn't muster the strength to view him yet. I waited a couple hours until it was time to leave, then trudged forward to view his body for the last time.

Next was the burial, which occurred in the Georgetwon Cemetery. Hundreds of people showed up for the dreadful, gloomy ceremony. A Catholic priest made some comments, and my dad gave a short speech quoting Shakespeare. "Good night sweet prince! And may flights of angels sing thee to thy rest!" Tears turned the dust into mud everywhere and after the ceremony, dozens of people went the Georgetown Hotel for drinks, an unacknowledged irony to my brother's death from a drunk driver.

Friends and parents I had known since childhood offered condolences, but there was no comfort, just unending agony and soul-crushing grief.

Dad stayed a couple days for moral support, then Victoria drove him to the airport to fly home to Los Angeles.

Aside from losing my brother and best friend, I also lost a significant part of my social circle, basically all his friends, because seeing them after his death was too difficult. His absence was too overwhelming.

I took off two weeks from work to deal with the aftermath. Rick had lived in a mobile home in Garden Valley a few miles from Georgetown, and his landlord compassionately informed us we would be charged a full month's rent if the mobile home was not empty and available for another renter by the first of August, less than three weeks away.

James Flemmons, one of Rick's friends from junior high school, volunteered to help us move, and my mom, Eric, Victoria, and I went to his house one Sunday and packed up his belongings. It was the most dismal, miserable task that only deepened our grief, as we packed his clothes, bass guitar, tools, camping gear, pictures, and other personal items. His girlfriend was so traumatized that she was unable to stay in the trailer and had begun living with friends, mostly out of contact with the world, but we could not wait. We were under the landlord's deadline to get

Rick's property removed, and we all had to return to jobs eventually and continue our shattered lives.

I went back to work after two weeks, still shocked and profoundly sad, but Hank needed my help, and I had lots to do, or they would find someone else. Everyone in the office quietly expressed their sad condolences. I stopped eating lunch at the office and instead went to nearby restaurants. After a month or so, I was ready to return to the lunchroom, but the topics of conversation were generally cheerless and muted, as no one wanted to seem too happy in the face of my continuing grief. That eventually wore off, and a few weeks later, secretaries were laughing and chatting as they had previously. I was doing my best to stay included, though still glum and depressed.

Fortunately, I had lots of work, and this helped distract from the pain and grief, but it was always there.

Mom started seeing a therapist, but she said it was no help. All she did was cry and talk about how sad she was and how her life had been wrecked, and the therapist sat and listened without any emotion and only a few brief comments. There really was not much else for him to say or do.

I was uninterested in any type of therapy. It wouldn't bring my brother back, and I was not interested in talking about my pain to someone I did not know or who did not know him.

I talked with friends about my grief. They were all very patient, compassionate, supportive, and tried their best to be helpful.

I read numerous books about life after death, but the most helpful was *When Bad Things Happen to Good People*. Author and Rabbi Harold S. Kushner discussed the death of his ten-year-old son, who had died from some horrible childhood disease and, like myself, he had gone on a quest to find moral and spiritual answers. After examining the tragedy from every conceivable moral, religious, and philosophical angle, he concluded that no one was to blame—including God. God had not punished either his son or him, or anyone else, and there was no rhyme or reason as to how or why these things occurred. There was no cause-and-effect relationship between bad behavior and death. Bad people lived into their nineties and innocent children, like his son, died early from diseases, but there was no logic, pattern, or plan to any of it. Therefore, there was no logical solution or way of avoiding it. It simply had to be accepted as a fact of life—like a rainy day or an earthquake, for which no one was to blame or hold responsible. That was at least a path to avoid further questioning, which I did because there was no satisfactory answer, and I was tired of searching.

I did my best to pick up the broken pieces of my life and continue. I stayed with Victoria for another year, but we broke up when the flame in the relationship died. There was no sense in trying to fake it after two years. She had helped me immeasurably through the shock and tragedy of my brother's death, and for that, I will always be grateful.

We remained friends.

GLOOMY DAYS

Life was much different with my brother gone. His absence always lingered in the background, casting an ever-present pall of sadness.

Folsom itself now seemed different. The whole town was a continuous reminder of my brother's life and legacy. The high school was filled with memories of his triumphs on the football field and wrestling mat. The streets he used to drive and fields where he used to camp now contained a ghostly vacancy. When the miniature train chugged through the city park near the zoo, the steam engine whistle had an even more lonely, forlorn sound far in the distance. In prior years, the whistle seemed to signal an arrival, but now it sounded a grim, lonely departure on Sunday afternoons.

Months later, I was still living at home, and my mom remained sullen and introspective. When Christmas arrived, we decided not to decorate or exchange gifts. Celebrating Christmas without Rick would be too difficult, so we celebrated in non-traditional ways for a few years. The first time, we took a road trip to visit my dad, who had moved to Monterey, did some sightseeing, visited some museums, and had a lazy Christmas holiday in a hotel.

Following Christmas, another dismal and dreary reminder arrived—Rick's birthday. We decided to go to a nice restaurant, like we used to, and have dinner in his honor, though it would be a hollow experience that left us sad and quiet.

We had his property, and we weren't sure what to do with it all. He had a Toyota 4Runner truck, which we sold. He had another old Ford truck that was in good shape; we sold that, also. We kept his large tool chest and some of his tools, bass guitar, bass amp, photo albums, a few pieces of clothing, and some personal items. Everything else was discarded, sold, donated, or given away.

After my one-year contract with TIER1 expired, Zack said the firm could not hire me as a full-time employee. He had checked with the higher-ups and was informed they didn't have the caseload. A recession was slowing the economy and, supposedly, the firm just didn't have enough work to hire me. He was sorry but thankful for all my efforts and contributions.

I wondered whether that was true.

Zack had told me about his days as a new attorney, working long hours and weekends. He seemed to imply that years of thankless toil was the price to higher status in a law firm. He was probably right, but I did not agree that I should stifle my opinions to avoid chafing someone's teetering ego. I thought we were professionals dedicated to serving the client, not contestants in a reality TV show. He may have sensed I was not the submissive 'yes man' law firms sought in new associates, and that was enough to hire someone else.

I had no personal conflicts with Zack, Kent, Hank,

or anyone else, but there was a subtle power dynamic I never liked or accepted—the presumption that their ideas were *better*, because they had trial experience. It was an unpleasant throwback to the situation I had experienced growing up—always considered inferior to my older brother by default. The seasoned attorneys usually utilized their experience as a signal that rather than voice my alternative views, I should defer to their proclamations and keep my thoughts to myself.

Law school had not prepared me for office politics and jealous elitism, just the opposite. They taught us to analyze the facts rigorously, identify all legal questions and zealously present arguments for each side. Shrinking away from an issue was the path to failure.

Perhaps my open satisfaction with winning the motion in the food poisoning case annoyed those I had doubted. The adage quoted by President John F. Kennedy, "Success has a thousand fathers, but defeat is an orphan," has no place in a multi-tiered law firm. Unless the credit is willingly shared with underlings, all glory for victory is reserved for the senior veterans, and taking any of it might be a serious and costly mistake.

I didn't pretend to know everything, but it was insulting to go through four years of law school, pass the bar exam, then be regarded as incompetent. That was the culture, and it effectively kept young lawyers in their place. I may have wandered across an invisible barrier. I'll never know.

Interestingly, when trial was approaching, everyone's opinion was welcome. Hank and Kent would meander around the office in a state of semi-panic, asking anyone who would listen to critique their trial strategies. How would the jury react to their cross-examination? Their closing arguments? They fretted about what witnesses would say, jury instructions, objections, and valued anyone's feedback, but the day after a verdict, they were again omniscient experts who needed no advice or consultation.

In their defense, Hank and Kent were excellent lawyers, and I wouldn't want to tangle with them in the courtroom. I just wish law firm culture had not been moored to a hierarchy where value was determined primarily by experience, but I suppose it was that way from the start and always will be.

When it came to work, I was a lot like my dad. I could be a great team player, but I didn't like laboring under pretenses of my inferiority, just like I didn't like comparisons to my brother, always coming up short. I understood the hierarchy and grudgingly accepted it, but I proved I could work under supervision, that my view of the law and facts could be right, and it had nothing to do with trial experience.

Even though I had done no jury trials, I thought I had enough litigation experience to get hired at another firm. I sent job applications and resumes all over Sacramento and received not a single letter, phone call, or interview. That was a shock. Maybe it *was* the recession, or maybe Dad's paralegal instructor, Ron Olendorf, had been right all along—the door to the 'good old boy' network was closed. I had simply been extremely lucky when I landed the law clerk job at TIER1—in the right place at the right time. My good fortune ran out, however, after my contract expired, and I had no connections that could lead to another job.

I had no choice; I had to start my own law practice.

I opened my new office in a nearly empty complex off Highway 50. The one-story building used to be full of lawyers, but the firm broke up, and now only a few offices were occupied. Some still had a desk and bookcase or two; phone wires dangled from the walls; square outlines of frames where pictures, degrees, and diplomas had once hung were visible. I had my pick of about fifteen empty offices and chose one in the back corner, shaded by a tall pine tree, where I would be isolated and free from any distractions. I expected the building to fill up soon with other tenants, but it never did.

The vacant suites all over the building seemed to accentuate the ghostly absence of my brother. I ignored the creepy emptiness and continued my work in solitude.

A receptionist worked at the front entrance, though there was not a lot for her to do. She received the daily mail and delivered it to the few attorneys in the building. She brought my mail already opened, which struck me as strange, but I thought she was providing an extra courtesy. One day, she delivered an opened envelope and letter that I was expecting to contain a check. Unknown to me, the client had sent cash. The letter made no mention of enclosing any money, so I was not aware that the payment was missing and only learned about the theft after my client asked a few days later if I had received it. Now I understood why the receptionist opened my mail.

I confronted the thief, and she denied taking any cash or that there had been any in the envelope. I was angry, but there was not a lot I could do. It was her word against mine. She pretended the envelope had arrived already opened, but I knew that was a lie. She had been opening my mail for weeks, and I was just too naïve to know that she was a criminal searching for money.

I located another cheap office in Folsom a few days later and moved. No one was ever allowed to open my mail again, and nothing ever went missing.

My new office in Folsom was closer, and I would no longer have the ten-mile drive to work in the morning.

Meanwhile, the grief just under the surface remained, like a layer of old paint below a fresh coat.

Despite the underlying anguish, I needed to grow my law practice. Private firms were everywhere, so success was attainable—but how?

Advertising supposedly was the answer, but that was expensive and again—what company would see my advertising and call? They already had corporate attorneys. Advertising would bring in mostly poor clients with weak cases—complaints about landlords, mean neighbors, used cars, tax liens, credit-reporting agencies, mortgage companies, work policies, all the types of cases that eat up time with tedious document review and time-soaking legal research, but pay little or nothing.

There were no fat cat clients knocking on my door, nor did I know where to find any.

I'd learned from Chase Powell & Glass that a personal injury law practice could be lucrative, but I needed lots of clients to build a caseload that yielded several sizeable settlements every month—that's where the money was, not suing neighbors over fence disputes or used car dealers.

I received most clients through word of mouth and referrals, but all the big corporate clients who paid huge retainers went to other attorneys.

Without a heavy caseload, I had enough time for classes at American River College a couple times a week. I thought courses in psychology, history, computer science, math, and English would be a good distraction and make me a better lawyer. I wondered whether firms had seen the absence of an undergraduate degree on my resume and deemed me unqualified—even though I had a law degree, had passed the bar exam the first try, and had a year of litigation experience. *Perhaps going to law school with only a paralegal certificate had been hasty*, I thought, but it didn't matter that much anymore. The hole in my soul wouldn't be healed by a high-paying job in a downtown law firm, and there was little urgency anymore. My brother wasn't coming back and wouldn't share in any of my good fortune.

A few months after Rick's funeral, Matt Murry showed up one night and asked if I wanted to go for a ride.

"Where?" I asked.

"Someplace special. I think you'll like it."

I put on my coat, left the house, and hopped in his Toyota truck.

We drove east toward Placerville, rising into the foothills on a two-lane road. Twenty minutes later, we turned onto a dirt path and continued traveling slowly upward to a peak rising high above the surrounding area. We parked at a chain-link fence and walked around it, continuing to the peak several hundred feet.

When we reached the top, I understood why Matt wanted to take me there. The view was astonishing. Below us we could see all of Sacramento County sprawling across the Central Valley. It was as if a scale model of Sacramento County had been constructed in a warehouse, and we were standing at the edge looking at the creation below us on the floor. Thousands of lights twinkled in the clear sky below us, and we could see familiar landmarks here and there—a great patch of darkness that was Folsom Lake, the horizontal stretch of Folsom Dam, the skyline of Sacramento, Highway 50 slicing through Rancho Cordova like a laser.

We stood in awe and silence gazing at the twinkling landscape. The vastness of the view, encompassing the town below where we had both grown up, seemed to be saying something, beckoning to us that we were part of something larger than ourselves we couldn't quite explain.

After absorbing the beauty of the view for a while, we returned to the truck and made our way back home. I thanked Matt for taking me to the peak, and he was glad I agreed to go.

The future I had expected shortly after becoming an attorney had turned to ashes in my hands. Any hope of receiving the generous, once-in-a-lifetime support from Jeff Keller had been buried with my brother. He had been Rick's close friend, not mine, though I had anticipated getting to know him better.

To pay the bills while waiting for my personal injury practice to flourish, I took a variety of unusual cases. I helped recover money for a young man who had been hurt as a small child, only to find out when he turned eighteen that his mother had previously withdrawn all the settlement funds from his trust account, about $30,000. The bank had improperly allowed numerous trust withdrawals over ten years, but I got it all back for him.

I represented a farmer in a lawsuit against some

people who had stolen several bags of walnuts from his orchard. They had been caught by police and prosecuted, but the grower was not satisfied. They settled for a modest sum, and my client's pride was restored.

A friend's dad was bitten by a vicious dog when he went into a backyard to do some electrical work, and he came to me with his hand bandaged, purple and swollen, fingers like sausages. A settlement was quickly reached with the owner's homeowner's insurance. I didn't charge the customary one-third, like most personal injury lawyers. I charged him for a few hours, and he kept a lot of money that would have gone into the pocket of another lawyer.

While getting a haircut, I told the stylist I was an attorney, and she told me she had been rear-ended and needed representation. I took her case and settled it for the arbitration award, which was more than twice the amount of the insurance company's prior offers.

I wrote short contracts for people, reviewed leases, drafted several simple trusts, helped a couple friends get divorced, handled a few drunk driving cases, and successfully handled a claim against a paint shop that did a poor job painting my friend's car.

I was still a long way from the future I had imagined.

MOVING ON

I still lived in the town where I had grown up, still saw people I knew, Rick's old friends, here and there around town—at the Sutter Club, Folsom Hotel, grocery store, gas station. It was awkward for a couple years. His absence was always overwhelming in any social situation among people he used to know. To avoid the clumsiness, I started avoiding people and began associating with friends I made after high school. I was tired of constant reminders of the past and all the ensuing pain. I was tired of being the poster boy for tragedy. My function in life was not to quiet rooms and receive sad condolences and sympathies everywhere I went. I had suffered, but I didn't like being defined by the suffering—as if that were my special cross to bear, while everyone else went on with their lives, dating, getting married, working in good jobs, taking vacations, enjoying life. In the beginning, I had appreciated everyone's condolences and sympathy. Years later, I didn't want it anymore. It felt out of place—like congratulating an adult for getting straight A's in sixth grade—an odd, poorly fitting, undesired anachronism.

Unfortunately, my personal injury practice had not grown at the rate I expected. A job at one of the prestigious downtown firms was out of the question. I checked ads occasionally and was tempted to apply, but I knew it would be fruitless. I didn't care anymore. I'd already worked at the bottom rung of an elite corporate firm and had been willing to sacrifice. Not anymore. Whatever ambiguous notions of the American Dream that had inspired me before law school had been shattered into a million pieces following my brother's death. I still wanted financial and career success, but it seemed as if a switch had been flipped, and I was suddenly done climbing corporate ladders, being a company man, working weekends on short notice. My priority was healing and fulfilling whatever destiny lay ahead, just not as a member of any corporate law firm, where they owned my time and controlled my future.

I eventually found a niche handling complicated, technical issues of statutory and regulatory interpretation. They were difficult to win, but I soon began triumphing.

My long-awaited success brought some satisfaction and material comforts, but nothing like I had expected before law school. The best part of my new life was charting my own course, deciding which cases to take, making my own decisions. I was in full control of my time and destiny, and when I won, the credit was all mine.

I eventually had enough good fortune to buy a house ten miles from Folsom and started new chapters in my life.

I still played guitar, joined a few bands, enjoyed performing in clubs around Sacramento but never again felt on the brink of greatness, as I had when Rick and I played together and anticipated a record deal with Jeff Keller's assistance.

My dad, girded and steeped in his faith, was never plunged into the long-term grief, misery, and suffering my mom and I experienced. Dad's faith told him Rick's soul was in heaven, safe and secure, and he would see him when he got there, and that was the end of the issue, no further discussion needed. I'm glad his faith brought him comfort.

For me, the pain was always hidden deep inside, where I ignored it like a sentimental artifact I could not throw away. That was the best choice—ignore the pain, ignore my brother's absence, ignore the memories, and plod forward. If I didn't think about him, I didn't get sad. That seemed to work—until his birthday arrived again, or Christmas. I'd be sad for a day, then go back to forgetting and living with unanswered questions, but ignoring my desire for answers.

It was a strategy that worked, though a part of me remained bitter and broken.

PLATO

I continued my policy of ignoring my grief and anger about my brother's death and remained sullen on his birthday and holidays, times that had previously been filled with laughter, joy, music, and love. I quit decorating during Christmas, as it was only a sad reminder of all the Christmases I had spent with him. As long as I refrained from thinking about the tragedy, I wouldn't become upset and depressed, and I could continue with my life. I would just ride out the rest of my time not dwelling or talking about it, and someday the whole fiasco would be over.

Back in the early '90s when I had been reading about spirituality and metaphysics, I picked up a book titled *PLATO, The Republic and Other Works.* I had heard of Plato and knew he was a famous ancient philosopher, but I had never read any of his writings. I figured any good lawyer needed to know something about Plato, so I bought the book, put it on a bookshelf, where it was soon forgotten and remained unread for several years.

One day I decided I was going to read Plato. I took the book off the shelf and began reading. I liked it from the start. The thoughts were dense and intricately detailed. I had to read some passages twice to understand them, but I studied every sentence carefully. When I reached page 487, I began a chapter called, "PHAEDO," which was Plato's argument that the soul was eternal. His argument was sheer genius.

His dialogue went, in part:

> And this is true of all opposites? And are we convinced that all of them are generated out of opposites?
>
> Yes....
>
> Well, and is there not an opposite of life, as sleep is the opposite of waking?
>
> True...
>
> And what is that?
>
> Death...
>
> And these are then generated, if they are opposites, one from the other, and have their two immediate processes also?
>
> Of course....
>
> Then, suppose that you analyze life-and-death to me in the same manner. Is not death opposed to life?
>
> Yes.
>
> And they are generated one from the other?
>
> Yes.
>
> What is generated from life?
>
> Death.
>
> And what from death?
>
> I can only say in answer – life.
>
> Then the living, whether things or persons, ... are generated from the dead?
>
> That is clear... Then the inference is that our souls are in the world below?
>
> That is true.

Plato's chain of reasoning about life, death, and the soul was something I had never heard. I had always understood that the soul was invisible and intangible, but the concept always hung out there, unrelated to any context, vague and unexplained. I was taught that when we died, our souls left our bodies and went to heaven or hell, depending on God's judgment of our lives. But what was the soul? Could anyone define it and explain what it was? Did it really exist? The books I read had not provided clear, definitive answers.

According to Plato, death is "generated" from life, because that *which is not life*, is death. The soul, whatever it is, is manifested in the living body. Therefore, the soul is an aspect of life, *not* death. It follows that since the soul has no *physical* existence but manifests during life, it *cannot die upon death of the physical body*. It has no physical body. Therefore, it must be immortal, according to Plato.

I wanted to know what happened to my brother. Did his soul survive? Would I ever encounter him again, even if in some other form?

And what about that most priceless gift, which filled me with confidence and security, his love? Did that die, too?

Perhaps bio scientists would say that what we call the soul is merely a collection of chemical reactions in the brain that manifest in ideas and feelings, but it is not necessary to debate the physical causes. Even if biochemical reactions cause feelings and emotions, those states still cannot be put into physical form, weighed, measured, and sold on a store shelf. This invisible, intangible aspect of human existence containing all of our thoughts, fears, feelings, and hopes must be the soul.

After contemplating Plato, I developed new insights. I now understood the time Matt Murry had taken me to the mountain peak to view the Sacramento Valley at night. I couldn't quite understand the powerful experience at the time, but thinking about it again, there was something about the change in perspective that was at the heart of the experience. As we stood on the peak, we could see Folsom in the distance. It appeared small, but it was surrounded by the twinkling lights of other neighborhoods. From the perspective of the mountain top, it was clear Folsom was part of a larger whole that stretched across the valley. That was the key; *from a different perspective*, we could see Folsom was not a separated, isolated town, unrelated to neighboring cities—it was connected to and part of a larger community—the same way redwoods appear to be separate but are connected by their root system, living as one giant entity—the same way humans appear to be distinct and separate beings, but are connected by the invisible realm of the soul in which all aspects of humanity are experienced.

I wondered if my strange, almost spooky, experience at the redwoods had a deeper meaning. Perhaps that disembodied feeling was meant to teach me that the invisible, intangible part of me was still connected not only to my brother, but to others—that our true essence is not our flesh and bones, but the part we call the soul, which never dies.

The metaphorical experiences at the redwoods and mountain peak with Matt seemed to indicate yes, beneath our skin and bones, we all share the same 'source' of life, as religions, poets, and mystics have taught and preached for millennia. That realization led eventually to another insight. If Rick could speak to me, I think he would say:

"Ben, don't ever think for a second that my love died. I've always loved you and always will. Love is like the soul. It's not made of cement, steel, wood, or atoms, like physical matter. You can't put some in a bottle or backpack and take it with you. It doesn't go sour, like a gallon of milk left in the sun for a week. How can something that never decays and has no physical existence ever die? It can't. Even though you can't put love on a scale and weigh it, you know it's real; you perceive it with your senses; you can *feel* it—anytime. It's always there for you. All the memories, experiences, feelings, joy and happiness love brought cannot be reversed or canceled. The truth of the bond is there to support you forever. Stop avoiding this truth. Accept that my love *will be with you always*. You just have to *choose* it. Embrace it. Rely on it. Know this, Ben. You *must* know this."

Based on everything I know about philosophy, logic, religion, and metaphysics, I think he'd be right.

Spiritual teachers say we have a choice between fear and love. I'd been choosing fear for a long time—fear of the reality and finality of my brother's death. I never found a way to cope with the horrifying fact. I couldn't bear the thought of his permanent absence. The cruelty and irrevocability of his removal from my life was unfathomable, and the thought of his 'nonexistence,' of never seeing or talking to him again, crushed me like a hammer smashing a grape. Ignoring the fear, however, never healed it.

I had bitterly and reluctantly accepted the fact that Rick was dead. He'd never walk, talk, or breath again on this earth—barring a divine resurrection. But there was more truth to consider than this grim reality.

His death had *not* somehow retroactively canceled or revoked his love. His departing had not changed the bond between us, nor had it changed the memories of our shared experiences. His absence never altered how I felt about him. Would anyone say I could no longer recount not only our mutual affection, but all the time we spent growing up, eventually maturing into best friends? Would anyone contend all that history was now irrelevant, empty and meaningless?

Previously, I looked at all my memories and sentiments with fear. They represented pain and unspeakable loss, but reading all the books about spirituality, metaphysics, life after suffering, and Plato, a new truth emerged: I have the option to choose love rather than fear.

We built our friendship into a wonderful thing. Rick's love was demonstrated over and over. Am I not allowed to treasure that and let it give me strength?

Am I not allowed to recount all the joy and

happiness we experienced together and let it warm and comfort me?

If he were here, wouldn't he support me through any challenge, any hardship? He'd be the first. He'd jump in front of a bullet for me, and I'd do the same for him.

I now *choose* to recognize the continuing existence of our connection, and I *choose* to draw strength, comfort and inspiration from it. Who can prove I'm wrong? Only a fool would try.

The bond with my brother remains a strong and real attachment, which I will always preserve and cherish.

His physical death is only a tiny fragment of the larger truth. Yes, he's gone, but his spirit and love survive, because that is what *I choose*.

All the unforgettable memories are stored safely in my heart—where they will always remain.

And when the pain resurfaces now and then, I remind myself, and then it seems obvious:

Love never was something you could put in a bottle.

THE LAST CHEERS

When I think of my brother, I often think of the last time I saw him alive. It was about two weeks before he died, after a short jam session in our new practice room on a Wednesday evening.

I had become busy at TIER1, and the forty-minute drive from Folsom to Marty's house for practice took too much time. We agreed to change locations so I could get to rehearsal after work on the way home. I had made the long drive for two years, and now my brother was willing to drive an hour after work to accommodate my schedule.

I located a storage business off the freeway on my way home from work that would rent us a 10 x 30 unit with electricity, and they didn't care if our band used it for practice. There were no apartments or houses nearby where people might complain about the noise.

After setting up our amps, cranking up the volume, and just the two of us jamming for half an hour, Rick said we should get a drink somewhere, so I gave him directions to Paradise Beach, a trendy bar in Citrus Heights and met him there a short while later. We did not intend to party into the night or chase women. It was a Wednesday evening, he had a girlfriend, and I was still involved with Victoria, who was a caring, wonderful person, but I knew the relationship was not destined to end in marriage.

Paradise Beach was one of the popular bars in the Sacramento area during the early 90s. It had a grand entrance with a tall, rectangular window to the left, formed by small squares of thick, opaque glass—like some tropical bar you might see on the Miami shoreline. Once inside the cavernous interior, there were several raised platforms, a large dance floor, a raised bar, a small counter on the far side of the room, and another bar outside next to a large, sand-covered volleyball court. It was always overflowing on the weekends, but not too busy during the week.

We arrived around 9:00 and went inside. It was mostly empty; a few people were scattered about having conversations. We ordered beers and sat at a table in the raised section overlooking the dance floor. We drank and chatted about plans for our next gig. It was the middle of summer, a great time to play festivals, parties, and bar gigs, and by now, we had a sufficient fan following to start thinking about playing the larger clubs in Sacramento and the surrounding areas. Plus, we had the ace in the hole, Jeff Keller, who was going to get us noticed by the record companies. Jeff was currently on tour with Diamond Blade, but Rick would be seeing him again soon, and the topic would be discussed.

As we sat talking and drinking our beers, a pretty young lady walked up the stairs to the raised section and sat at the bar overlooking the dance floor, ten feet away from our table. We were the only three in this area of the bar. I thought she would probably be meeting someone, so I waited for a man to arrive. She had thick, long dark hair, muscular legs stretching the fabric of tight jeans, a lean, flat midsection, toned arms, long painted fingernails, and high-heeled shoes. She was pretty, with dark eyebrows and dark eyes. *Surely a man would be joining her any moment*, I thought.

After fifteen minutes of waiting, the girl remained alone at the bar. I was sure she was alone, as no fool would keep her waiting this long.

Suddenly, I felt emboldened to talk to her. My brother and I had been eyeing her, silently acknowledging her attractiveness, and Rick's presence seemed to filter away and displace fear and replace it with confidence and optimism—that was his effect on people.

I got up and walked to the girl, sat down next to her, introduced myself. She took my hand, smiled. Her name was Karla, and she was not waiting for anyone; she was alone; she liked going there Wednesday evenings. Our conversation flowed smoothly for about ten minutes. Rick eventually came over quietly and sat to my left; Karla was to my right. He remained still and quiet.

I continued talking to Karla, who seemed to like me, then decided to introduce my brother. I had expected him to intervene, but he had remained unusually silent. After I introduced him, he turned on his usual charm and began a discussion. She seemed to like him, also.

I sat back, not jealous at all, and figured if he wanted Karla, he could have her, because I was more concerned about his happiness than getting her for myself. It wasn't clear whether she liked him better than me, but she seemed to enjoy talking to him, so I withdrew from the banter and let them talk.

Oddly, as if noticing my retreat, Rick suddenly went quiet, giving me a chance to talk again. I engaged Karla, and she was responsive, friendly, and still seemed interested.

Rick then seemed to restrain himself from further conversation.

I would have dated Karla without question, but I just wasn't sure if he wanted her—even though he had a girlfriend. It was his choice, I decided. If he wanted her, he could have her, and the rest would be between him, Karla, and his girlfriend—or ex-girlfriend.

It was getting late, and Rick still had to drive to Garden Valley, which was almost an hour's drive from the bar, so we said goodbye to Karla. She smiled warmly and shook our hands, then we left the bar and walked outside.

It seemed we both had been so deferential toward the other that neither had gotten Karla's phone number. That was regrettable, but I figured I would come back and get her number on another Wednesday, when my brother was not there—as long as he was not interested. He still had a girlfriend, so I was probably in the clear, but I wanted to be sure.

In the parking lot, he told me I should have gotten Karla's phone number. I told him I thought he was interested, but he said no and encouraged me to get her number if I saw her again. I told him I would.

We said we would talk later about scheduling another practice, shook hands, and said goodbye. I watched as he got into his Toyota 4Runner, started it, and drove away.

I felt so proud. After twenty-six years, any doubt that ever existed was dissolved and swept away forever. Rick and I, although different people with different personalities, were complete equals who trusted each other, wanted the best for the other, and would sacrifice our own interests for that purpose.

I had finally reached the place I always wanted. I loved my brother, and he loved me.

Nothing and no one can ever change that.

Through all the growing-up years, jealousies, anger, resentments, joys, triumphs, and later tragedy and soul-searching, I found a few helpful answers. The weight of science, logic, and reason suggests that our souls are immortal, that something survives our physical death, though I cannot explain with any concrete details. Human experience, reasoning, and analogies provide the best understanding, for me, anyway.

Thinking over my life growing up in my brother's shadow finally made me realize that he made me who I am. When he gloated about his success, it inspired me to do better and equal or surpass his achievement. When he excelled as a running back, I chose quarterback. When he picked up a welding torch and made a beautiful gate, I picked up a guitar and learned how to play Van Halen. When he joined friends and went fishing for the weekend in the mountains, I reflected about my upcoming essay and wrote a story that delighted Ms. Pinchot. Had I not experienced his influence, I might have grown into a lazy onlooker in life, undistinguished, undeveloped, unmotivated to achieve or excel beyond average, blending into the background, talents unused, but his influence and later his love brought out the best in me.

And from all the memories grand and bitter, cherished and forgotten, all I can say is this:

Where I find love, I will find my brother.

Made in the USA
Middletown, DE
13 November 2023

42625192R00265